New C~~~~~~~ ~~~~

Series Editors
Kofi Campbell
Department of English
Wilfrid Laurier University
Waterloo, ON, Canada

Shalini Puri
Department of English
University of Pittsburgh
Pittsburgh, PA, USA

New Caribbean Studies series seeks to contribute to Caribbean self-understanding, to intervene in the terms of global engagement with the region, and to extend Caribbean Studies' role in reinventing various disciplines and their methodologies well beyond the Caribbean. The series especially solicits humanities-informed and interdisciplinary scholarship from across the region's language traditions.

More information about this series at
http://www.palgrave.com/gp/series/14752

Nicole N. Aljoe • Brycchan Carey
Thomas W. Krise
Editors

Literary Histories of the Early Anglophone Caribbean

Islands in the Stream

Editors
Nicole N. Aljoe
Department of English
Northeastern University
Boston, MA, USA

Brycchan Carey
Department of Humanities
Northumbria University
New Castle-Upon-Tyne, UK

Thomas W. Krise
Pacific Lutheran University
Tacoma, WA, USA

New Caribbean Studies
ISBN 978-3-030-10081-0   ISBN 978-3-319-71592-6   (eBook)
https://doi.org/10.1007/978-3-319-71592-6

Cover illustration: CPC Collection / Alamy Stock Photo

Printed on acid-free paper

This Palgrave Macmillan imprint is published by the registered company Springer International Publishing AG part of Springer Nature.
The registered company address is: Gewerbestrasse 11, 6330 Cham, Switzerland

Contents

Notes on Contributors

Nicole N. Aljoe is Associate Professor of English and African American Studies at Northeastern University. She is co-director of *The Early Caribbean Digital Archive* and editor of *Caribbeana: The Journal of the Early Caribbean Society*. Author of *Creole Testimonies: Slave Narratives from the British West Indies, 1709–1836* (Palgrave 2012), she also co-edited *Journeys of the Slave Narrative in the Early Americas* (UVA 2014).

Brycchan Carey is Professor of English at Northumbria University. He is the author of *British Abolitionism and the Rhetoric of Sensibility: Writing, Sentiment, and Slavery, 1760–1807* (Palgrave, 2005) and *From Peace to Freedom: Quaker Rhetoric and the Birth of American Antislavery, 1658–1761* (Yale University Press, 2012). His edition of Olaudah Equiano's *Interesting Narrative* was published by Oxford World's Classics in 2018.

Richard Frohock is an associate professor in the Department of English at Oklahoma State University, USA. He is the author of *Buccaneers and Privateers: The Story of the English Sea Rover, 1675–1725* and articles in *The Journal of Early American Literature* and *Eighteenth Century Studies*. His areas of interest and expertise include early American, early Caribbean and eighteenth-century British literature.

Jo Anne Harris is an assistant professor at the Georgia Gwinnett College, USA. Her teaching and research focus on cultural and digital representations of the Caribbean through development of online resources such as The Virtual Caribbean Cybrary.

Thomas W. Krise is President Emeritus and Professor of English at Pacific Lutheran University in Tacoma, Washington. A former president of the Early Caribbean Society and the Society of Early Americanists, he is the editor of *Caribbeana: An Anthology of English Literature of the West Indies, 1657–1777* (University of Chicago Press, 1999).

Keith Sandiford is a professor in the Department of English at Louisiana State University, USA. His areas of interest include eighteenth-century British literature and cultural studies and eighteenth-century Atlantic intellectual history. He received his Bachelor's degree from Inter-American University of Puerto Rico and a Master's degree and PhD from the University of Illinois, Urbana-Champaign.

Cassander Smith is Assistant Professor of English in the Department of English at the University of Alabama, USA, where she teaches undergraduate and graduate courses in early African American, American and Caribbean literatures. Both her teaching and research focus on representations of black Africans in early Atlantic literature, emphasizing the racial-cultural ideologies that helped shape English encounters with the early Americas and helped shape the literature produced about those encounters. Her work has appeared in several edited collections and journals including *Early American Literature* and *Studies in Travel Writing*. She is the author of *Black Africans in the British Imagination: English Narratives of the Atlantic World* (2016).

Sue Thomas is an associate professor in the Department of English at La Trobe University, Melbourne, Australia. She is the author of *Telling West Indian Lives*. Her recent research ranges across decolonizing literatures, nineteenth- and twentieth-century writing and histories of representation of racial difference, including "whiteness" as a historical racial category. In the field of decolonizing literatures, her special areas of interest are Caribbean writing, the transculturation of modernism, and transcultural and transhistorical textual traffic. Her scholarship is highly attentive to historical and cultural contexts, and histories of genre and representation. She is a member of the editorial board of *Postcolonial Studies* and of the National Advisory Board of the Australian Modernist Studies Network.

Candace Ward is an associate professor in the Department of English at the Florida State University, USA. She specializes in eighteenth-century British literature, early Anglo-Caribbean literature and culture, and early women's fiction. She has also worked on the editorial staff of *College*

English (1990–1992) and *South Atlantic Review* (1992–1993) and at Dover Publications (1993–1996). In 2002–2003, she was awarded a Fulbright Fellowship to the University of the West Indies, Jamaica, and an American Association of University Women postdoctoral fellowship. Her book, *Desire and Disorder: Fever, Fictions, and Feeling in English Georgian Culture* (2007), explores one of the eighteenth century's most persistent tropes, the fevered body. She is the co-editor with Tim Watson of the Broadview edition of the 1827 novel *Hamel, the Obeah Man*.

Tim Watson is an associate professor in the Department of English at the University of Miami, USA. He is the author of *Caribbean Culture and British Fiction in the Atlantic World, 1780–1870* and the co-editor with Candace Ward of the Broadview edition of the 1827 novel *Hamel, the Obeah Man*.

Kelly Wisecup is Assistant Professor of English at the Northwestern University, USA, and the author of *Medical Encounters: Knowledge and Identity in Early American Literatures* (2013). With Toni Wall Jaudon, she edited a special issue on obeah for *Atlantic Studies* (2015).

LIST OF FIGURES

CHAPTER 1

Introduction

Nicole N. Aljoe, Brycchan Carey, and Thomas W. Krise

This volume of essays on the subject of early Caribbean literature aims to provide scholars and readers with a sense of the richness and complexity of more than two centuries of English language literary works by and about people in a region marked by being the first place that the Old and New worlds collided, where a near-complete genocide was followed by the largest forced migration in history; where mass-scale deforestation was followed by the world's first monoculture; where previously unimaginable wealth helped fuel the industrialization and imperial expansion of Europe; and where those empires clashed violently and traded territories more than in other parts of the imperialized globe.

Each of the terms in "Early Caribbean Literature" is open to debate. For our purposes, "early" describes the period from the first written accounts of European contact with the Caribbean region, from 1492 onwards, until the age of Emancipation in the nineteenth century. Given

N. N. Aljoe
Department of English, Northeastern University, Boston, MA, USA

B. Carey (✉)
Department of Humanities, Northumbria University, New Castle-Upon-Tyne, UK

T. W. Krise
Department of English, Pacific Lutheran University, Tacoma, WA, USA

© The Author(s) 2018
N. N. Aljoe et al. (eds.), *Literary Histories of the Early Anglophone Caribbean*, New Caribbean Studies,
https://doi.org/10.1007/978-3-319-71592-6_1

1

that our focus is on the English-speaking colonies of the Caribbean, the main time period runs from the first permanent English settlement in St. Christopher in 1624 until the few decades that followed the British Emancipation Act in 1833. Our second term, "Caribbean," describes the islands in and close to the Caribbean Sea, as well as those continental societies that consider themselves (both in the early period and today) as being part of Caribbean society; for example, the modern states of Guyana and Belize. Finally, we define "Literature" very broadly to include the full range of both descriptive and imaginative texts written in the Caribbean region or about it, from poems, plays, and novels on the one hand to biographies, voyages, and scientific writings on the other. This expansive definition allows for texts from *The Tempest* to *Robinson Crusoe* to *Treasure Island*, but, in practice, we tend to focus on those by writers with more direct experience of the region, such as James Grainger's *The Sugar Cane*, J. W. Orderson's *Creoleana*, or Mary Seacole's *Wonderful Adventures*.

Despite this broad definition, we do acknowledge limitations to our project. In particular, the texts considered in these essays are mostly confined to those written in English. This may reflect our own interests and abilities, but it also reflects a more widespread cultural reality. While the Caribbean is home to literatures in English, Spanish, French, Dutch, Papiamento, Haitian creole, as well as a wide range of patois and creoles arising from the contact of African languages with various imperial ones, each language group tended (then and now) to pay more attention to others from their own language group than to closer neighbors who speak other languages. For instance, people in Jamaica (in the early period and today) pay closer attention to culture and events a thousand miles away in Barbados than they do to the same issues in nearby Haiti or Cuba. Similarly, French speakers in Martinique are more aware of far-away French Guiana and Haiti than they are of nearby St. Lucia or Dominica. Certain issues and events, however, such as the Haitian Revolution, drew much attention in the English-speaking Caribbean and sparked a large body of literature in English, and therefore make their way into our realm of early Anglophone Caribbean literature. Likewise, some texts and ideas were too important to remain confined to any single language community and had a wider distribution through translation, imitation, and inspiration, and chapters of this volume touch on translations from French, Spanish, German, and Dutch texts.

While we contend that early Caribbean literature is a rich and diverse body of writing, the need for this volume exists because of the relative lack of literary and textual studies of the early Caribbean. And while some Caribbean-based scholars such as Elsa Goveia, Kamau Brathwaite (writing as a trained historian), Barbara Lalla, Verene Shepherd, and Hilary McD Beckles, engaged in important foundational explorations of early Caribbean cultures, that work was often difficult to access. Historians have always accorded the region an important role in the making of the modern world but, until recent decades, literary scholars tended to treat writing concerned with the early Caribbean as a subsidiary of British or American studies. Some literary critics from the region question whether literary texts written by colonizers and slavers in the early period should be included within the definition of "Caribbean Literature" at all, and prefer to assign the literary production of the colonial period to the national and imperial literature of the colonizers, in this case, to British literature. While this is a reasonable position, in practice scholars of British literature have generally located early Caribbean writing within the category of American literature. In turn, Americanists have long tended to focus attention on the literary works by and about people living in the North American colonies that eventually became the United States. The result has been that early Caribbean literature is often overlooked by literary scholars and sometimes deliberately ignored.

The material conditions of early Caribbean publishing have had something to do with this state of affairs. When compared with the prodigious and expanding output of printing houses in eighteenth-century London, Edinburgh, Dublin, Boston, and Philadelphia, published works from the Caribbean may seem sparse; imaginative literature and *belles lettres* especially so. The relatively limited production of these texts in the Caribbean no doubt contributed to the failure of literary scholars to accord early Caribbean literature its due place in literary history, but the largely metropolitan and high-cultural interests of academics in the established universities of the English-speaking world also tended to relegate this literature to the margins until late in the twentieth century. There has nevertheless been a modest increase in academic attention to early Caribbean writing in recent years, prompted in part by broader historical and scholarly events and debates. The majority of the United Kingdom's Caribbean colonies achieved independence between 1958 and 1983 and this coincided with a period of sustained immigration into the United Kingdom from the Caribbean. Interest in the history and culture of the region improved in British universities as a result, albeit more slowly than it might have done, at the same time that scholars from across the world developed the field of postcolonial literary studies. In North America, and particularly in the United States, the twentieth-century development of early American studies, with its attendant analysis of non-literary texts via the lens of literary studies, opened the disciplinary door to treating the natural histories, travel accounts, pro- and antislavery polemics, sermons, political texts, and elements of visual culture as worthy subjects of literary attention. These developments on both sides of the Atlantic, although often more concerned with later periods and other regions, also promoted further study of the literature of the early Caribbean, albeit at their margins. There remains, however, some distance to travel before early Caribbean literature achieves the attention it deserves.

Another context for the relatively slow development of the study of early Caribbean literature has been the tendency of scholars of contemporary Caribbean literature to date the origins of the field to the earliest postcolonial writers such as C. L. R. James in the 1930s, followed by John Hearne, George Lamming, Edgar Mittelholzer, V. S. Naipaul, Samuel Selvon, Derek Walcott, and others in the post-Second World War period. Contemporary Caribbean literary critics also often restrict the definition of "Caribbean writer" to those born of Afro- and Indo-Caribbean ancestry who also continue to live and work in the region. This definition can exclude writers like Jean Rhys and V. S. Naipaul: Rhys because she was of European ancestry and left Dominica when she was 18 years of age, and Naipaul because he also left Trinidad as a young man, never to return as a permanent resident. A further complexity is that Caribbean literature has played an important role in the development of national and regional identities as the former colonies of the Caribbean became independent states. In contrast to many larger countries, however, "national" identity in the Caribbean can often be transcended by "regional" identity. In this way, achievements such as Marlon James's receipt of the 2015 Man Booker Prize for his novel, *A Brief History of Seven Killings* (2014), is a cause for great pride not just in James's Jamaica, but throughout the region. This means that defining what constitutes Caribbean literature has very real implications for the identity and sense of value of more than seven million people living in the nearly two dozen nations, colonies, and territories that make up the English-speaking Caribbean. With so many layers of complexity and importance, scholars of the early Caribbean need to be sensitive to the contemporary impact of their work.

At an organizational level, literary study of the early Caribbean arose in the context of early American studies on the one hand and early modern and eighteenth-century British literary studies on the other. In the early 1990s, early Americanist literary scholars in the United States created two societies devoted to ensuring that the colonial and early national period of American literature received attention in the American Literature Association and the American Society for Eighteenth-Century Studies (ASECS). Those two early American literature societies merged under the name of the Society of Early Americanists in 1999. Meanwhile, Caribbean literature of the twentieth century began to draw attention from the 1980s onward. Issues of postcolonialism and other literary theories, as well as the subjects of race, class, and gender, made the Caribbean a site of particular interest and complexity. Literature departments across North America and in the United Kingdom, Australia, and New Zealand began to hire Caribbean specialists. Scholars of eighteenth-century Britain and colonial North America also began to take notice of the Caribbean as a nexus for theoretical issues that gained interest in the 1980s and 1990s. Using the model of the Society of Early Americanists, a group of scholars interested in the early Caribbean founded the Early Caribbean Society (ECS) in 2002 to promote the representation of the Caribbean in various scholarly society conferences throughout the Caribbean, the United States, the United Kingdom, and elsewhere. In the early 2010s, the ECS conducted a series of symposia, which included scholars from Australia, the Caribbean, the United Kingdom, and the United States meeting in St. James, Barbados; San Juan, Puerto Rico; and London, United Kingdom. Research presented at these symposia contributed substantially to the essays included in the present volume.

The ECS fulfils an important scholarly need. Early Caribbeanists, like Early Americanists, tend to be somewhat isolated institutionally. Universities rarely have more than one such specialist on the faculty, making the international scholarly association all the more important to the exchange of ideas and the support for individual scholars' research agendas. Despite this apparent isolation, however, many other scholars of British, American, or literatures in English are finding connections between their scholarly interests and texts from the early Caribbean. The present volume was accordingly conceived as a way to provide both dedicated early Caribbeanists as well as scholars and readers with related or even tangential interests with a set of literary historical essays to orient their research into the early literature of the region and to provoke questions for further study. As a relatively new field of literary inquiry, early Caribbean literature is beginning to develop anthologies and editions of texts for use in classrooms, and some Caribbean texts have been included in standard classroom anthologies of British and American literature over the past decade or so. At the same time, there is increasing recognition of the part that the Caribbean has played more broadly in the development of literatures in English from the early modern and eighteenth-century periods onwards. As the essays in this volume demonstrate, early Caribbean literature touches on issues that transcend the early modern world and have important implications for classroom and civic discussions about issues including colonialism and neo-imperialism, racism and ethnic identity, religion and ideology, capitalism and trade, and exploitation and warfare. The region also plays an important role in the development of academic disciplines and literary genres from natural history to journalism, and from the novel to the georgic. Some of the most potent portrayals of race, racism, slavery, piracy, and adventurers also originate in the Caribbean. As an emerging field of academic study, early Caribbean literary history has immense potential to transform our understanding of both the early Caribbean itself and the many broader discourses which it generated and sustained.

Literary Histories of the Early Anglophone Caribbean: Islands in the Stream builds on the important work of earlier Caribbean-based scholars and comprises work by scholars from Australia, the Caribbean, North America, and the United Kingdom. Some of the authors come to the field of early Caribbean literature from a position of expertise in other regions and specialties, yet all have early Caribbean studies at the heart of their research. The collective goal of this volume is to provide other scholars and readers with considerations of the literary historical context within which to situate key issues for further study. To facilitate this, the collection brings to bear a wide range of theoretical and methodological approaches, as well as offering readings of a broad selection of texts from across the Caribbean world in the seventeenth, eighteenth, and nineteenth centuries.

The opening chapters of the volume seek to recover lost or overlooked facets of the early Caribbean, from indigenous cultures to medical discourse and the evangelical experience. In Chap. 2, Keith Sandiford explores memory and rememory. Reading the pre-Columbian archives collected in the work of Ricardo E. Alegría (1978) and Louis Allaire's work on the Island Caribs of the Lesser Antilles (1973) alongside Father Ramon Pane's *Relación Acerca de las Antigüedades de los Indios* (1498) and William Earle's *Obi; or, The History of Three-Fingered Jack* (1800),

Sandiford uses current notions of memory as an analytical tool to explore a paradigm of early Caribbean literary history that privileges the mythic consciousness and material culture of indigenous Caribbean people, and the occult knowledge and revolutionary imaginary of transplanted African slaves. In Chap. 3, Sue Thomas examines early Caribbean evangelical life narratives, reading a range of these narratives dating from 1768 to 1835, to show that they offer evidence of the historical soundscapes of plantation slavery cultures and the complex processes of creolization and translation in the inscription of lives. She thereby highlights the literary and historical significance of a genre of West Indian writing usually overlooked in accounts of the early Caribbean. In Chap. 4, Kelly Wisecup focuses on botanist and physician Hans Sloane's case studies of disease in his *Voyage to Jamaica* (1707–25), Benjamin Moseley's medical tracts, and James Grainger's georgic poem *The Sugar Cane* (1764) to call for new methodologies for studying the medical cultures of the early Caribbean that attend to Afro-Caribbean knowledge and practices and to colonists' strategies of domination, as well as to moments when African knowledge shaped not just the content but also the form of colonial writing.

The essays in the central section of the volume are largely concerned with strategies of testimony, reportage, and representation. In Chap. 5, Jo Anne Harris examines *Caribbeana*, a collection of entries first printed by Samuel Keimer in the *Barbados Gazette* (1732–38), to argue that as creoles challenged imperial authority and responded to London's metropolitan discourse, they acquired the legal, political, and cultural means to act as agents for their own economic interests and that the changing tone and shifting viewpoints of the essays, poetry, and debates published in both the *Barbados Gazette* and *Caribbeana* reflected the genesis of a literary metamorphosis from imperial to creole. In Chap. 6, Nicole N. Aljoe, reads "The Speech of John Talbot Campo-Bell," a response to "The Speech of Moses Bon Sa'am" (1736), which was reported to be that of a Maroon leader exhorting a crowd that included slaves to retaliate against the system of enslavement by attacking Jamaican plantation owners, to argue that the narrative reveals the importance of slave voices to early print culture in the Caribbean as well as important details about slave lives, and that the fact that its message is profoundly mediated should not inhibit close readings of the text. In Chap. 7, Richard Frohock looks beyond the celebrated story of female pirates Anne Bonny and Mary Read to consider how stories of female captives are used to articulate the attributes of male captors. Reading Woodes Rogers's *Cruising Voyage Round the World* (1712),

Exquemelin's *Buccaneers of America* (1678), and Charles Johnson's *A General History of the Pyrates* (1724), Frohock argues that looking beyond Bonny and Read generates new insights about the role of women and the limits of egalitarian qualities of piratical societies as represented in key eighteenth-century piracy narratives.

The last three chapters of this volume consider questions of literary form and literary genre. In Chap. 8, Candace Ward and Tim Watson examine two early novels in English produced by authors resident in the Caribbean, Cynric Williams's *Hamel, the Obeah Man* (1827) and E. L. Joseph's *Warner Arundell: The Adventures of a Creole* (1838), to show that their attempts to produce an expansive account of Caribbean society forced them to include a wide array of characters, voices, and points of view, including ones that were ostensibly at odds with their authors' political positions, but this expansiveness reiterates the need to consider these works as a crucial part of Caribbean literary history. In Chap. 9, Brycchan Carey surveys the treatment of the early Caribbean in a wide range of satirical literature and argues that the eighteenth-century satirists who represented the Caribbean increasingly saw the region as a location of vice that stood in need of correction, and that as the eighteenth century progressed the chief iniquities they calumniated were slavery and the slave trade. Thus, satirists became as much a part of the literary proto-abolitionist movement as did the sentimental poets and novelists whose work has been more intensively studied. In Chap. 10, the closing essay of this volume, Cassander Smith asks what is the critical and historical relationship between early Caribbean literature and modern-day Caribbean literature, for whom does it matter, and how do the meanings of authorship and authority transform when we consider texts that register multiple voices and experiences that do not simply appear in the texts but help to shape those very texts? To answer these questions, she examines two narratives that relate the legend of "Inkle and Yarico," Richard Ligon's *A True and Exact History of the Island of Barbadoes* (1657) and Beryl Gilroy's novel *Inkle and Yarico* (1996). She concludes her essay, and the volume as whole, by arguing that when we approach early Caribbean literature from multicultural perspectives, we construct a literary history that matters not just to a narrow group of mostly American and European scholars working in the early modern period but also for those who study in and about the region today.

Taken together, these essays offer new perspectives and original research into a broad range of writing concerning the early Caribbean, and it is our hope that they will stimulate further discussion, exploration, and scholarly collaboration. Indeed, a volume such as this is a truly cooperative venture, and many people have contributed to its publication. The editors would like to thank all the contributors for their enthusiasm for this project and their patience in seeing it come to fruition. We would also like to thank our institutions, Northeastern University, Northumbria University, and Pacific Lutheran University, for their support and encouragement. We are grateful to the scholarly societies within which the Early Caribbean Society has developed, especially the American and British Societies for Eighteenth-Century Studies (ASECS and BSECS) and the Society of Early Americanists (SEA). We thank Palgrave Macmillan, and in particular our editors Brigitte Shull, Tomas Rene, and Shruthi Ramakrishna. And New Caribbean series editors Shalini Puri and Kofi Campbell, for having confidence in our project and seeing the manuscript through to publication. Finally, we would like to extend a special vote of thanks to all the members of the Early Caribbean Society, past, present, and future, for their enthusiasm and collegiality in the ongoing project of defining and promoting the field of early Caribbean literary history.

CHAPTER 2

"Memory, Rememory, and the Moral Constitution of Caribbean Literary History"

Keith Sandiford

The project of elaborating a literary history is a work of remembering. It is so in a threefold permutation of what it means to remember. First, the editors and essayists of the project will remember in the common meaning of revisiting the Caribbean past, to look again at its archives, to recollect the voices found therein, and to make those voices speak anew to the present. Second, that enterprise will remember as a river remembers. Especially when they have been channelized, straightened, diverted, or otherwise turned away from their natural courses, rivers, in their episodes of periodic flooding, compel us to acknowledge that rivers too remember. As Toni Morrison reminds us, they are always trying to get back to where they were.[1] In like manner, editors and contributors to this anthology will by conscious acts of will, mind, and imagination be trying to restore the subjects of early Caribbean texts to the proper status of agency which history has often denied them. This kind of remembering will trace the streams of indigenous Caribbean and diasporic African peoples' consciousnesses back to their mythic sources, to understand their true relation to time and mind, to help them "get back to where they were." Third, a literary history conceived in these terms will perform the work of remembering in a

K. Sandiford (✉)
Department of English, Louisiana State University, Baton Rouge, LA, USA

© The Author(s) 2018
N. N. Aljoe et al. (eds.), *Literary Histories of the Early Anglophone Caribbean*, New Caribbean Studies,
https://doi.org/10.1007/978-3-319-71592-6_2

very originary sense of the word: it will perform the very patient work of recovering and putting together again the scattered parts (the membra, in the literal Latin etymology) of bodies that primordially reproduced their ontologies and cosmologies through oral, ritual, and artifactual practices, then had these relationships written into European consciousness by European subjects, and still later wrote accounts that attempt to contest, correct, and resist colonial representations, and begin the long process of redeeming their consciousnesses on their own terms. Positioned at this juncture in the early twenty-first century, this volume continues that process in the ways the essayists seek to codify, document, interpret, critique, and theorize the archives of Caribbean consciousness. Most importantly, though, these practitioners seek to advance how we understand those archives in ways that help us to rethink the archives' imaginary nature, and to define the greater cultural imaginary in which they were produced.

Invoking the expansive category of the "greater cultural imaginary" provides certain opportunities and foregrounds certain issues, conflicts, and contradictions that underlie and trouble the possibilities of a construct called "Caribbean literary history." From these issues I want to formulate the following questions that this essay will address. What relations to history should such a project establish? What relations to literature should it define? Given the power of hegemonic colonialities to determine historiographical and literary practices, and given the power of colonized masses to subvert and contest these practices, where should a critic look to fix the inflection point of these agonistic powers, and thence define a set of relevant models for this project? How might that inflection point suggest sources and alternatives (forms and contents) that would articulate with those models? Respecting the disparate ethnogeneses of indigenous Caribbean and Afro-Caribbean peoples, how best to represent the implicit cultural differences? How best to valorize appropriately the experiential commonalities, the material, mythic and metaphysical linkages that may be recovered from exploring their signifying systems?

For the guidance of readers, I supply here a descriptive outline of the essay's main parts. Immediately following this roadmap, I provide an introduction to the primary texts I have chosen to illustrate the conceptual and theoretical issues laid out in the essay's foregrounds. Following that section, I will sketch out some central definitions for memory and rememory, with key identifications of certain theorists and intellectual sources who offer suitable foundations for the arguments I develop in this essay. Next, I will advance some approaches to the major questions framed for the essay and engage some of the relevant critical positions to be found in the writings of Caribbean authors and other intellectuals who have addressed issues of literature and history of specific relevance to the region's peoples. This engagement will foreground some key conceptual terms with which to define Caribbean literary history. And finally, I will select thematic and structural aspects of the essay's primary reference texts, using them to illustrate the implications of the questions laid out in the preceding parts, with the objective of verifying the consistency of textual contents with the strategic and theoretical contents of the essay.

The primary reference texts which this essay will introduce shortly and focus on more substantively in the final section are spread wide apart in historical provenance, and differ significantly in genre and thematic contents. The first is Father Ramon Pane's (pronounced Pah-nay) *Relación Acerca de las Antigüedades de los Indios* (*An Account of the Antiquities of the Indians*), completed in his Spanish original in 1498, and first translated into English by Edward Gaylor Bourne in 1906).[2] The second is William Earle, Jr's *Obi; or, The History of Three-Fingered Jack* (1800), an epistolary novella written by English hands.

A Jeronimite father, Ramon Pane arrived in the Indies in 1494 and lived among the Taino for two years.[3] Following instructions from Columbus, Pane collected information about their language, mores, myths, and cosmology that clearly served the interests of the Catholic Church and the imperial Spanish state. The *Antiquities* hold the distinction of being the first ethnographic records of an indigenous Caribbean (or Latin American) community, setting down certain defining origin narratives (of the Taino, their gods, the cosmos) with equally essential accounts about their rites, and their beliefs about sex, gender, and healing, among other things.

The biographical record on William Earle is perplexingly sparse.[4] Probably born in England in 1781, he was the son of a well-known London bookseller. Author of two dramatic works, *Natural Faults* (1799) and *The Villagers* (date unknown), Earle appears to have sought and found spectacular public notoriety very early in life: he became embroiled in a controversy alleging that he had plagiarized the play *First Faults*. For defaming a respectable tradesman he spent six months in prison. A reputed abolitionist sympathizer, he is also believed to have spent time in Jamaica. Earle's *Obi; or, The History of Three-Fingered Jack* is a narrative of slavery, rebellion, witchcraft, terror, and brutal death, capturing the profound climate of revolutionary angst hanging over Britain and her West Indian colonies at the turn of the century.

While I treat it more substantively in the essay's final section, I will preview here my rationale for pairing these two very disparate texts. Though specifically produced under Spanish auspices, the contents of Pane's *Antiquities* were collected at the foundational moment for the formulation of European ideologies of conquest, colonization, and empire; ideologies that legitimated the subjugation of the Taino and other indigenous populations, and the enslavement of the diasporic African communities who came later. As Pane's text brought Europeans face-to-face with ethnic diversity in cultural practices (especially the Taino's mystifying worship of zemis), so Earle's novella brought English readers face-to-face with the occult practices of African-derived obeah and a protagonist-practitioner who threatened to use it to revolutionize the colonial system in Jamaica at the onset of abolition. As Earle's text marked a destabilizing moment for the slavocratic system, so Pane's text marked a destabilizing moment for the Taino, who would face appropriation of their homelands and ultimate existential decimation and, equally, a paradoxical destabilizing of European consciousness about the geography and ethnography of the world.

That the indigenous Taino and the transplanted Africans should figure a problematic relationship to history is unsurprising. Both groups entered European historical consciousness by acts of forcible propulsion: the first by accidental "discovery" and opportunistic conquest, the second by coerced diaspora and dehumanizing slavery. Their separate and collective experiences under colonialism produced accounts that defined their relationships to history in terms of archaism, oblivion, rupture, invisibility, erasure, and nightmare. Columbus and successive Spanish chroniclers repeatedly constructed the Caribbean indigenous in terms of unsophisticated culture, docility, and nakedness, traits which marked them as existing outside of Western time, civilization, and consciousness, and therefore ripe for political subjugation and incorporation into those categories. Columbus' early journal entry prefigures these motives: "Weapons they have none, nor are acquainted with them, for I showed them swords which they grasped by the blades, and cut themselves through ignorance. They have no iron … They all go completely naked… It appears to me, that the people are ingenious, and would be good servants and I am of opinion that they would very readily become Christians, as they appear to have no religion."[5] This foundational assessment, followed by the implementation of Spanish colonial policies that produced starvation, disease, and large-scale slaughter, easily validated a narrative of absolute existential erasure. What developed into a practically universal consensus about Taino extinction has over the past three decades become the subject of re-evaluation and revision.[6] The absence of letters and their concomitant scribal codes and institutions functioned equally to place early Caribbean colonized peoples at a distinct disadvantage for reading, interpreting, critiquing, or making formal literate responses in cases where interpretation, debate, and discursive skill would otherwise be valued forms of engagement. The presentation of the Requerimiento (1513) to illiterate native people, and Fr. Ramon Pane's resistance to Taino narrative authority provide two categorical illustrations of silencing, exclusion, and inequality which would define the relationships of the colonized to literature. The official proclamation of Spain's rights of conquest, appropriation, and enslavement, and the duty of the natives to submit and obey on penalty of imprisonment or death, the Requerimiento was typically read in Latin or Spanish, to people who neither spoke nor understood either of those languages, and sometimes, absurdly, to empty beaches and deserted villages. Pane's research established him as the first ethnographer of the Americas. But the undisputed value of his book's contents aside, his representation of the Taino reveals some of his limitations as a European observer who cannot escape his ethnocentric biases and preconceptions. In Chapters 2–6, Pane records a narrative in which a man called Guahayona abducts a large number of women to another island, persuading them first to abandon their husbands and later their children. It is a complicated and mystifying story of deception and treachery, overweening greed, and carnal desire. Clearly confounded by the opacities of the different language and cultural beliefs shaping the story, and resisting the power accorded to myth, fable, and the irrational in the narrative, twice within those chapters Pane attributes his failure to comprehend meanings not to barriers posed for him by language or cultural difference but to the illiteracy of the Taino. He wrote "And because they have neither letters nor writing, they do not know how to tell such fables well, nor can I write them well. Therefore, I believe I put first what ought to be last and the last first."[7] Coming from a non-native laboring under the disadvantages mentioned above, his responses of incomprehension and incredulity, and his critique of incommensurability define the nature of the problem. They all confirm the reader's skepticism about his competency to judge Taino story-telling skills.

His ethnographic commentary carries a number of presuppositions that prejudice the credibility of the Taino as tellers of their own stories and therefore impugn their relationship to language. First, the commentary presupposes that narrative skill is dependent on the existence of literate (scribal) models. Second, his commentary suggests that he had some a priori knowledge of the story's plot. Third, that there exist some normative (universal?) criteria on which the truth value of a story (even a story from a wholly unfamiliar culture) may be determined. Here, then, lie certain answers to the question of early Caribbean literary relations: when mediated through the agency of a state, church, or some other ideological interest, those relations are almost always shaped by the designs of those interests. Commonly, the authority of native voices is dialogized by inhospitable or downright hostile reluctance to native truth claims. Almost always, too, the impetus to disseminate stories from the indigenous or the colonized transplants is mediated by an intent to control the production and circulation of such stories.

For its relevance to memory and to memory's narrative and ideological functions in this essay, I will invoke David Scott's scholarship on the archive and the archival.[8] Scott's formulations serve not merely to mark points of authority and concurrence for this discussion, but also to indicate how the re-emergence of memory as a postcolonial practice can be harnessed to underwrite the methodological criteria for a project of Caribbean literary history.

My preoccupation in this essay with the ways memory and myth interpenetrate one another draws on Wilson Harris' vision of this complex relation. In his fiction and essays, Harris always assigns intrinsic value to the capacity of rites to unveil the power of myth in the continuum of time. He searches in his ideology of mythic consciousness for "a philosophy of history [that] may well lie buried in the arts of the imagination," specifically naming limbo, vodun, Carib bush-baby omens, Arawak zemi, Latin, and English inheritances. He emphasizes, "my concern is with epic stratagems available to Caribbean man in the dilemmas of history which surround him."[9] The uses of the imagination, memory, and myth strongly argue that in this project we are embarked on nothing less than a history of consciousness fashioned from the memories of Caribbean peoples' traumas, from the power of their unfettered imaginations to recover narratives from the past to inform the present and envision the future.

William Earle's reproduction of Three-Fingered Jack as a subject of memory suggests the possibility that his novella may serve as its own critique of theory. The will to remember should find one archetype in Three-Fingered Jack's purposeful determination to honor his father's moral legacy first by the patient reception of his father's narrative bestowed on him as an oral gift by his mother. With him patience quickly hardened into the unbending resolution of filial duty. The private pact he made to remember the crimes of slave traders against his father launched him on a career where the sacred piety of bequeathed memory doggedly pursues the secular motives of a materialist history. Jack's willingness to spread terror and disrupt the regime of slave power inscribes itself on the public consciousness as an inerasable fact with the force of a rememory—persistent, repeatable, indelible.

On Toni Morrison's dramatic emplotment of the concept in *Beloved* I am going to ground the transhistorical continuities of rememory in both Pane's *Antiquities* and Earle's *Three-Fingered Jack*. Morrison defines rememory as an object, something that can lie in wait for you, that you could bump into in a random place. It is traumatic memory which may materialize as a persona, place, or other phenomenon, animated by its own volition, capable of being shared by many who have experienced it in common.[10] The elements of trauma, ancestral materialization, and the sacralization of place and object in Taino rites and beliefs illustrate the self-evidence of rememory. Sethe delivers her apprehension of its meaning with a mystifying heuristic intentionality: "If a house burns down, it's gone, but the place – the picture of it – stays, and not just in my rememory, but out there, in the world. What I remember is a picture floating around there outside my head. I mean, even if I don't think about it, even if I die, the picture of what I did, or knew, or saw is still out there."[11] That indomitable will becomes action in the protracted standoffs and murders Jack staged from his local retreats in caves and mountains of Jamaica, in the sensational plays and pantomimes based on his life and produced on various Atlantic stages (mainly Fawcett and Arnold's pantomime in London and New York, extending from 1800 through the 1830s). Jack's relationship to the mythic values of caves and to the cultural flows of circum-Atlantic productions will in the analysis to follow be established as a certifiable Caribbean episteme.

The Caribbean social theorist Sylvia Wynter identifies Caribbean epistemes as "flows of creative energy related to myth and ontology."[12] The Caribbean episteme may be deployed as an explanatory tool for the illumination of obeah as a religion, a politics, and a metaphysics in Three-Fingered Jack's case. Similarly, the practices of obeah, myal, and marronage among the Maroons, and ritual practices of Maroon fete men and fete women involving spirit possessions and visitations, as well as elements associated with Kromanti play manifest certifiable epistemic power.[13] These categories name a complex of cosmological systems which would help to define the moral constitution I am attempting to reconstruct. What interests me most about these systems is the way they secrete themselves even across colonial societies sharply divided along racial, ethnic, and class lines. Jack personified both the public expression of shared memory and the elusive mystification of hidden knowledge and occult power. In Maroon narratives concerning eighteenth- and nineteenth-century events (in war, tracking fugitive slaves, battling enemy spirits), Kromanti practitioners test their spiritual power against that of other adversarial forces in what Kenneth Bilby calls contests to assert "Maroon spiritual superiority," each contest a veritable "life or death struggle."[14] We are hardly likely to bump into an episteme as a physical artifact, not even on a literal archaeological dig. Still, none of this should deter theorists and critics engaged in the labor of producing a literary history from foundations grounded in creative flows of ontology and myth.

Turning next to the compound question, where to fix the inflection point between hegemonic discursive power and delegitimized but subversive power, one confronts the issue of defining relevant models for a project like this. Relevant here need not mean new; indeed, as often happens, the search for alternatives may take us back to sources and origins, to the known but perhaps forgotten, to the familiar but perhaps overlooked. The codes of the Requerimiento and of colonial ethnography demonstrate a patent complicity between history and literature that renders their related methods and presuppositions suspect for what should be a decolonizing praxis. Attempting to pursue such a praxis, it is instructive to recollect the original statements and subsequent debates among Caribbean intellectuals that have framed the consequences of the history/literature complicity as a "quarrel with history," as defined by Derek Walcott.[15] Consistent with the signs of indigenous intentionality in Pane's account, a strong impetus has emerged from those debates to find alternatives in non-scribal and non-literary sources to what might otherwise be paralysis or impasse. Stipulating to the persistence of the "quarrel," Walcott has chosen to circumscribe it by deeming history "irrelevant" and declaring his own independence from it. Abjuring the nostalgia for monuments and ruins, Walcott turns to the Caribbean's geography, vegetation, and common scenes for ruins and of diurnal life to honor buried lives of slaves and to recover memories of the past. In his poem "Almond Trees," Walcott indicates not that history is unimportant or totally absent, but rather to be found in the subtle, not always visible, interplay of humans, animals, light, seascape, landscape which can together produce a painterly effect that seems to "amaze the sun" itself.[16]

As an alternative to literature, and to the literariness of history, the Caribbean debate and a strong current in postcolonial thought privilege orality and often find the composite term "orature" better suited to define the region's narrative forms. Cultural theorist and rare poetic imagination, Kamau Brathwaite exemplifies this approach to orality and orature in the evolution of his original poetic technique as well as in his critical essays. His thesis is that the essential resources of Caribbean language are to be found not in canonical texts but submerged within the spoken word, sound, song, story, and noise of the people and their environment. These resources he denominates as "nation language," a category to be distinguished from the highly individualized practices of "literate" reading, and the institutions and technologies that support and perpetuate it. Brathwaite writes:

> Reading is an isolated, individualistic expression. The oral tradition, on the other hand, makes demands not only on the poet but also on the audience to complete the community: the noise and sounds that the poet makes are responded to by the audience and are returned to him. Hence we have the creation of a continuum where the meaning truly resides. And this total expression comes about because people live in the openair, because people live in conditions of poverty, because people come from a historical experience where they had to rely on their own breath patterns rather than on paraphernalia like books and museums. They had to depend on immanence, the power within themselves, rather than the technology outside themselves.[17]

Some cultural scholars extend Brathwaite's multivoiced language to include ritual practices, dance, movement, and folktales. The telling of folktales and the performance of dance and ritual movement require a dedicated investment in memory and in the power of the imagination.

Both memory and the imagination are central to the methodologies and the archival matrices embedded in the principal illustrative texts of this essay. Memory and the imagination persist in the conceptual categories of alternatives given in Caribbean critical and theoretical writing. In his highly original and provocative essay on the subject of the "quarrel with history," Edward Baugh situates imagination above history, ascribing to imagination an obligatory function in the production of cultural identity: "Histories can reside in places other than monuments or written texts."[18]

As has been demonstrated in the Taino narrative tale, and as will be shown in Earle's novella, memory can often be found to reciprocate and collude with processes that promote the durability of myth. The uses of the imagination, memory, and myth strongly argue that in this project we are embarked on nothing less than a history of consciousness fashioned from the memories of Caribbean peoples' traumas, from the power of their unfettered imaginations to recover narratives from the past to inform the present and envision the future.

Pairing the indigenous and diasporic communities in this essay to theorize the grounds for a literary history should highlight both commonalities and linkages as well as cultural differences. Because the commonalities offer the strongest tools for the task at hand, I will quickly sketch out some significant differences and then return to devote more space and emphasis to the similitudes.

That the Taino indigenous and the African implanted held categorically different relationships to the land springs foremost to mind in this comparison. Claims of birth and ancestry legitimized the one, where the uneasy conditions of alienation and diaspora shaped the consciousness of the other. But the differentiating factor of the journey (the Middle Passage) marks a critical condition separating the colonial experiences of the two groups. The rigors and traumatic consequences of a long journey inspired and reproduced diasporic memories in ways that set the Africans apart from the indigenous. Without any desire to minimize the experiences of the indigenous or to adduce arbitrary criteria for a false equivalency, this selection from a list developed by Monica Schuler emphasizes the distinctive consequences of captivity followed by a long oceanic voyage: separation from family and familiar surroundings; sensory and physical deprivation; long periods of physical immobility; dehydration; depression and probable hallucinations. On the side of similitudes, there is no need here to recite the widely documented particulars of uprooting, dispossession, the atrocities of torture, rape, and murder, and the loss of freedom and patrimony. These are now largely undisputed. Thus we can advance the discourse by crystallizing from the particulars some persistent themes, thence establishing a conceptual vocabulary with which to think through the issues on this side of the divide.

First, there is an inescapable principle of unity binding the two colonized communities that is ratified by their oppressed conditions, by their sharing the same living spaces (sometimes collusively, sometimes adversarially), and by the ways they leveraged proximity into contacts that shaped the region's diverse history. These relations inscribe a unity that over time became inherent, indivisible, organic. I interpret Kamau Brathwaite's epigrammatic "the unity is submarine" not only as an allusion to the originary role of the sea in connecting these people, but also as a reference to the often unrecognized (invisible, imperceptible) flows and currents of blood, language, custom, and cuisine that evidence the two peoples' cultural exchanges over time and space. Invoked above, the figure of collusion reminds us that cohabitation in adjacent neighborhoods (in Jamaica, Cuba, and Hispaniola) facilitated strategic cooperation to confront the common threat of European oppression. These connections, accidental or deliberate, should make us more mindful of what Edouard Glissant calls this "complicity of relation," which should drive us "back to the point of entanglement from which we were forcefully turned away."[19] This would appear to be a rich conceptual space from which to recover forms of subjectivity and intersubjectivity illustrating the dynamic processes of ethnogenetic formation that creolized the identities of the two groups. Glissant's figure suggests a forceful deflection or diversion; it emphasizes the persistent themes of loss and absence that permeate the groups' consciousnesses. Separation from material objects and meaningful social relationships shaped them as subjects of mourning and nostalgia; by some measures of more drastic accounting, separation rendered both peoples victims of "kidnapped memory," and therefore "condemned to amnesia."[20] But the intelligent use of these projects should remind us that not all kidnappings are fatal, and that some amnesias are indeed reversible. Our resources for imagining the theoretical possibilities of freeing kidnapped memories and reversing amnesias may be significantly enriched by considering the paradoxical uses of a strategy Gregorio Kohon calls "retroactive interpretation of events." By retroactively inscribing the Conquest and its deprivations into their precolonial omens and messages from the gods, Kohon writes, pre-Columbian Caribbeans ascribed to colonial events the character of inevitability "and this allowed them an easier acceptance of whatever events happened to take place since they had been announced."[21]

I pass now to the final movement of this essay, in which I want to illustrate how Pane's *Antiquities* and Earle's epistolary fiction *Three-Fingered Jack* would furnish a fertile casebook for the definition of a new literary history on the terms I have set out earlier in this essay. My strategy will invoke memory, aggregating to it and supplementing it with the compelling power of rememory, to explore how these together inform the thematic ideas, comparative mentalities, and shared imaginaries represented in the texts.

The habits of orality deployed in the Taino's cosmogonic imagination of the narrative past establish memory for the Taino as the portal to consciousness and the unconscious, the magical access to time, timelessness, and myth. Narrative memory frames the paradigms of tribal belief about the origins of time, the genesis of men and women (with specific accounts of their gender differentiation), the characters of their deities and chiefs, and the emergence of floral and faunal species, among other phenomena. Besides these explanatory functions, memory serves the moral objectives of admonishing the people against disobedience to gods and parents,[22] and against negligence and inattention to social duties.[23] Transmitted musically through the medium of songs (areitos) to the accompaniment of music, the laws of their society are codified in popular form for the guidance of their children and the governance of their men and women: "Like the Moors, they have their religion set forth in ancient chants by which they are governed, as the Moors are by their Scripture. When they sing their chants, they play an instrument called mayohavau that is made of wood and is hollow, strong, yet very thin, an ell long and half as wide."[24] But one pervasive theme that shapes the imaginary of the Taino and projects them through the timelessness of their own myths into the time of modernity inaugurated by colonialism is the theme of loss and absence. Some instances of this theme suggest ways to recover the processual meanings of Taino action and belief in the recurrence of certain subthemes: exodus and migration are exemplified in Guahayona's abduction of the women, patricide and filicide are both bound up in the fable of a son who wants to kill his father, Yaya, but is exiled and subsequently killed by his father. Founded both in the revealed foreknowledge of Yucahuguama (Yucahu), one of the highest Taino deities, and in the powerful indicia of narrative foreshadowings, the contingencies of migration, exile, and societal disruption all presage the invasion of colonizing forces. Yucahu was reported to have told a cacique "that those who remained alive after his death would enjoy their dominion for but a brief time because a clothed people would come to their land who would overcome them and kill them, and they would die of hunger."[25] Notwithstanding the dread of this prognostication and the dire inconvenience of its historical truth, the theme of loss and absence still exerts certain salutary and socially redemptive consequences when located within the workings of myth and metamorphosis. Four identical brothers entered Yaya's (the main god's) cave, took and ate the fishes contained in a gourd but could not rehang the gourd in its proper place. The gourd fell to the earth, spilling its contents, which were the incarnation of Yaya's son. Those fishes were transformed and filled the earth with water which became the ocean.[26] Disobedience and dereliction of duty bring retributive justice. For returning late to his post as night watchman of the Taino cave of origins, Macacoel was abducted by the Sun and turned into stone. Others from the tribe were captured and turned into hog plum trees.[27] In another transgressive fable, Yahubaba was sent out to pick a certain plant used by the people to bathe themselves. Venturing out before dawn (apparently prohibited), he was caught by the Sun and turned into a bird (a nightingale). While scholars of Caribbean ethnology and archaeology have shown these myths and fables to have been susceptible to manipulation both by the Taino tellers and by the Spanish researcher, it is evident that for the Taino they represented a coherent narrative of cosmographic and ontologic origins, of the roots of conflict and rebellion, of the fluid relations of humans with nature.[28] What is even more instructive is that these vagaries and transformations belie the Western narrative of these early societies as being frozen in archaic stasis without the possibility of change or development before the conquerors came. Metamorphosis, to paraphrase Wilson Harris, is a conceit with which to escape the absolutisms and fixities, the traumas and losses, to imagine the present and future as the gifts of a fluid inheritance. In one of his essays where he relates loss to metamorphosis, Harris writes:

> The loss of absolute quantity in the nothingness of the past or in multiplications of meaninglessness in the future is a failure to encompass numbers in material exactitude. But the shadow that flows through such loss or failure transforms itself into music or rhythm which seems to take us beyond the grasp of words. And yet it brings most closely to attention the scope of language to find a Presence out of partial liberation combining and recombining into trial and metamorphosis. Nothing is taken for granted, nothing is final, in the pursuit of a Presence that lives through apparent negatives, it seems, which harbor 'levitation and change,' or transfigured things in the vulnerable, awakening consciousness of humanity.[29]

The tropes of combining, recombining, and metamorphosis are stabilized aesthetically as phases in the re-membering of loss and absence that is the whole object of memory.

As the Taino children received the law through song narratives from their elders, so Jack inherited a narrative legacy that assumed for him the force of law. Powerfully operating on Jack's imagination from his tender boyhood days, memory is the central animating impulse for all his life's willed heroic actions. And it must be emphasized that his mother is the source through whom he receives the narrative of the legacy he was sworn to honor, the account of those crimes against his kindred he was determined to avenge. Born after his father's (Makro's) death at the cowardly hands of Captain Harrop, and three months after his mother entered slavery in Jamaica, he heard the narrative surrounding those events from her compelling lips. Upon that foundation he layers successive accretions of narratives both precedent to and contemporaneous with his parents' personal narratives. He processed and made his own Amri's retelling of the perfidy of the Europeans who captured her and Makro, in spite of their generosity and hospitality toward the white strangers in Gambia. Amri unhesitatingly re-members to her son the separate infliction of five hundred stripes upon her and his father. Jack re-members in his own body another five hundred he personally suffered after his arrest as a fugitive slave. The live burning of his grandfather Feruarue, charged with practicing obeah and leading a slave revolt, cooperated with all these to reproduce the transgenerational nature of traumatic memory from parent to child, from slave to slave. These are the materials from which he later constructs the very real essentials of a Feloop imaginary. Two theoretical abstracts can be derived from this family narrative. First, Amri's role in prefiguring the agenda for Jack's agency in secular history and symbolic memory establishes the role of the slave mother in mediating the course of her child's initiation into the knowledge of social duties and into the part he must play in what Walter Benjamin calls the "theatre of the social mind."[30] What Amri inscribed in her son's memory effectively takes on the character of an episteme, capable of displacing or disrupting the master narratives of history, science, and imperialism.[31] Hers is a conscious act of the will, the likes of which are repeated by Sethe in Morrison's *Beloved*. In his focus on that novel, Satya Mohanty reads the gesture of remembering as a key feature of the moral and historical imagination.[32] What Jack does with it positions his agency at the nodal points where flows converge. He adopts it as a personal obligation to avenge crimes against family. That obligation is experienced as an internal prompting, an inner voice that validates the memory as his own, stamps the memory as coherent with his own identity. If these conditions are sometimes understood as the grounds on which individuals "imagine" identities, Jack demonstrates the will to transform private memory into a social and cultural imaginary. Earle's epistolary narrator draws this portrait of the young slave: "His youthful fiery soul led him to imagine himself the destroyer of all Europe; he saw in the warlike picture his fancy drew, the course he was to follow, and the transport of his heart was often visible by the uncommon hauteur of his manners."[33] Coming within the first two pages of the narrative, this clear statement of a resolve to reverse and revise the order of history signifies a very early moment of transcendence; it is the moment when his memory quest is transformed from the status of an individual vendetta to the status of an imperative to achieve a social objective. Jack's passionate embrace of the identity marker "Feloop" (somewhat problematic, but not surprising, what with the blurrings of ethnicity that slavery caused) redefines the nature of his quest in terms that are patriotic and nationalistic.[34] The imaginary, Kerwin Lee Klein tells us, has an express agency in "securing perpetual affective bonds."[35] The Feloop imaginary would be fueled from the streams of collective memory which have the power to heal trauma and to dictate the terms of revisionist history.

In both Pane and Earle, rememory bears its own relations to collective memory and to revisionist history. Here revisionist history is a term for those practices and mentalities that privilege countermemory. Revisionist history decolonizes the imaginaries of the colonized of those very discourses that subject and exclude the colonized. In both texts, rememory is identified in episodes of past overlapping present, in the dramatization of ancestral or contemporary traumas, and in the materialization of myth in sites meaningful to persons and communities. Pane's primary record folds these manifestations into a straightforward description, though never neglecting to interpolate the orthodox critique of his enlightened European mind and his Catholic fear of idolatry and heresy:

All or the majority of the people of the Island of Hispaniola have many zemis of various sorts. Some contain the bones of their father and mother and relatives and ancestors; they are made of stone or of wood. And they have many of both kinds, some that speak, and others that cause the things they eat to grow, and others that make it rain, and others that make the winds blow. Those simple ignorant people believe that those idols—or more properly speaking, demons—make such things happen because they have no knowledge of our holy faith. When one of them is sick, they take him to the behique[shaman], who is the aforesaid ... in such fashion that they do not know what they are doing; and thus they say many senseless things, affirming therein that they are speaking with the zemis, and that the latter tell them that the sickness has come from.[36]

For the Taino, the ubiquity of zemis in their habitations, their gathering places, and diffused around their landscapes shows how ineradicably they imagined continuity between the beginnings of the cosmos, the origins of their gods, and the personification of those gods in their caciques. Summarizing this persistence, Irving Rouse explains that the Taino believed zemis lived in trees and rocks; that women prayed to them for safe delivery in childbirth; that the tribe decorated their pots with them and offered them food for propitiation.[37] Zemis defined rememory in the sense of a memory by which the Taino not only made continuously present the memory of the gods, but also the memory of the zemi's owners who had passed it on to their successive heirs, all along to the present owner.[38] To underscore this loop of lineal continuity, it should be emphasized that the zemi was both the name of the god and the artifact representing that god. When the cacique died, his zemi was transferred to a temple where it was venerated as a symbol of the cacique's ancestors. Of rememory materialized in this way, Caroline Rody writes that it emphasizes "the interconnectedness of minds, past and present and thus neatly conjoins [*Beloved*'s] supernatural vision with its aspiration to communal epic … to 'rememory' is to use one's imaginative power to realize a latent, abiding connection to the past."[39] In Chapters 17 and 18 of Pane's *Antiquities*, rememory is staged as the persistence of past trauma in episodes involving violence and friction inflicted on family members. The episodes dramatize human rage, sacerdotal fallibility (or deceit, as Pane seems to think), and partiality on the part of the zemis. Rememory is evidenced in the indelibility of the perceived trauma (the picture of the dead man and the memory of that picture), in the behique's embodiment of the traumatized family's sense of injury, and the partiality of the zemis. As it switches between present and past tense, Pane's narration reproduces those events in memory and reinforces the transgenerational obligation to re-member the circumstances of the death and to seek to avenge it.

The centrality of caves in the Taino imaginary Illustrates the materialization of myth in their daily life as depicted in Pane's *Antiquities*. Notice has been taken earlier of the caves' role in explaining the origins of the gods and the origins of the people, of their conception as sacred entrances to the underworld, as repositories for zemis, as places for burial and shelter. Now I want to draw attention to an articulation between caves and trees, specifically the ceiba tree (*ceiba pentandra*, or the silk cotton tree). Pane does not name the ceiba specifically but his description of trees with close identical features of massive size, and used for secular and ritual

purposes, suggests the ceiba (Chapter 19). From other colonial chroniclers and secondary sources, we learn that the ceiba was used to make
zemis, coffins, and canoes—all objects that figured in cave burials.[40]

Among many pre-Columbian peoples, the ceiba was considered the
principal spirit tree, and was known variously as the "world tree," and the
"God tree." Taino worldview situated and valorized the ceiba as the connecting link between the two cosmic spheres, the underworld of the cave
(the world of the dead), and the world of the sky.[41]

Caves and trees articulate dynamically in the Taino construction of a
worldview that made their relationship to the gods, the earth, and themselves a continuous conversation with the natural world and the supernatural.[42] Though separated by nearly three centuries from the encounter
between Pane's Taino and Columbus, the literary representation of Earle's
Three-Fingered Jack's confrontation with the Jamaican colonial authorities replicates the continuity and interconnectedness of rememory with
unerring consistency. In Earle the three categorical locations defined for
this section can be identified in discrete historical, political, and cultural
relations of the narrative. However, for strategic purposes, I am going to
switch the order in which I develop them in the forthcoming discussion. I
will place the dramatization of ancestral and contemporary traumas first
because that provides some useful definitional lights with which to read
the other two, and then I will combine the categories of past overlapping
present and the materialization of myth.

Its status as a relatively recent neologism notwithstanding, rememory is
not an artificial or merely imaginary thing. All the narratives of terror Jack
received from his mother and from or about members of his extended
family (Makro, Feruare, Bashra, and Mahali) are internalized as shared
memory. They exist in his mind as reifications of very real, palpable things
and steel Jack's resolve for revenge. They persist in Jack's consciousness as
transgenerational trauma, as a psychic haunting of memories collected
about father, mother, grandfather, and in fact about all their shipboard
mates.[43]

Mystification has its value in deepening the concept, but these are some
concrete objects that reproduce rememory: the girdle Makro left with
Amri for Jack to inherit[44]; the stripes imprinted on his body and the bodies
of his kin; Jack's own two fingers and later his hand and head severed in
the encounters with Maroon bounty hunters[45]; his father's body tossed
ingloriously to the surging waves, to deepen by one more artifact the sub-
terranean archive Walcott sources as the locus of Caribbean history. The

definition is amplified by the addition of place to the catalog. This will get its own development in the paragraphs to follow.

Combining temporality with myth in this critical theorizing of pertinent issues in *Three-Fingered Jack* emphasizes how rememory may be accessed at sites that have preserved both their secular and sacralized uses across time, and have so figured the interpenetration of these uses as to occupy the space of myth. As physical settings for certain dramatic events in *Three-Fingered Jack*, as for the analogous struggles of Maroon slaves across the Caribbean, caves, cells, huts, mountain fastnesses, and the terrific beetling precipice on which Jack fought his last battle with Quashee and Sam, uniquely constitute the conditions for the fortuitous and sustained experiences of rememory.[46] The place where his mother was to be burned alive and the spot where his grandfather was burned alive would both retain the memories and hold in place the palpable pictures and associations of those past events; they would "rememory," a kindred consciousness, in Caroline Rody's verbalization (in the technical linguistic sense) of the concept, "to use [his/her] imaginative power to realize a latent, abiding connection to the past."[47] For their capacity to transcend time and to figure mythic allusiveness, caves deserve yet another separate treatment with respect to Earle's topographies. In *Three-Fingered Jack*, caves repeat their functions as sites of rememory as they spectralize the transgenerational memories of Taino and African cultural rituals, political resistance, and physical and psychic traumas. In *Three-Fingered Jack*, they are the sanctuaries of choice for fugitive slaves and for assortments of social outcasts and desperadoes (Bashra, a victim of yaws, lived in a cave which also sheltered a band of robbers). Jack lived in a cave described as "noisome, dark and dismal ... a stifling vapour proceeded from the earth, and the lamp burnt but dimly."[48] In Bashra's cave "Snails drew their slimy train upon his shrivelled feet, and lizards and vipers filled the air of his hut with foul uncleanliness. His dwelling was the receptacle of robbers, and he gave them Obi, to protect them from the wounds of their assailants."[49] These spectral places conjure up images of the ominous lurking evil that obeah suggested in the minds of plantation whites. But caves also bear an especial potency as religious and political sanctuaries for obeah practitioners and acolytes, including Jack's grandfather, his mentor Bashra, also an obeah man, and his rebel comrade Mahali. First, caves represent counterhistorical sites in this narrative because they are the liminal spaces that mark the point of rupture between the slave's relationship to an unfree social ethos and an autonomous site of freedom. Second, they represent for Jack the ambivalence of loss, traumatically in their persistent implications in the deaths of his significant kin, and discursively as the sites where he imagined and executed critical acts of retribution and revolutionary will. The caves' persistence in Jack's existential traumas is illustrated when he (with Mahali's assistance) snatched his mother from the flames where she was to be burned alive and tried to take her to the safety of his cave. (She expires on the way.) They are immanent too in the similarly brutal deaths of his grandfather and mentor who had used cave spaces for resistance and survival. Jack's cave is positioned paradoxically in that it serves as a physical symbol of his absolute rejection of plantation political and economic discourses, while at the same time accommodating his volitional immersion in the potencies of memory and rememory. In his rhetorical harangue to a slave audience trembling with fear and reluctance, that rejection rings in the terms of disavowal and in the impulses to re-member all the causes for which rebellion is now justified (dislocation, disaffiliation, freedom, and even an imaginary of Pan-African nationalism): "Remember the struggle is for liberty; to destroy the power of our enemies, to regain the privileges of our native land .... Who is there would not, for the sake of themselves, their wives, their children and the country, rise into a firm body, cemented by the ties that bind us to each other? Who is there would not rise to repel the bold invaders of those rights dear to an African, and to every man who loves his country and his tender offspring?"[50]

This speech was delivered after his daring attempt to kill Captain Harrop, for which he was whipped and imprisoned. Escaping that captivity, he hunted down Harrop and held him as his private prisoner in his cave. Thus, for Jack, the cave becomes the site of rememory in being the repository of his memories of his own acts, his memories of close kin, and their memories. Characterizing corresponding episodes of flight in African American slavery as "stealing away practices," Saidiya Hartman theorizes the appropriated spaces as giving voice to the need to "make counter claims of freedom, humanity and the self ('a reconstructed self that negates the dominant terms of identity and existence'),"[51] and the traces of memory circulating within the spaces are recovered as "a sentient recollection of connectedness experienced at the site of rupture, where the very consciousness of disconnectedness acts as a mode of testimony and memory."[52] In an essay that defines volition as one of its primacies, Monica Schuler shows that these sites are multiple in their semiosis: they are material, functional, and symbolic; they are objectifications of the will to remember.[53] They reproduce flight as a very intentional political act. They are deeply disruptive to the stability of the slavocracy, in that they mark separation from ruling epistemes; they mark a crucial moment when the revolutionized consciousness is radically delinked from European epistemic systems and repositioned in Caribbean-specific epistemes. Ascribing to memory so deployed the status of a defensive "authentic mode of discourse," Kerwin Lee Klein intuits its potential to become "a form of counterhistory that challenges the false generalizations in exclusionary 'History.'"[54] The implication is that the emergence of memory as a category of academic discourse is a healthy result of "decolonization."[55] To recover forms of space and modes of memory in a project like this is to rediscover a past that suffuses its vital energy into the present; to experience archives whose use is fundamentally "to block the work of forgetting."

CONCLUSION

To conclude, the invocation of forgetting returns us to its antonym, the point at which we began and the core concern of this essay. Memory and re-membering have been proposed as the very active tools and agencies for imagining and producing a project of literary history consistent with the cultural experiences of Caribbean peoples. Differentiated from the formal requirements of scribal histories, a memory-based objective depends heavily on the re-membered truths of shared mythic spaces, shared losses, shared strategies for survival, and the persistence of consciousness through time. While "history," traditionally conceived, imposes its own rationalist rules and positivist restrictions, memory at once invites the arts of the imagination and the self-creating processes of imaginaries to engage both material and metaphysical sources to recover a new object. Grounded in a set of coherent memory traditions that place historically affiliated communities at the center, this kind of project will recover political power where Derrida locates it, in the archives of people's consciousness. Produced at this historical moment, of both postcoloniality and decoloniality, these projects must be purposefully aligned with the new emerging intellectual practices which have the power to illuminate past truths and create their own traditions.[56] These practices reimagine memory as a particular kind of knowledge, a particular kind of theory, a particular kind of criticism that will be re-membered in our traditions in ways that will re-enchant their connections to origins and sources in both cosmic and terrestrial spaces.

NOTES

1. Quoted in Daniel McCool, *The Fall and Rise of America's Rivers* (New York: Columbia University Press, 2012), 167.
2. I am using a modern English translation by Susan C. Griswold, ed. Jose Juan Arrom (Durham and London: Duke University Press, 1999), hereafter referred to as *Antiquities*.
3. Jose Juan Arrom's Introduction to the *Antiquities* (pp. xi–xxix) provides valuable biographical and other backgrounds to Pane and his text.
4. These sources throw modest light on Earle's biography: Andrew Kippis and William Godwin, eds. *The New Annual Register, or General Repository of History, 1814–15* (London, 1780–1825), 23–4. On Earle's authorship, see David Erskine Baker, Isaac Reed, and Stephen Jones, *Biographia Dramatica, or Companion to the Playhouse* (London: Longman, Hurst, Rees, 1812), 1:214; and Samuel Austin Allibone, *A Critical Dictionary of English Literature and British and American Authors*, 4 vols (Philadelphia, 1801), 1:539.
5. Christopher Columbus, Journal entry for October 11, 1492, http://www.historyguide.org/earlymod/columbus.html (accessed July 11, 2014).
6. For representative scholarly opinion, see William F. Keegan, "Destruction of the Taino," *Archaeology* (January/February, 1992): 51–56; Lynne Guitar, "Documenting the Myth of Taíno Extinction" *KACIKE: The Journal of Caribbean Amerindian History and Anthropology*. Retrieved July 11, 2014, http://www.kacike.org/GuitarEnglish.html; Maximilian C. Forte, "Extinction: The Historical Trope of Anti-Indigeneity in the Caribbean" http://indigenouscaribbean.files.wordpress.com/2008/05/forteatlantic2005.pdf (accessed July 11, 2014).
7. Pane, *Antiquities*, 11.
8. Scott, "Archaeologies of Black Memory, an Interview with Robert Hill," *Small Axe* 5 (1999): 82–83.
9. Harris, "History, Fable and Myth in the Caribbean and Guianas," *Selected Essays of Wilson Harris*, ed. A. J. M. Bundy (New York: Routledge, 1999), 151.
10. Morrison, *Beloved* (New York: New American Library, 1987), 35–36.
11. *Beloved*, 36.
12. Sylvia Wynter, "The Ceremony Must Be Found: After Humanism," *Boundary 2* (Spring/Fall 84): 20.
13. Kenneth Bilby, *True Born Maroons* (Gainesville: University Press of Florida, 2008), 74–76; 326–329.
14. Bilby, 289–290.
15. The "quarrel" has been widely historicized by leading Caribbean authors and scholars. For a distinguished critical essay, see Edward Baugh, "The West Indian Writer and his Quarrel with History," *Small Axe* 16 (2012): 60–74.

16. Walcott, "The Almond Trees," in *Castaway and other Poems* (London: Cape, 1965), 36–37.
17. Edward Kamau Brathwaite, "History of the Voice," *Roots: Essays in Caribbean Literature* (Ann Arbor: U of Michigan P, 1993), 259–304.
18. Baugh, "Quarrel with History," 61.
19. Edouard Glissant, *Caribbean Discourse: Selected Essays* (Charlottesville: University of Virginia Press, 1992), 25.
20. Eduardo Galeano, *Memory of Fire, I: Genesis*, trans. Cedric Belfrage (New York: Pantheon Books, 1985), XV.
21. Gregorio Kohon, "The Aztecs, Mazada and the Compulsion to Repeat," in Rozine Josef Perelberg, *Time and Memory* (London: Institute of Psychoanalysis, 2007), 114.
22. Pane, *Antiquities*, 13.
23. Pane, *Antiquities*, 8–9
24. Pane, *Antiquities*, 20.
25. Pane, *Antiquities*, 31.
26. Pane, *Antiquities*, 14.
27. Pane, *Antiquities*, 6.
28. See Warner, *Fantastic Metamorphosis*, 31–32; and William F. Keegan, *Taino Indian Myth and Practice: The Arrival of the Stranger* King (Gainesville: University Press of Florida, 2007), 42–43.
29. Wilson Harris, "Merlin and Parsifal: Adversarial Twins," in *Selected Essays of Wilson Harris: The Unfinished Genesis of the Imagination*, ed. Andrew Bundy (London: Routledge, 1999), 64.
30. Benjamin, "A Berlin Chronicle," in *One Way Street* (Verso: London, 1997), 314–316.
31. Kerwin Lee Klein, "On the Emergence of Memory in Historical Discourse," *Representations* 69 (2000):136, 138.
32. See also Satya Mohanty, "the epistemic holds particular power for the oppressed," in "The Epistemic Status of Cultural Identity: On Beloved and the Post Colonial Condition," *Cultural Critique* 24 (Spring 1993): 65, 72.
33. Earle, *Three-Fingered Jack*, 72.
34. An uncommon African ethnicity, it appears to have been a European invention to label the Jola people who occupied an area on the west coast of Africa between the Gambia and the Casamance rivers. Mungo Park also uses this marker to identify the same people in his *Travels in the Interior Districts of Africa* (Edinburgh: Oliver Boyd, 1816), 1:15–16.11. Three-Fingered Jack claims ethnic kinship with them and legitimizes his nationalistic and revolutionary aspirations in their name.
35. Kerwin Lee Klein, "Emergence," 136–137; see also Scott, "Archaeologies," XIV.

36. Pane, *Antiquities*, 21.
37. Irving Rouse, *The Tainos: Rise and Decline of the People Who Greeted Columbus* (New Haven: Yale University Press, 1994), 13–14.
38. Jose J. Arrom, *Taino: Pre-Columbian Art and Culture from the Caribbean* (New York: Museo del Barrio, 1997), 106.
39. Caroline Rody, "Toni Morrison's *Beloved*: History, "Rememory," and a "Clamor for a Kiss," *American Literary History*, 7 (Spring 1995):101.
40. Ceiba wood was used to make the zemi of the Taino god Baibrama, an image discovered in Jamaica in 1757; see Nicholas Saunders, *The Peoples of the Caribbean: An Encyclopedia of Archaeology and Traditional Culture* (Santa Barbara: ABC Clio, 2005), 146, 159.
41. Saunders, 289; and Keegan, *Talking Taino*, 95.
42. Recorded in Pane, *Antiquities*, Chapter 19, a myth involving a Taino man, a talking tree, and a behique (shaman) is illustrative of this kind of anthropomorphism.
43. For an illuminating source on transgenerational trauma and the obligations it imposes on blood relations, see Jacques Derrida, *Specters of Marx, the State of the Debt, the Work of Mourning, & the New International*, trans. Peggy Kamuf (New York: Routledge, 1994), 9–10.
44. Pane, *Antiquities*, 90.
45. Pane, *Antiquities*, 143.
46. Pane, *Antiquities*, 157.
47. Rody, "Toni Morrison's Beloved: History, "Rememory," and a "Clamor for a Kiss," *American Literary History*, 7 (Spring 1995):101.
48. Pane, *Antiquities*, 122.
49. Pane, *Antiquities*, 104.
50. Pane, *Antiquities*, 110
51. Saidiya V. Hartman, *Scenes of Subjection: Terror, Slavery, and Self-Making in Nineteenth-Century America* (New York: Oxford University Press, 1997), 72.
52. Hartman, 74.
53. Monica Schuler, "Enslavement, the Slave Voyage and Astral and Aquatic Journeys," in Jose C. Curto, and Renee Soulodre-LaFrance, *Africa and the Americas: Interconnections during the Slave Trade* (Trenton, New Jersey: Africa World Press, 2005), 193.
54. Klein, "On the Emergence of "Memory," 137.
55. Pierre Nora, *Les Lieux de Memoire* (*Realms of Memory*) (New York: Columbia University Press, 1996–1998), 19.
56. Melanie Newton urges the need for these anti-marginalizing and decolonializing practices in her essay, "Returns to a Native Land: Indigeneity and Decolonization in the Anglophone Caribbean," *Small Axe* 17(2013):110.

BIBLIOGRAPHY

Allibone, Samuel Austin. *A Critical Dictionary of English Literature and British and American Authors*, 4 vols. Philadelphia, 1801.

Arrom, Jose J. *Taino: Pre-Columbian Art and Culture from the Caribbean.* New York: Museo del Barrio, 1997.

Baker, David Erskine, Isaac Reed, and Stephen Jones. *Biographia Dramatica, or Companion to the Playhouse.* London: Longman, Hurst, Rees, 1812.

Baugh, Edward. "The West Indian Writer and His Quarrel with History." *Small Axe* 16 (2012): 60–74.

Benjamin, Walter. "A Berlin Chronicle." `In *One Way Street.* 293–346. Verso: London, 1997.

Bilby, Kenneth. *True Born Maroons.* Gainesville: University Press of Florida, 2008.

Brathwaite, Edward Kamau. "History of the Voice." In *Roots: Essays in Caribbean Literature.* 259–304. Ann Arbor: U of Michigan P, 1993.

Columbus, Christopher. Journal entry for October11, 1492. Accessed July 11, 2014. http://www.historyguide.org/earlymod/columbus.html.

Derrida, Jacques. *Specters of Marx, the State of the Debt, the Work of Mourning, & the New International,* trans. Peggy Kamuf. New York: Routledge, 1994.

Forte, Maximilian C. "Extinction: The Historical Trope of Anti-Indigeneity in the Caribbean." *Issues in Caribbean Amerindian Studies,* 6, no. 4 (August 2004–August 2005). Accessed July 11, 2014. http://indigenouscaribbean.files.wordpress.com/2008/05/forteatlantic2005.pdf.

Galeano, Eduardo. *Memory of Fire, I: Genesis,* trans. Cedric Belfrage. New York: Pantheon Books, 1985.

Glissant, Edouard. *Caribbean Discourse: Selected Essays.* Charlottesville: University of Virginia Press, 1992.

Guitar, Lynne. "Documenting the Myth of Taíno Extinction." *KACIKE: The Journal of Caribbean Amerindian History and Anthropology.* Accessed July 11, 2014. http://www.kacike.org/GuitarEnglish.html.

Harris, Wilson. "History, Fable and Myth in the Caribbean and Guianas." In *Selected Essays of Wilson Harris.* Ed. A. J. M. Bundy. 152–166. New York: Routledge, 1999a.

Harris, Wilson. "Merlin and Parsifal: Adversarial Twins." In *Selected Essays of Wilson Harris: The Unfinished Genesis of the Imagination.* Ed. Andrew Bundy. 57–64. London: Routledge, 1999b.

Hartman, Saidiya V. *Scenes of Subjection: Terror, Slavery, and Self-Making in Nineteenth-Century America.* New York: Oxford University Press, 1997.

Keegan, William F. *Taino Indian Myth and Practice: The Arrival of the Stranger King.* Gainesville: University Press of Florida, 2007.

Kippis, Andrew, and William Godwin, eds. *The New Annual Register, or General Repository of History, 1814–15.* London, 1780–1825.

Klein, Kerwin Lee. "On the Emergence of Memory in Historical Discourse." *Representations* 69 (2000): 127–150.

Kohon, Gregorio. "The Aztecs, Mazada and the Compulsion to Repeat." In *Time and Memory*. Ed. Rozine Josef Perelberg. 103–127. London: Institute of Psychoanalysis, 2007.

McCool, Daniel. *The Fall and Rise of America's Rivers.* New York: Columbia University Press, 2012.

Mohanty, Satya. "The Epistemic Status of Cultural Identity: On Beloved and the Post Colonial Condition." *Cultural Critique* 24 (Spring 1993): 41–80.

Morrison, Toni, *Beloved.* New York: New American Library, 1987.

Newton, Melanie. "Returns to a Native Land: Indigeneity and Decolonization in the Anglophone Caribbean." *Small Axe* 17 (2013): 108–122.

Nora, Pierre. *Les Lieux de Memoire—Realms of Memory.* New York: Columbia University Press, 1996–1998.

Pane, Ramon. *An Account of the Antiquities of the Indians*, trans. Susan C. Griswold, ed. Jose Juan Arrom. Durham: Duke University Press, 1999.

Park, Mungo. *Travels in the Interior Districts of Africa.* Edinburgh: Oliver Boyd, 1816.

Rody, Caroline. "Toni Morrison's *Beloved*: History, "Rememory," and a "Clamor for a Kiss." *American Literary History* 7 (Spring 1995): 92–119.

Saunders, Nicholas. *The Peoples of the Caribbean: An Encyclopedia of Archaeology and Traditional Culture.* Santa Barbara: ABC Clio, 2005.

Schuler, Monica. "Enslavement, the Slave Voyage and Astral and Aquatic Journeys. In *Africa and the Americas: Interconnections during the Slave Trade*. Ed. Jose C. Curto, and Renee Soulodre-LaFrance. 185–214. Trenton, New Jersey: Africa World Press, 2005.

Scott, David. "Archaeologies of Black Memory, an Interview with Robert Hill." *Small Axe* 5 (1999): 82–83.

Walcott. "The Almond Trees." In *Castaway and Other Poems*. 36–37. London: Cape, 1965.

Warner, Marina. *Fantastic Metamorphoses, Other Worlds: Ways of Telling the Self.* London: Oxford University Press, 2002.

Wynter, Sylvia. "The Ceremony Must Be Found: After Humanism, *Boundary 2*. Spring/Fall (1984): 19–70.

CHAPTER 3

Early Caribbean Evangelical Life Narrative

Sue Thomas

The Caribbean life narrative which reached the widest audience during the plantation slavery period was that of Cornelius (1727, by his reckoning, to 1801), a "Negro-Assistant" in the Moravian mission on St Thomas. A master mason, he purchased his freedom from slavery on the Royal Plantation in 1767, having already bought his wife's freedom; he subsequently progressively purchased the freedom of his six children. He had been baptized a Moravian (United Brethren) in 1749 and became an assistant in 1754. Drawing on "a blend of Moravian and African practices" the appointment of "Negro-assistants" by missionaries, Jon Sensbach argues, "created a lattice of spiritual mentors and fictive kin who helped incorporate Africans into the evangelical family," "rebuild[ing] kin connections" for "people whose intricate tendrils of kinship had been ripped apart by the slave trade." It proved a "revolutionary" system which "would come to form the marrow of black Christian fellowship in the Protestant Atlantic world."[1] Indeed Sylvia R. Frey and Betty Wood attribute the phenomenal success of the evangelical revival among African diasporic peoples in the American south and the West Indies by 1830 to a creolization of forms of worship and the way "evangelical institutions came to constitute important loci wherein African peoples could develop a sense of belonging and

S. Thomas (✉)
La Trobe University, Melbourne, VIC, Australia

© The Author(s) 2018
N. N. Aljoe et al. (eds.), *Literary Histories of the Early Anglophone Caribbean*, New Caribbean Studies,
https://doi.org/10.1007/978-3-319-71592-6_3

assert a cultural presence in the larger society through the creation of their own moral and social communities."[2] More recent research has high-lighted the centrality of oral narration of lives and evangelical print cultures to evangelical community-building and to the emergence of an evangelical public sphere.[3] In English alone, Cornelius's "Life" was published with slight variations in *Periodical Accounts Relating to the Missions of the Church of the United Brethren, Established among the Heathen* in 1803, in the *Methodist Magazine* in 1805, as a pamphlet in Antigua in 1820 for a Sunday School and literacy project, and in the (Anglican) Church Missionary Society journal, the *Missionary Register*, in 1823.[4] The *Methodist Magazine* had an audience of around a hundred thousand people at the turn of the nineteenth century.[5] The "Life" would also have been read aloud to congregations and classes. Moravian genres of life narrative included speaking at meetings and love feasts, exhorting, participation in "speakings" (spiritual counselling), and the *Lebenslauf* or life course (largely self-authored or self-dictated spiritual memoirs read at funerals and meetings). Though literate in Creole, Dutch, Danish, German and English, Cornelius pointedly did not write an account of his life, insisting that the salvation of his "soul ... alone" was "worth speaking of."[6] Moravian missionaries in St Thomas pieced together a written "Life" of Cornelius from memories of his oral relatings of his life in the faith (a stock feature of exhorting), missionary records, accounts of his deathbed and funeral witnessed by missionaries and a transcription of a speech to the catachumens at the Moravian mission at New Herrnhut in St Thomas, which had already been published in German in 1877 in Christian Oldendorp's *Geschichte der Mission der evangelischen Brüder auf den Caribischen Inseln S. Thomas, S. Croix und S. Jan*. For Cornelius, Christianity represented the possibility of a making "whole" of a "a people scattered and peeled.—A nation meted out and trodden under foot."[7] His biblical reference is to Isaiah 18:7.

His "Life" is part of a very dispersed archive of extant Caribbean evangelical life narratives that is scarcely known today, and, as such, part of under-researched oral storying, and vast and local print cultures. In this essay I read a range of early Caribbean life narratives alongside and against the grain of exemplary texts of the evangelical mission in the West Indies of the plantation slavery period. I take as my core examples of this mission texts by Thomas Coke (1747–1814), the founder of the Wesleyan Methodist overseas missionary network, and a range of written and visual material by Moravian missionary Lewis Stobwasser (1785–1832) from the

1810s and 1820s.[8] The life narratives of Cambric Dracott, "Harry the Black" and an unnamed black woman who recited his life to missionaries in 1819 offer evidence of the historical soundscapes of plantation slavery cultures and complex processes of creolization and translation in the inscription of lives. Simon Gikandi argues that missionary discourse constitutes a "third text" of the "archive of enslavement," being "written by people who were neither masters nor slaves, observers whose relationship to the institution of slavery was tenuous, and whose intentions were driven by goals that were sometimes at odds with the systematizing function of the archive of enslavement." For him the records of masters produced a vindication of "the authority of natural history, the key to the ideology of white power. Here, in the archive, the African could be reduced to the world of nature and the prehuman … fix[ed] … as an object, as chattel, as property, and indeed as the symbol of the barbarism that enabled white civilization and its modernist cravings."[9] His example of a third text is Oldendorp's history in which Cornelius figures. Missionary discourse fixes Africa as a symbol of heathen darkness from which human souls are salvageable through mission enterprise. The life narratives of converts more typically represent plantation slavery culture as a corrupting and traumatizing darkness. They convey a richer sense of the historical meanings of the lived experience of evangelical community and creolization processes.

Christian missionary work in the Caribbean became central to efforts to ameliorate the conditions in which enslaved people lived and laboured. In 1808, Beilby Porteus, the Bishop of London, whose diocese included the West Indies, anticipated in *A Letter to the Governors, Legislatures, and Proprietors of Plantations in the West India Islands* a new phase of "truly Imperial works" for the "English nation" in the wake of its abolition of its slave trade a year earlier: a "*universal benevolence*" to be realized "in assisting and protecting the distressed, and in meliorating the condition of distant countries, by communicating to them in various ways, the blessings of the Christian Revelation."[10] In his "Dedication" of *A History of the West Indies, Containing the Natural, Civil and Ecclesiastical History of Each Island* (1808–11) to the "*Subscribers towards the West India Missions*," Coke represents as sublime "[t]he sacred monument, which, under God, you have been instrumental in raising to the efficacy of the divine grace, among the swarthy inhabitants of the torrid zone" and extols "the evidences of Christianity" that have rewarded their "liberal exertions" "as a conspicuous demonstration, that those who are sunk in heathenish darkness, are not outcasts of the divine mercy."[11] Seeking funding to establish

Methodist missions outside England in 1786, Coke had written of that divine mercy in the West Indies as a "compensation" for the immiseration of enslavement: "Our country is enriched by the labours of the poor slaves who cultivate the soil, and surely the least compensation we can make them, is to endeavour to enrich them in return with the riches of grace. But the grand consideration to the children of GOD, is the value of the souls of these negroes, a set of people utterly despised by all the world, except the Methodists and Moravians."[12] The first Moravian mission in the Caribbean was established in St Thomas in 1732; Methodist evangelization began in Antigua in 1760, and expanded during the 1780s. The Moravian mission in Antigua had been established in 1756. Writing to Christian Ignatius La Trobe, the Secretary to the Moravian church in Britain, in 1814 Lewis Stobwasser, a missionary then based in Antigua, opined that the "slave trade ... has been the means of bringing many thousands from darkness into the saving light" of Christian redemption.[13] Moravian missionaries were instructed to teach that "God, for wise reasons, permits his children to experience many hardships and difficulties in this world. But he also comforts them richly, and gives them something infinitely better instead thereof. ... Our Lord Jesus Christ himself experienced very great difficulties in this world, but he bore them patiently. We, through his grace, are to do the same."[14] In an appeal for funds for Moravian missions in 1824, Stobwasser anticipated that evangelization would "make" "Negroes" "good faithful and obedient subjects, and satisfied with their state, as appointed by Providence."[15] Coke described missionaries as "extending ... the hand of Christian friendship"[16]; Christocentric Moravians write of "Jesus as the Friend of sinners."[17]

The usability of evangelical life narrative to support missionary endeavours is amply demonstrated by the reach of Cornelius's "Life." For the 1803 Moravian audience Cornelius's history exemplified the virtue of quietism, a "whole ethos of self-yielding, self-abasing resignation to the will of God and the will of the community."[18] The authors of his "Life" report that his funeral was attended "by a very large company of Negroe-brethren and Sisters" and "a great many white people, as a pleasing proof, how much this venerable Negro-brother was esteemed and beloved by persons of all ranks and colours."[19] Mary Prince, a Moravian convert, whose slave narrative *The History of Mary Prince, a West Indian Slave, Related by Herself* was published by Thomas Pringle, the Secretary of the Anti-Slavery Society in Britain in 1831, by contrast with the Cornelius of the "Life," found such quietism around enslavement "a hard and heavy task,"[20] and identifies with the biblical figure of Jeremiah in his anguish in trenchantly denouncing slavery and slaveowners in biblical terms. Indeed the identification is represented as enabling the retrospective account of her life.[21] For her the condition of the enslaved person is not grace, rather being "disgraced and thought no more of than beasts."[22] By 1805, the *Methodist Magazine* (formerly the *Arminian Magazine*) regularly featured lives of exemplary evangelical Christians as "evidences" of divine grace. The Methodist hierarchy also published life narratives in pamphlet and book form; in 1768, John Wesley himself edited for publication the diary of white Creole Mary Gilbert (1751–1768), the daughter of the founder of Methodism in the Caribbean, Nathaniel Gilbert.[23] Based from 1813 in Antigua, William Dawes (1762–1836), appointed the Superintendent of Church Missionary Society Schools in the West Indies in 1820, published the "Life" as a pamphlet that year as part of an evangelical Sunday School and Creole benevolent project which by the mid- to late 1820s was shaping female anti-slavery activism in Britain. The project drew particular inspiration from his "free coloured" Methodist sister-in-law Anne Hart Gilbert (1768–1834),[24] whose spiritual memoir of her niece, Dawes's god-daughter, Grace Gilbert Hart, he also published in 1821.[25] It is the first known publication of an African-Caribbean woman and is in the genre of the happy death, a record of a life "well spent in disciplined holiness" capped off by a "death, free from anguish and uncertainty" about the prospect of spiritual resurrection.[26] A heavily and unsympathetically edited version of her "A Short Account of Peregrine Pickle (Now Baptised Peter) a Negro Belonging to His Majesty and Employed in the Naval Yard at English Harbour, Antigua" was published in the *Methodist Magazine* in 1821, and subsequently in *Missionary Notices* and the *Christian Secretary*.[27] Dawes's ecumenical cross-racial cooperation with Methodists led to a major falling out with the Church Missionary Society (CMS) in the late 1820s, and he has been written out of official CMS histories.[28] Dawes forwarded the pamphlet to the CMS in London. The "Life" was published in the CMS *Missionary Register* in April 1823 as an "instructive and affecting narrative" while the British parliament was considering measures to ameliorate the lives of enslaved people, including promotion of Christianization, especially through legislating for an episcopal establishment in the West Indies.[29]

In this context, and in the wake of a major slave rebellion in Demerara, in 1824 a "proposal for forming a separate fund for the Moravian missions in the West Indies" which included material by Stobwasser was widely advertised in evangelical journals. In writing of "Negroes," Stobwasser represents racial difference as "moral depravities ... so deeply rooted that a mere cessation of slavery would not cure them in the least of their laziness, impertinence, lying, stealing, and lasciviousness." The proposal invoked an ideal of the well-ordered plantation[30]; Moravian missions, which did own slaves,[31] would boast that among their converts on estates "Church discipline" and not the whip was "used ... as a means of helping the slaves do their duty."[32] This is an argument that emphasizes the perceived commercial, prudential, managerial and humanitarian reach of Christian discipline.

Idealized visual representations of the well-ordered plantation and enslaved population were used to illustrate the value of missionary enterprises. In Thomas Coke's *A History of the West Indies*, for instance, a pastoral scene in Grenada includes three emblems of natural increase of the enslaved population: enslaved black mothers nursing black babies. The plantation owner, a white woman at his side, looks through his telescope at the commercial prosperity and production signified by the ships in the harbour.[33] The emblems of natural increase are testimony to the way in which after 1807, as Joan Anim-Addo shows, "the relative well-being of the enslaved woman and her reproductivity became crucial."[34] Coloured engravings made from Stobwasser's drawings of Antiguan mission stations at Spring Gardens, Gracehill, Gracebay and Cedarhall were published as *Ansichten von Missions-Niederlassungen der Evangelischen Brüder-Gemeinde, Vues des Établissements missionnaires fondés par la Communauté évangélique des Frères-Unis*, usually dated as having been published in 1830[35]; Stobwasser was stationed in Antigua, his first missionary posting, from late 1812 to 1822. Details of the first three of the engravings in washed-out greys illustrate *A Small Place* (1988) by Jamaica Kincaid, a jeremiad against the legacies of plantation slavery and neocolonial corruption.[36] The engravings of Gracehill, Gracebay and Cedarhall show converts at work or walking to work with mission buildings in a picturesque middle distance. Those of Gracehill and Gracebay include a black woman with a baby. The view of Spring Gardens, the main mission in St John's, shows black women and girls with hair covered by headscarves or hats, talking around the sandbox tree (otherwise called the possumwood, jabillo or monkey no-climb), under which the Moravian mission in Antigua had first been promulgated. Men are working and talking around the neatly ordered mission buildings. Mary Prince, converted in c. 1822, belonged to the Spring Gardens congregation.[37] Salome Cuthbert (c. 1732–1828), whose *Lebenslauf* was published in *Periodical Accounts Relating to the Missions of the Church of the United Brethren* in 1829, became a "negro-assistant" at Gracehill in 1791, moving there in 1807, having been bequeathed her freedom by her then owner Mrs Cuthbert.[38] The vertical hierarchies of Stobwasser's drawings place the congregation members under the protection of the mission stations (emblematized by the buildings and sandbox tree). In the self-authored section of his *Lebenslauf*, written when he was 42, around the time he took up a posting to Berlin in 1827, he acknowledges that the growth of a sense of vocation in Antigua ("engage[ment]" in winning souls" for his "Saviour") helped discipline his "own disordered heart, agitated as it was by alternations of despondence and presumption."[39] For Count Nicolaus Ludwig von Zinzendorf, the leader of the Moravian revival in the eighteenth century, "religion was a living 'impression' (*Eindruck*) made on the heart and soul (*Gemüt*) of the individual."[40] Stobwasser records: "The crowds of negroes who frequented the meetings in the large congregation at St John's, especially on festival days, when they appeared clad in white, made a deep impression on me; and I was forcibly reminded of a remark made by Brother Ganson, as I was laboring to express myself to him in English:—that the negroes in Antigua would soon open my mouth." His sustaining comradeship with fellow missionaries is individualized; in a further instance of hierarchization the congregations are a "scene of labour."[41] Both Prince's slave narrative and Cuthbert's *Lebenslauf* highlight, by contrast, the roles of female "negro-assistants," also called godmothers, in community leadership, mediation of disputes, and education; roles which accommodate other-mothering practices, which have been crucial in African diasporic cultures. Patricia Hill Collins highlights community education and the inculcation of "the ethic of caring and personal accountability" as the core of other-mothering.[42]

The illustrations occlude the "iniquity," "complicated ills," "abominations," "miseries" and "cruelties" of slavery. These are the terms free coloured Methodist leader Elizabeth Hart, later Thwaites (1771–1833), Anne Hart Gilbert's sister, uses in a 1794 letter.[43] In *A History of the West Indies*, Coke does describe the slave trade as a "most abominable traffic, (for the abolition of which every Christian will bless the love of God),"[44] and embeds short slave narratives, for example, missionary Edward Turner's "biographical sketch" of Cambric Dracott "take[n] down from her own mouth" in Tortola,[45] and included with "no apology" in a form— a History—he "denominate[s]" "*the memory of the world*."[46] Coke writes that the "striking ... detail" in the memorial of Cambric Dracott "affords us a more pointed comment on the situation of a slave, than a whole volume of abstract reasoning."[47] The sketch was reprinted as an extended footnote in Captain Thomas Southey's *Chronological History of the West Indies*, under the year 1798, the date of Coke's visit to Tortola, where, as on other islands, the coloured and black members of the Methodist congregation (2723) massively outnumbered the white members (16), a demographic that underpins the creolization of forms of evangelical worship and lay organization.[48] Southey, the brother of poet Robert Southey, describes "[t]he history of the West Indies" as "present[ing] little more than a melancholy series of calamities and crimes. The islands have been laid waste by hurricanes and visited by pestilence; but the sufferings which have arisen from natural causes are few and trifling in comparison with those which moral and political circumstances have produced."[49] Cambric—her last name in the sketch is the family name of her third owners—was born in Barbados, c. 1735, "the property of Henry Evens Holdin, Esq.," the child of people designated simply "a Mulatto man and a Mestee woman," and was in 1798, in Turner's view, a sister of "deep piety and good sense ... fast verging towards the grave," "bid[ding] fair to end her life in peace," confident of grace. Turner solicited from Cambric, who had "intirely forgot" the "little proficiency in reading" she acquired in early schooling "to read and work," an "account" of "her life."[50] The account or experience was a Methodist genre of life narration, with which Cambric would have been familiar, experiences being narrated orally at Methodist class meetings and love feasts.

Cambric's account, as developed by Turner, is not typical of the genre, which usually focuses more tightly on conversion, the conversion process, and the effect of "God's grace" on "the heart."[51] The description of her conversion is perfunctory and framed in stock Methodist discourse which acknowledges her as a volitional subject: during a difficult third "marriage" to an "enemy of godliness," she "hear[d] the Methodists ... was convinced of sin, and induced to join the [Methodist] society." Turner explains that legal "matrimony ... is universally denied to slaves," who "may unite, but only by private contract." The narrative draws out in visceral detail Cambric's trauma at having been sold away from the surviving of her two children, white first husband (a smith by trade) and family in Barbados by an unnamed second owner, who was enraged by his failure to "seduce his slave," "notwithstanding he was a married man," and sought calculated "revenge," both by separating her from the child and the husband to whom she was faithful and maliciously "blacken[ing] her character … to give a sanction to the inhuman treatment she was to undergo."[52] Cambric's refusal of her master asserts a right over her sexualized body and to "affective individualism," the right "to feel love and erotic desire" for her "conjugal mate," and to have the permissible private contract respected.[53] In Saidiya Hartman's terms, such "aspirations" proved to be "wildly utopian, derelict to capitalism."[54] Turner's interest in her account and his acknowledgement of the human legitimacy of the aspirations created the "conditions of possibility" for Cambric to have put on written record the laceration of her maternal feeling and her grief over loss of her child and husband,[55] that for around "thirty years" she had no "intelligence" of the fate of her child (who had died in the interim), the depravity of her second owner, and her good character both in Barbados and Tortola (where the Dracotts "from their confidence in her rectitude" allow her "to act without control" as their domestic servant). She had no further children in Tortola, despite a 16-year marriage to a "Dutchman" who died. The identity of the second owner would be discoverable by Barbadian readers of the *History* through the detail of her ownership as a commodity recorded there. Turner editorializes on her "treatment" as a bondswoman with terms such as "inhuman" and "shocking separation."[56]

In 1787, in the then Dutch colony St Eustatius (Statia), where English was very widely spoken, Coke met an enslaved man, Harry, who had been converted to Methodism in north America and had begun exhorting and holding prayer-meetings on the island after his arrival there in 1785. In Methodist historiography he is represented as having been "raised up" by Jesus to "prepare" the way for Coke,[57] an allusion to the biblical recognition of John the Baptist having prepared the way for Jesus by "crying in the wilderness."[58] Coke writes in his journal that "Harry did so grieve in spirit at the wickedness of the people around him, that at last the fire broke forth, and he bore a public testimony for Jesus."[59] Methodist minister Rev. Dr Wycherley Gumbs has written a short novel, *Black Harry "A Slave Redeemed"—A Man of Destiny* (1996), celebrating "his passion to proclaim the Gospel, his indomitable will, his unflagging zeal, and his love for those under the yoke of slavery."[60] Recently, John Neal has proclaimed Harry "an Afro-American pioneer missionary sent by Christ … [D]espite being a slave Black Harry discipled when he was transported and can therefore be described as a missionary. … Black Harry is a prototype for Methodist pioneers who illustrate that 'Mission in the way of Christ is a mission "from below.""'[61] By the mid-nineteenth century, the story of his persecution by Governor Rennolds, as pieced together from Coke's writings, was being retold for advanced Sunday School students.[62] Coke had unsuccessfully petitioned the Dutch government to "obtain protection" for Harry's congregation. Rennolds banished Harry from Statia, after having him publicly whipped, before Coke's second visit in 1789. In the standard historiography, Coke emerges as the founder of Methodism in Statia by licensing Harry as a class leader on his first visit and as a defender of the denomination and religious "*prayer*, the great key to every blessing."[63] Coke would meet Harry again in America in 1796; Coke's 1817 biographer Samuel Drew includes his reflection after the renewal of contact that back in America Harry had not "been exposed to that brutality which he had suffered in former years. Through all these changes, and the lapse of time, he seemed to have retained his piety and his zeal. He is useful in the society, of which he is a member, at the prayer-meetings and other private assemblies." Coke read this as "an answer … from heaven to the petitions of many thousands in England" in support of Methodist evangelization in Statia.[64]

In 1819, missionaries in St Bartholomew took down part of "recital of a Black Woman" who had been a member of Harry's congregation—her story is at odds with Coke's on significant points—and sent it back to London; the manuscript is in the Wesleyan Methodist Missionary Archives at the School of African and Oriental Studies at the University of London.[65] Contextualizing the discrepancies and fuller detail of everyday life in the congregation in her narrative displaces the authority accorded Coke's version of Harry and draws out some of the meanings of the authorization of Harry's and the woman's experiences. The recital deals with Harry's founding and management of the congregation, the stakes of having and keeping an "island" of "sound sanctification" in a slave-labour economy, Harry's "heart work" and powers of prophecy, and the narrator's own journeys in the faith.[66] Sanctification, "an ecstatic and sensible experience," was a Methodist ideal, promising "dependence and self-emptying, freedom from inbred sin," and a sense of sustaining well-being.[67] The informant had no news of Harry after his banishment; she reports that on his deathbed Rennolds (rendered phonetically as Runnels) "said he had a dispute with a man on religion and he was heard to say: oh! That blood, that blood! And many suppose he meant father Harry. His last words were, hell-fire!"[68] Jesus's "cover" of Methodist souls is a major theme of the recital; ironically it was Harry's recital of Charles Wesley's "Jesus, lover of my soul," a hymn which extols that cover, which led to the whipping and the banishment.

The first-person narrator describes in Harry a charismatic speaker venerated in his Methodist community in the language of family as "old father Harry," "old father" and "uncle Harry." He was illiterate; his power of speech is "all heart work," a characterization which emphasizes, not only his use of prodigious memory as a resource, but also the performative dimension of his leadership, and its effect on his audience. He appointed a literate steward "to do all his writing business." A rival literate Methodist exhorter raised up to "confound" Harry failed in his mission: in a valorization of oracy, "his form of religion soon dwindled to nothing, for he had only the letter and our good old Harry had the Spirit which made him so prosper."[69] The phrase "sound sanctification" highlights the crucialness of oracy and voice to the achievement of the Methodist ideal of sanctification. Harry's approach to using scribes is instrumental, as was that of Robert Wedderburn (1762–1835), the free coloured radical British Spencian activist, born in Jamaica, and also an evangelical convert. He noted "that he could not write, but that he had caused his ideas to be committed to writing by another person."[70] Srinivas Aravamudan urges that the "conflation of the category of subjecthood with the agency that comes from the complex technology of literacy" is a relatively recent phenomenon. "Humanism [as it has developed in the academy] seizes on literacy as self-exposure and makes it a foundational act on which it builds an aesthetic edifice."[71] The standard of literacy of Anne Hart Gilbert and Elizabeth Hart Thwaites was exceptional among West Indian converts. Literacy and education were affordable and highly prized in their family, and put freely in the service of the illiterate and of bondspeople. The sisters, for instance, initiated their long careers of other-mothering by teaching enslaved children in the period 1787–88. Their father, Barry Conyers Hart, a free coloured man, was probably the illegitimate, but recognized son of John Hart, former Governor of Maryland (1714–20) and Captain-General of the Leeward Islands (1721–27). Barry Hart was the owner of Hart's Estate, and "distinguished as an able writer," "often [taking] part in newspaper controversy, the 'poet's corner' being frequently filled with pieces of poetry of his own composition." His wife, Ann, a free coloured woman, had reportedly had "a very superior education in England." The Hart family pastimes included reading of the Bible, such poets as John Milton, Edward Young, William Cowper and Thomas Moss, and Hannah More on cross-class social obligation and bonding.[72]

In the recital, Harry having "the Spirit" suggests confidence in divine inspiration and protection of his "right way." After a group of "wild young men" heckle him, the one who "pelted him with rotten eggs" suffers the summary "judgment of God": "his hand and arm became dead to his body," and on his deathbed which closely follows he anticipates damnation.[73] Rennolds banned Harry from public speaking, in Coke's account, because of the excessive enthusiasm of his converts. Methodist converts often enacted the process by sinking to the ground in preparation for the experience of new birth.[74] Coke noted that members of Harry's audience would sometimes "remain in a state of stupor" on the ground "for some hours." The ban was prompted, in Coke's narrative, by 16 doing so during one particular meeting.[75] Ann Taves observes that in 1739 John Wesley had represented such acting out as "'signs and wonders ... done by the name ... of Jesus,'" the "'presence of his majesty'":

> In the context of class meetings, bands, love-feasts, and watch nights, Methodists sang the hymns of Christian experience written by Charles Wesley and testified to their own "experience." By locating experience in this context, Methodists did two things that set them apart from their Congregationalist and Presbyterian contemporaries. First, they created a quasi-public space in which they expected that they might physically experience the power of God. Second, by locating such experience in communal lay-led spaces and linking authenticity with observable "fruits" rather than nuanced philosophical distinctions, they democratized the process whereby such experiences were authenticated.[76]

Rennolds's ban on Methodist worship was pitched against such democratization and authentication of public voice and empowerment through lay leadership. In the woman's recital, while Rennolds was present at one of Harry's meetings, Harry

> began to exhort very much against the sin of fornication at the same time the Governor had an eye on a coloured young woman that was in Society [that is, a congregation member]. This same Governor had been once a Clergyman, and he saw himself so reproved by a black man that he did not know A from B, this heightened his prejudice, and he then said that this man would make the blacks too wise.[77]

He banned Harry from public speaking and decreed that "if he was found in the act of prayer he should be put into the fort, and the free people also and fed upon bread and water; and the poor slaves were to be whipped." Harry's meetings were then held under cover of distance from patrolling guards in the town "in country places and behind the mountains" "and the Lord always graciously visited us." In town, meetings were held under cover without "singing" which might draw the attention of the guards.[78] Harry recited the hymn the woman calls "Jesus Cover of my soul" as an intervention in a debate among congregation members about its meanings; calling this a prayer, guards arrested him for holding an illegal meeting. In the hymn the I of the singer implores Jesus to "Cover my defenseless head/With the shadow of thy wing" and affirms that "Plenteous grace with thee is found, Grace to cover all my sin."[79]

Cover is formulated in the woman's narrative as the "Lord" being on "the side" of the congregation. Faith covered Harry, authorizing him and his converts to fulminate against the moral corruptions of a plantation slavery and busy trading colony, rather than African darkness; the corruptions represent "the wrath to come." Sold on from north America to Mr Godette in Statia, Harry wove the cover of an evangelical family. Harry used to hold prayer-meetings and classes in the woman's family home; when she was 15 her father "thought it fit" that she should join the congregation. She acknowledges that during "our persecution" by Rennolds, being "among" the congregation ("them") provided a cover for her having "only the form of godliness," meaning that the "vital godliness,"[80] of "ecstatic ... experience"[81] eluded her. The "love of Christ" offered Harry the cover of "patient forbearance" during the punishment. After the whipping the woman's story tells, though, that he prophesied "dreadful calamities" for Statia. Even during the whipping of Harry, the woman reports that "the island was shook with a severe earthquake" that drove a good number of onlookers from the spectacle. His prophecies, including that "the market place should be covered" in "grass,"

> did come to pass. The first trouble that came on the land was a severe fire, which lasted a whole day, and that fire first began in the market, the very place where he was whipped. The next trouble was a violent flood which washed all oer the land, and no one was hurt but the man that took hold of Harry to carry him to the fort he was washed away in the flood. And after that they have been known to want bread and water; and they have indeed been troubled by caterpillars in their houses, though before they only came through the streets.[82]

Harry's experience and the woman's witness of its reach and repercussions are represented as "cosmic dramas."[83] The use of the word "nothing" in the narrative suggests the stakes of "sound sanctification": without it the congregation would "sink into nothing"; "sound sanctification" is a "fire" within the heart that "blaze[s] out" and "refresh[es]," and makes one "anew." An analogy with fire being "entirely outed" (ashes) suggests an awful prospect of damnation[84]; in the terms of Wesley's hymn, loss of the "haven" or "refuge" of resurrection of the "soul" under "cover" of Jesus.[85] Visionary capacity and prophetic utterance were integral to the experience of nineteenth-century African-American spiritual leaders, Methodists Rebecca Jackson, Elizabeth, Jarena Lee and Amanda Smith, and Baptist Nat Turner, and to West Indian spiritual leaders Sarah Moore, Jr and Robert Wedderburn.[86] Spirit possession and a sense of the efficacy of prophecy, spiritual visions, and of a mystical Providence characterize both Sub-Saharan African and Methodist spiritual idioms of this period, albeit that their meanings are culturally contingent.

Early Caribbean evangelical life narrative draws attention to the negotiation of agency by converts in lived cultures of life story within the public and quasi-public spaces of their communities. These cultures have historically also had a broader reach through dissemination of written narratives in global evangelical print cultures to promote the amelioration of slavery. Missionary discourse, exemplified in this essay by publications of Methodist Thomas Coke and Moravian Lewis Stobwasser, is part of the cognitive social and political terrain of modernity which shaped the emergence of modern forms of subjectivity in plantation slavery cultures. While missionary discourse constructed Africa in spiritual terms as heathen darkness, converts would find spiritual darkness a usable and powerful concept to critique and expose the material iniquities of plantation slavery and colonial trading cultures. The lay structures of evangelical missions enabled African diasporic leadership and community-building through oracy, mentoring and education.

NOTES

1. Jon Sensbach, *Rebecca's Revival: Creating Black Christianity in the Atlantic World* (Cambridge, MA: Harvard University Press, 2005), 93.
2. Sylvia R. Frey and Betty Wood, *Come Shouting to Zion: African American Protestantism in the American South and British Caribbean to 1830* (Chapel Hill, NC: University of North Carolina Press, 1998), 118.

3. See Ann Taves, *Fits, Trances, & Visions: Experiencing Religion and Explaining Experience from Wesley to James* (Princeton: Princeton University Press, 1999); David Hempton, *Methodism: Empire of the Spirit* (New Haven: Yale University Press, 2005); D. Bruce Hindmarsh, *The Evangelical Conversion Narrative: Spiritual Autobiography in Early Modern England* (Oxford: Oxford University Press, 2005); Phyllis Mack, *Heart Religion in the British Enlightenment: Gender and Emotion in Early Methodism* (Cambridge: Cambridge University Press, 2008); Maureen Warner-Lewis, *Archibald Monteath: Igbo, Jamaican, Moravian* (Kingston: University of the West Indies Press, 2007); Sue Thomas, *Telling West Indian Lives: Life Narrative and the Reform of Plantation Slavery Cultures, 1804–1834* (New York: Palgrave Macmillan, 2014); Jennifer Snead, "Print, Predestination, and the Public Sphere: Transnational Evangelical Periodicals, 1740–1745," *Early American Literature* 45, no. 1 (2010), 93–118.

4. "Life of Cornelius, a Negro-Assistant in the Brethren's Mission in St Thomas, as Related in the Diary of Newherrnhut," *Periodical Accounts Relating to the Missions of the Church of the United Brethren, Established among the Heathen* 3 (1801–05), 181–90; "The Life of Cornelius, a Negro Assistant in the Brethren's Mission in the Island of St Thomas," *Methodist Magazine* 18 (1805), 385–90; *The Life of Cornelius: A Negro Assistant in the Moravian Church at St Thomas* (St John's: Loving & Hill, 1820), a twelve-page pamphlet; and "Memoir of Cornelius, an Aged Negro, Assistant [*sic*] in the Brethren's Church at St Thomas, Who Died in November 1801," *Missionary Register*, April 1823, 161–64. The pamphlet is mentioned in Don Mitchell, *Mitchell's West Indian Bibliography: Caribbean Books and Pamphlets*, 11th ed., 2012, accessed September 30, 2011, www.books.ai.

5. Hempton, *Methodism*, 67.

6. "Life of Cornelius," *Periodical Accounts*, 182.

7. "Life of Cornelius," *Periodical Accounts*, 189–90.

8. An English translation of Stobwasser's *Lebenslauf*, "Memoir of Brother John Henry Lewis Stobwasser, Missionary in Antigua, Who Departed This Life at Berlin, January 9, 1832," was published in *Periodical Accounts Relating to the Missions of the Church of the United Brethren, Established among the Heathen* and reprinted in the *United Brethren's Missionary Intelligencer and Religious Miscellany* 6 (1837): 38–44, 49–55.

9. Simon Gikandi, "Rethinking the Archive of Enslavement," *Early American Literature* 50, no. 1 (2015), 93, 92.

10. Beilby Porteus, *A Letter to the Governors, Legislatures, and Proprietors of Plantations in the British West-India Islands* (London: T. Cadell, T. Payne, & F.C. and J. Rivington, 1808), 33–34.

11. Thomas Coke, *A History of the West Indies, Containing the Natural, Civil and Ecclesiastical History of Each Island*, vol. 1 (Liverpool: Nuttall, Fisher, and Dixon, 1808), iv–v.

12. Thomas Coke, *An Address to the Pious and Benevolent, Proposing an Annual Subscription for the Support of Missionaries in the Highlands and Adjacent Islands of Scotland, the Isles of Jersey, and Guernsey, and Newfoundland, the West Indies, and the Provinces of Novi Scotia and Quebec* (London: n.p., 1786), 8.

13. Lewis Stobwasser to Christian Ignatius La Trobe, 8 November 1814, Antigua Archives Book 122/3, Letters from Antigua 1811–18, Moravian Church Archive and Library, London.

14. *Instructions for the Members of the Unitas Fratum, Who Minister in the Gospel among the Heathen* (London: n.p., 1784), 47.

15. "Proposal for Forming a Separate Fund for the Moravian Missions in the West Indies," *New Evangelical Magazine and Theological Review*, 1824, 360.

16. Coke, *A History of the West Indies*, vol. 1, 184.

17. "Life of Cornelius," *Periodical Accounts*, 184.

18. Hindmarsh, *Evangelical Conversion Narrative*, 175.

19. "Life of Cornelius," *Periodical Accounts*, 188–189.

20. Mary Prince, *The History of Mary Prince, a West Indian Slave, Related by Herself*, ed. Sara Salih (London: Penguin, 2004), 37.

21. Thomas, *Telling West Indian Lives*, 122–23.

22. Prince, *History of Mary Prince*, 37.

23. Mary Gilbert, *An Extract of Miss Mary Gilbert's Journal*, ed. John Wesley, 5th ed. (1768; London: G. Whitfield, 1799).

24. Free coloured was a historical racial category in the West Indies.

25. The memoir is transcribed in William Dawes to Rev. Josiah Pratt, 1 and 5 May 1821, in *Church Missionary Society Archive. Section V: Missions to the Americas. Part 1: West Indies Mission, 1819–1861* (Marlborough: Adam Matthew, 1999), Reel 2, C W M1.

26. Hempton, *Methodism*, 85.

27. Anne Gilbert, "A Short History of Peregrine Pickle (Now Baptised Peter) a Negro Belonging to His Majesty and Employed in the Naval Yard at English Harbour, Antigua," Wesleyan Methodist Missionary Society/West Indies/Correspondence/Box 116/Fiche Box 3, Archives and Special Collections, School of Oriental and African Studies, University of London; "West Indies," *Methodist Magazine* 44 (1821): 947–49.

28. Thomas, *Telling West Indian Lives*, 11–63. Dawes is not mentioned in Eugene Stock's *The History of the Church Missionary Society, Its Environment, Its Men and Its Work*, 4 vols. (London: Church Missionary Society, 1899–1916).

29. "Memoir of Cornelius, an Aged Negro, Assistant [*sic*] in the Brethren's Church at St Thomas, Who Died in November 1801," *Missionary Register*, April 1823, 161.

30. "Proposal for Forming a Separate Fund for the Moravian Missions in the West Indies," *New Evangelical Magazine and Theological Review*, 1824, 361. A shorter version of the proposal was published as "Moravian Missions in the West Indies," *Christian Guardian and Church of England Magazine*, 1824, 435–37. Material from the proposal was reused in *Particulars of the Sunday Schools for Negro Children, &c under the Direction of the Moravian Missionaries in the West Indies* (n.p., 1826).

31. *Slave Registers of Former British Colonial Dependencies 1812–1834* (Provo, UT: ancestry.com, 2007), online database. Antiguan slave returns show, for instance, that the Moravian missions on the island owned nine slaves in 1821.

32. G. Oliver Maynard, *A History of the Moravian Church, Eastern West Indies Province* (n.p.: n.p., 1968), 39.

33. Coke, *A History of the West Indies*, vol. 2 (Liverpool: Nuttall, Fisher, and Dixon, 1810), fold-out plate after page 46.

34. Joan Anim-Addo, "Sister Goose's Sisters: African-Caribbean Women's Nineteenth-Century Testimony," *Women: A Cultural Review* 15, no. 1 (2004), 37.

35. Johann Heinrich Lewis Stobwasser, *Ansichten von Missions-Niederlassungen der Evangelischen Brüder-Gemeinde, Vues des Établissements missionnaires fondés par la Communauté évangélique des Frères-Unis* (Basel: Publié au profit des Missions Évangéliques par une Société d'amis de l'Evangile, 1830?), Archive of Early American Images, John Carter Brown Library, Brown University, online collection. The descriptions of the images in this archive do not recognize that the buildings are mission stations.

36. Jamaica Kincaid, *A Small Place* (London: Virago, 1988), [1], [21], [40], [75]. The cover image—in colour—is a reversal of a segment of Stobwasser's *Vue de Gracehill dans l'Isle d'Antigoa aux Indes occidentales*.

37. Prince, *History of Mary Prince*, 29. Spring Gardens was the Moravian mission in St John's.

38. Salome Cuthbert, et al., "Memoir of the Life of the Negro-Assistant SALONE [*sic*] CUTHERT [*sic*], a Member of the Congregation at GRACEHILL (Compiled in part from her own narrative)," *Periodical Accounts Relating to the Missions of the Church of the United Brethren, Established among the Heathen* 11 (1829–31): 103–6.

39. Stobwasser, et al., "Memoir," 50.

40. Katherine Faull, introduction to *Moravian Women's Memoirs: Their Related Lives, 1750–1820* (Syracuse: Syracuse University Press, 1997), xxi.

41. Stobwasser, et al., "Memoir of Brother John Henry Lewis Stobwasser," 50.

42. Patricia Hill Collins, *Black Feminist Thought: Knowledge, Consciousness, and the Politics of Empowerment* (Boston: Unwin Hyman, 1990), 147, 129.

43. Elizabeth Hart Thwaites, "Letter from Elizabeth Hart to a Friend," October 24, 1794, in *The Hart Sisters: Early African Caribbean Writers, Evangelicals, and Radicals*, ed. Moira Ferguson (Lincoln, NE: University of Nebraska Press, 1993), 107, 109, 111.

44. Coke, *History*, vol. 1, 38.

45. Coke, *History*, vol. 3 (Liverpool: Nuttall, Fisher, and Dixon, 1811), 121.

46. Coke, *History*, vol. 1, 19. Nicole Aljoe draws attention to the number of West Indian slave narratives that are "embedded in other texts such as travel narratives, diaries, and journals or appear in records kept by legal, medical, and religious institutions." *Creole Testimonies: Slave Narratives from the British West Indies, 1709–1838* (New York: Palgrave Macmillan, 2012), 13.

47. Coke, *History*, vol. 3, 121.

48. The statistics are recorded by Coke, *History*, vol. 3, 121.

49. Captain Thomas Southey, *Chronological History of the West Indies*, vol. 3 (London: Longman, Rees, Orme, Brown and Green, 1827), 147–49. The quotation is from p. 616. The congregation membership is given by Coke, *History*, vol. 3, 121.

50. Coke, *History*, vol. 3, 121–23.

51. Paul Wesley Chilcote, introduction to *Her Own Story: Autobiographical Portraits of Early Methodist Women* (Nashville: Kingswood Press, 2001), 40.

52. Coke, *History*, vol. 3, 122–23.

53. Katherine Binhammer, *The Seduction Narrative in Britain, 1747–1800* (Cambridge: Cambridge University Press, 2009), 8, 2.

54. Saidiya Hartman, "Venus in Two Acts," *Small Axe* 26 (June 2008): 12.

55. David Scott, *Conscripts of Modernity: The Tragedy of Colonial Enlightenment* (Durham, NC: Duke University Press, 2004), 119.

56. Coke, *History*, vol. 3, 122–23.

57. John A. Vickers, ed., *The Journals of Dr. Thomas Coke* (Nashville: Kingswood Books, 2005), 37. Extracts from Coke's journals had been published in 1793 and 1816.

58. Matthew 3:3 (AV).

59. Vickers, ed., *Journals*, 37.

60. Rev. Dr Wycherley Gumbs, *Black Harry "A Slave Redeemed"—A Man of Destiny* (U.S. Virgin Islands: Wycherley Gumbs, 1996), 2.

61. John Neal, "'In the beginning…': Gender, Ethnicity and the Methodist Missionary Enterprise," Methodist Missionary Heritage Project, accessed 2 February 2016, http://www.methodistheritage.org.uk/missionary-history-neal-in-the-beginning-2011.pdf.

62. [Abel Stevens], *Sketches & Incidents: A Budget from the Saddle-Bags of a Superannuated Itinerant* (New York: G. Lane and P.P. Sandford, 1844), 94–102.

63. Vickers, ed., *Journals*, 110. 3 February 1789.

64. Samuel Drew, *The Life of the Rev. Thomas Coke, LL.D. Including in Detail His Various Travels and Extraordinary Missionary Exertions, in England, Ireland, America, and the West-Indies: With an Account of His Death on the 3d of May, 1814, While on a Missionary Voyage to the Island of Ceylon, in the East-Indies. Interspersed with Numerous Reflections; and Concluding with an Abstract of His Writings and His Character* (London: n.p., 1817), 176.

65. "Some Account of Harry the Black Mentioned in Dr Coke's History: Taken from a Recital of a Black Woman in St Bartholomew January 1819," Wesleyan Methodist Missionary Society/West Indies/Correspondence, Archives and Special Collections, School of Oriental and African Studies, University of London. In developing the novel *Black Harry*, Gumbs has not known of this source.

66. Hempton writes of Methodists "sustaining 'islands of holiness' in an otherwise raucous environment, and … building a grander Christian family out of their manifold and diverse families." *Methodism*, 139. The term "sound sanctification" is used in "Some Account of Harry the Black."

67. Mack, *Heart Religion*, 13, 130.

68. "Some Account of Harry the Black."

69. "Some Account of Harry the Black."

70. Robert Wedderburn, *The Horrors of Slavery and Other Writings by Robert Wedderburn*, ed. Iain McCalman (New York: Marcus Wiener Publishing, 1991), 139.

71. Srinivas Aravamudan, *Tropicopolitans: Colonialism and Agency, 1688–1804* (Durham, NC: Duke University Press, 1999), 270–71.

72. Rev. John Horsford, *A Voice from the West Indies: Being a Review of the Character and Results of Missionary Efforts in the British and Other Colonies in the Caribbean Sea* (London: Alexander Heylin, 1856), 190, 193.

73. "Some Account of Harry the Black."

74. Taves, *Fits, Trances, & Visions*, 72.

75. Vickers, ed., *Journals*, 37.

76. Taves, *Fits, Trances & Visions*, 72, 75.

77. "Some Account of Harry the Black."

78. "Some Account of Harry the Black."

79. Charles Wesley, "Jesus, Lover of My Soul," Hymnary.org, accessed January 15, 2016, http://www.hymnary.og/text/jesus_lover_of_my_soul_let_me_to_thy_bos.

80. "Some Account of Harry the Black."

81. Mack, *Heart Religion*, 13.

82. "Some Account of Harry the Black."
83. Hempton, *Methodism*, 60.
84. "Some Account of Harry the Black."
85. Charles Wesley, "Jesus, Lover of My Soul."
86. For a very brief discussion of the African-American visionaries, see Jean McMahon Humez, introduction to *Gifts of Power: The Writings of Rebecca Jackson, Black Visionary, Shaker Eldress* (Amherst: University of Massachusetts Press, 1981), 6–7. On Sarah Moore, Jr and Robert Wedderburn, see Thomas, *Telling West Indian Lives*, 66–81, 97–117.

BIBLIOGRAPHY

Aljoe, Nicole. *Creole Testimonies: Slave Narratives from the British West Indies, 1709–1838.* New York: Palgrave Macmillan, 2012.

Anim-Addo, Joan. "Sister Goose's Sisters: African-Caribbean Women's Nineteenth-Century Testimony." *Women: A Cultural Review* 15, no. 1 (2004): 35–56.

Aravamudan, Srinivas. *Tropicopolitans: Colonialism and Agency, 1688–1804.* Durham, NC: Duke University Press, 1999.

Binhammer, Katherine. *The Seduction Narrative in Britain, 1747–1800.* Cambridge: Cambridge University Press, 2009.

Chilcote, Paul Wesley, ed. *Her Own Story: Autobiographical Portraits of Early Methodist Women.* Nashville: Kingswood Press, 2001.

Church Missionary Society Archive. Section V: Missions to the Americas. Part 1: West Indies Mission, 1819–1861. Marlborough: Adam Matthew, 1999.

Coke, Thomas. *An Address to the Pious and Benevolent, Proposing an Annual Subscription for the Support of Missionaries in the Highlands and Adjacent Islands of Scotland, the Isles of Jersey, and Guernsey, and Newfoundland, the West Indies, and the Provinces of Nova Scotia and Quebec.* London: n.p., 1786.

Coke, Thomas. *A History of the West Indies, Containing the Natural, Civil and Ecclesiastical History of Each Island.* 3 vols. Liverpool: Nuttall, Fisher, and Dixon, 1808–11.

Collins, Patricia Hill. *Black Feminist Thought: Knowledge, Consciousness, and the Politics of Empowerment.* Boston: Unwin Hyman, 1990.

Cuthbert, Salome, et al. "Memoir of the Life of the Negro-Assistant SALONE [*sic*] CUTHERT [*sic*], a Member of the Congregation at GRACEHILL (Compiled in Part from Her Own Narrative)." *Periodical Accounts Relating to the Missions of the Church of the United Brethren, Established among the Heathen* 11 (1829–31): 103–6.

Drew, Samuel. *The Life of the Rev. Thomas Coke, LL.D. Including in Detail His Various Travels and Extraordinary Missionary Exertions, in England, Ireland, America, and the West Indies: With an Account of his Death on the 3d of May,*

1814, While on a Missionary Voyage to the Island of Ceylon, in the East Indies. Interspersed with Numerous Reflections; and Concluding with an Abstract of His Writings and His Character. London: n.p., 1817.

Faull, Katharine. Introduction to *Moravian Women's Memoirs: Their Related Lives, 1750–1820.* Syracuse: Syracuse University Press, 1997.

Frey, Sylvia R. and Betty Wood. *Come Shouting to Zion: African American Protestantism in the American South and British Caribbean to 1830.* Chapel Hill, NC: University of North Carolina Press, 1998.

Gikandi, Simon. "Rethinking the Archive of Enslavement." *Early American Literature* 50, no. 1 (2015): 81–102.

Gilbert, Mary. *An Extract of Miss Mary Gilbert's Journal.* Ed. John Wesley. 5th ed. 1768; London: G. Whitfield, 1799.

Gumbs, Rev. Dr Wycherley. *Black Harry "A Slave Redeemed"—A Man of Destiny.* U.S. Virgin Islands: Wycherley Gumbs, 1996.

Hartman, Saidiya. "Venus in Two Acts." *Small Axe* 26 (June 2008): 1–14.

Hempton, David. *Methodism: Empire of the Spirit.* New Haven: Yale University Press, 2005.

Hindmarsh, D. Bruce. *The Evangelical Conversion Narrative: Spiritual Autobiography in Early Modern England.* Oxford: Oxford University Press, 2005.

Horsford, John, Rev. *A Voice from the West Indies: Being a Review of the Character and Results of Missionary Efforts in the British and Other Colonies in the Caribbean Sea.* London: Alexander Heylin, 1856.

Humez, Jean McMahon, ed. *Gifts of Power: The Writings of Rebecca Jackson, Black Visionary, Shaker Eldress.* Amherst: University of Massachusetts Press, 1981.

Instructions for the Members of the Unitas Fratum, Who Minister in the Gospel among the Heathen. London: n.p., 1784.

Kincaid, Jamaica. *A Small Place.* London: Virago, 1988.

King James Bible.

"Life of Cornelius, a Negro-Assistant in the Brethren's Mission in St Thomas, as Related in the Diary of Newherrnhut." *Periodical Accounts Relating to the Missions of the Church of the United Brethren, Established among the Heathen* 3 (1801–05): 181–90.

Mack, Phyllis. *Heart Religion in the British Enlightenment: Gender and Emotion in Early Methodism.* Cambridge: Cambridge University Press, 2008.

Maynard, G. Oliver. *A History of the Moravian Church, Eastern West Indies Province.* n.p.: n.p., 1968.

"Memoir of Cornelius, an Aged Negro, Assistant [*sic*] in the Brethren's Church at St Thomas, Who Died in November 1801." *Missionary Register*, April 1823, 161–64.

Mitchell, Don. *Mitchell's West Indian Bibliography: Caribbean Books and Pamphlets*, 11th ed., 2012, accessed September 30, 2011, www.books.ai.

"Moravian Missions in the West Indies." *Christian Guardian and Church of England Magazine*, 1824, 435–37.

Neal, John. "'In the beginning...': Gender, Ethnicity and the Methodist Missionary Enterprise." Methodist Missionary Heritage Project, accessed 2 February 2016, http://www.methodistheritage.org.uk/missionary-history-neal-in-the-beginning-2011.pdf.

Particulars of the Sunday Schools for Negro Children, &c Under the Direction of the Moravian Missionaries in the West Indies. n.p., 1826.

Porteus, Beilby. *A Letter to the Governors, Legislatures, and Proprietors of Plantations in the British West-India Islands*. London: T. Cadell, T. Payne, & F.C. and J. Rivington, 1808.

Prince, Mary. *The History of Mary Prince, a West Indian Slave, Related by Herself.* Ed. Sara Salih. London: Penguin, 2004.

"Proposal for Forming a Separate Fund for the Moravian Missions in the West Indies." *New Evangelical Magazine and Theological Review*, 1824, 358–61.

Scott, David. *Conscripts of Modernity: The Tragedy of Colonial Enlightenment*. Durham, NC: Duke University Press, 2004.

Sensbach, Jon. *Rebecca's Revival: Creating Black Christianity in the Atlantic World*. Cambridge, MA: Harvard University Press, 2005.

Slave Registers of Former British Colonial Dependencies 1812–1834. Provo, UT: ancestry.com, 2007, online database.

Snead, Jennifer. "Print, Predestination, and the Public Sphere: Transnational Evangelical Periodicals, 1740–1745." *Early American Literature* 45, no. 1 (2010): 93–118.

"Some Account of Harry the Black Mentioned in Dr Coke's History: Taken from a Recital of a Black Woman in St Bartholomew January 1819," MS, Wesleyan Methodist Missionary Society/West Indies/Correspondence, Archives and Special Collections, School of Oriental and African Studies, University of London.

Southey, Captain Thomas. *Chronological History of the West Indies*, vol. 3. London: Longman, Rees, Orme, Brown and Green, 1827.

[Stevens, Abel]. *Sketches & Incidents: A Budget from the Saddle-Bags of a Superannuated Itinerant*. New York: G. Lane and P.P. Sandford, 1844.

Stobwasser, Lewis. *Ansichten von Missions-Niederlassungen der Evangelischen Brüder-Gemeinde, Vues des Établissements missionnaires fondés par la Communauté évangélique des Frères-Unis*. Basel: Publié au profit des Missions Évangéliques par une Société d'amis de l'Evangile, 1830? Archive of Early American Images, John Carter Brown Library, Brown University, online collection.

Stobwasser, Lewis, et al. "Memoir of Brother John Henry Lewis Stobwasser, Missionary in Antigua, Who Departed This Life at Berlin, January 9, 1832." *United Brethren's Missionary Intelligencer and Religious Miscellany* 6 (1837): 38–44, 49–55.

Stobwasser, Lewis. To Christian Ignatius La Trobe, 8 November 1814. Antigua Archives Book 122/3, Letters from Antigua 1811–18, Moravian Church Archive and Library, London.

Stock, Eugene. *The History of the Church Missionary Society, Its Environment, Its Men and Its Work*, 4 vols. London: Church Missionary Society, 1899–1916.

Taves, Ann. *Fits, Trances, & Visions: Experiencing Religion and Explaining Experience from Wesley to James.* Princeton: Princeton University Press, 1999.

Thomas, Sue. *Telling West Indian Lives: Life Narrative and the Reform of Plantation Slavery Cultures, 1804–1834.* New York: Palgrave Macmillan, 2014.

Thwaites, Elizabeth Hart. "Letter from Elizabeth Hart to a Friend," October 24, 1794. In *The Hart Sisters: Early African Caribbean Writers, Evangelicals, and Radicals.* Ed. Moira Ferguson. Lincoln, NE: University of Nebraska Press, 1993.

Vickers, John A., ed. *The Journals of Dr. Thomas Coke.* Nashville: Kingswood Books, 2005.

Warner-Lewis, Maureen. *Archibald Monteath: Igbo, Jamaican, Moravian.* Kingston: University of the West Indies Press, 2007.

Wedderburn, Robert. *The Horrors of Slavery and Other Writings by Robert Wedderburn.* Ed. Iain McCalman. New York: Marcus Wiener Publishing, 1991.

Wesley, Charles. "Jesus, Lover of My Soul." Hymnary.org, accessed January 15, 2016, http://www.hymnary.org/text/jesus_lover_of_my_soul_let_me_to_thy_bos.

Wesleyan Methodist Missionary Society Archive. Archives and Special Collections, School of Oriental and African Studies, University of London.

"West Indies." *Methodist Magazine* 44 (1821): 947–49.

CHAPTER 4

The Promise of the Tropics: Wealth, Illness, and African Bodies in Early Anglo-Caribbean Medical Writing

Kelly Wisecup

In the introduction to his enormous *Voyage to Jamaica … Wherein is an Account of the Inhabitants, Air, Waters, Diseases, Trade &c of that Place* (1707), physician, natural historian, collector, plantation owner, and eventual secretary of the Royal Society Hans Sloane detailed the dangers that Jamaica held for British colonists' health. European inhabitants of the island, he explained, often changed color "from white to that of a yellowish colour"[1] and faced death from "ill Air."[2] The tropics also consumed bodies, for Sloane pointed out that the "Air here being so hot and brisk as to corrupt and spoil Meat in four hours after 'tis kill'd, no wonder if a diseased Body must be soon buried."[3]

In addition to these cases of colonial immoderation, *Voyages* is a natural history of the islands Sloane visited; indeed, the text is devoted primarily to describing and classifying the botanical productions of the Caribbean. Sloane's accounts of the Caribbean's illnesses and its botanical wealth produce an image of the tropics as a place both of great natural and medical

K. Wisecup (✉)
Department of English, Northwestern University, Evanston, IL, USA

© The Author(s) 2018
N. N. Aljoe et al. (eds.), *Literary Histories of the Early Anglophone Caribbean*, New Caribbean Studies,
https://doi.org/10.1007/978-3-319-71592-6_4

61

bounty and of frightening diseases. This contradictory image is a key feature of medical caribbeana, or poetry or prose from and about the West Indies, its diseases, and its medicinal plants. In addition to Sloane's *Voyages*, texts such as William Hughes's *The American Physitian; or a Treatise of the Roots, Shrubs, Plants, Fruit, Trees, Herbs &c. Growing in the English Plantations of America* (1672), Thomas Trapham's *Discourse of the State of Health in the Island of Jamaica* (1679), and Benjamin Moseley's 1804 *Medical Tracts* indicate physicians' concern with describing the Caribbean climate and its effect on health. Moreover, medical practice and an interest in plants that held immense medical and commercial value in England often overlapped, as indicated by the titles of physicians' books: from Trapham's *Some Observations on the Bermuda Berries* (1694) and Henry Stubbe's *The Indian Nectar, Or a Discourse Concerning Chocolata* (1692) to James Grainger's *The Sugar-Cane* (1764) and Moseley's chapter "On Sugar" in *Medical Tracts*.[4]

British physicians' dual focus on both plants and climate reflected long-standing European views of the Caribbean as a site of great wealth and of great danger to European bodies.

Classical western philosophies and geographies had indicated that the Caribbean should be uninhabitable: it was located in a tropical zone, one characterized by extreme heat that would presumably produce great mineral wealth yet that would also be hostile to life and produce monstrous forms of life. Sixteenth-century European travelers to Africa expected to meet certain death as they traveled farther south: as Anthonie Anes Pinteado noted in his account of his travels to Africa, printed by Richard Eden in 1555 as "The first voyage to Guinea," he warned his men not to travel further into Guinea, because of the "smotherynge heate with close and cloudy ayer and storminge wether of suche putrifyinge qualitie that it rotted the cotes of theyr backs."[5] Explorers such as Christopher Columbus began to revise these theories when they found the Caribbean to be habitable. As Nicolás Wey Gómez has shown, Columbus was instrumental in redefining views of the tropics, which "underwent a transformation from a forbidding inferno to prodigal paradise," a place that generated not only gold but also spices and valuable plants and that would not be fatal to Europeans.[6] However, as Wey Gómez explains, Columbus did not alter the classical philosophies predicting that monstrous, weak-willed people would be found in hot places. This revision of only part of the conceptions of the Caribbean justified promotions of colonization in the West Indies on the basis that gold would be found, even while allowing the concomitant enslavement, dispossession, and mistreatment of Native and African peoples, who, as people indigenous to tropical places, were expected to be barbarous and uncivilized.

Despite Columbus's revision, conceptions of the tropics as dangerous to Europeans' lives and bodies did not fully disappear from writing about the Caribbean. Colonial travelers paired accounts of natural fecundity with descriptions of horrible illnesses, rotting flesh, and degraded morals; descriptions that came to seem definitive of Caribbean literatures, on the one hand, and traits expected of people returning from a stay in the tropics, on the other. This contradiction—descriptions of medical wealth and of extreme forms of death—is a key element of medical caribbeana, for these texts collect, describe, and provide instructions for using the medical bounty of the tropics, and they warn readers about the dangers of living in the tropics and consuming its foods. Moreover, this contradiction was exacerbated by the transatlantic slave trade and the presence of Africans in the Caribbean. While British colonists argued that Africans were suited to the tropical climate given their original, southern location, and thus that they made ideal laborers, colonists also confronted—and attempted to disavow—the fact that their ability to safely extract and benefit from the Caribbean's botanical wealth depended directly on the immoderate labor and treatment of Africans.

In her transhistorical work, *Consuming the Caribbean: From Arawaks to Zombies*, Mimi Sheller shows that the image of the Caribbean "as a tropical paradise in which the land, plants, resources, bodies, and cultures of its inhabitants are open to be invaded, occupied, bought, moved, used, viewed, and consumed in various ways" is a very old and ongoing trope, one that originated with Columbus and was developed by British colonists.[7] As she points out, Europeans consumed not only goods and commodities from the Caribbean, but also "entire natures, landscapes, cultures, visual representations, and even human bodies."[8] This sort of "consumption 'at a distance'" was made possible by the mobility of European bodies and of Caribbean plants, resources, and images and by the immobility of African bodies.[9] Sheller traces across several centuries the processes whereby the "imaginative and material structures that span the Atlantic-Caribbean world enabled these unequal transformations of one person's sweat and blood into another's sugar, one person's provision ground into another's playground."[10]

Drawing on Sheller's argument, I examine medical writing from the late seventeenth through early nineteenth centuries in which British colonists sought to describe the Caribbean as a site of wonder, prime for material and epistemological consumption. I expand Sheller's argument by showing that such descriptions were inextricably linked to deep anxieties about the effects of consumption on British bodies and about the relation between slavery and European consumption. As Keith Sandiford has shown, acts of distancing were especially important for colonial Creoles whose social status was tainted by Caribbean forms of consumption, specifically, Creole society's "central relation to slavery and its marginal relation to metropolitan cultures."[11] Sandiford shows that absenteeism constituted one key strategy with which Creoles removed their bodies from the "physical scene of production,"[12] relocated them to the metropole, and then filled the metropole with the "epistemologies of colonization, and its particular productive underpinnings in sugar."[13] I follow Sandiford by taking colonists' fraught relation to Europe and their allegedly compromised bodily and cultural identities as a defining factor of Caribbean writing, but I depart from him by examining texts that are obsessed not with remaking Creole selves in the metropole but with maintaining the health and the status of people in the Caribbean, in spaces in which they faced directly the relation between slavery and the consumption and production of epistemological, economic, and social wealth.

In doing so, this chapter joins recent scholarship that has challenged previous views of the early Caribbean as producing little of literary or scientific value, by showing that British medical writers not only sought to ensure the health of their patients by providing useful information about harmful and healthful plants, herbs, and foods, but that they also used the rhetorical and material forms of their texts to advocate what they framed as moderate modes of consumption—of food and of texts about the Caribbean.[14] They accomplished this task by cataloging things, from plants and herbs to diseases, in short entries that provided descriptions and instructions for use or cures. In addition, the material form of the text— the short, repetitive entries, alphabetical indexes or tables, and glossaries of unfamiliar terms—restrained readers' exposure to these objects by first allowing them to glimpse it and its properties but then limiting that observation, providing notes for appropriate use or treatment, and by organizing tropical objects in familiar categories. These material forms moderated the consumption of Caribbean foods, plants, and rarities by transforming these potentially dangerous entities into objects of knowledge. In this way, colonists presented epistemological rather than physical consumption as an appropriate means of engaging with the tropics. Such forms of physical and textual moderation also worked to obscure the immoderate labor of enslaved Africans, labor on which colonists' consumption of products like sugar and rum depended, either by avoiding any mention of Africans or by transforming experiences in the Caribbean into objects of knowledge that could be safely consumed in England. However, as I explain below, Africans highlighted the effects of their immoderate labor on their bodies, by presenting symptoms of their enslavement and forced work, symptoms that disrupted colonists' rhetorical forms.[15]

I first examine William Hughes's 1672 *American Physitian*, a text that promises to offer descriptions of the "*Roots, Shrubs, Plants, Fruit, Trees, Herbs &c. Growing in the English Plantations of America.*"[16] Before Hughes begins his catalog of Caribbean botanical bounty, however, he takes a detour to describe several "remarkable" "rarities." He transforms such rarities into objects of knowledge to model a strategy with which readers might control their consumption of Caribbean flora, fauna, and food—a strategy that rests upon the effacement of immoderate forms of labor from the text. Next, I consider Sloane's introduction to *Voyage to Jamaica*, in which he catalogs not plants but diseases, in a section of case studies titled "*Of the Diseases I observed in* Jamaica, *and the Method by which I used to Cure them.*"[17] Sloane attempted to contain even unfamiliar tropical diseases in familiar narrative forms, thus demonstrating his medical expertise. However, he struggled to diagnose the illnesses that affected enslaved Africans: he found it difficult both to identity and to heal the diseases, and he admitted that Africans possessed their own powerful theories about their maladies. Africans' illnesses exposed the connections between colonists' ability to consume the Caribbean in moderation, on the one hand, and the effacement of immoderate labor and enslaved peoples' bodily illnesses, on the other. Finally, my conclusion shows how seventeenth- and eighteenth-century medical writing about moderation provided a foundation for nineteenth-century plantation medical treatises and novels, both of which idealize moderate planters and, consequently, shore up pro-slavery arguments.

"Rarities," Objects of Knowledge, and Immoderate Labor

In his *American Physitian*, Hughes sought to temper readers' access to Caribbean flora and fauna and thus to demonstrate how measuring one's physical and mental exposure to the tropics could maintain bodily health. On the title page, Hughes claimed to offer a treatise of American plants, roots, and trees. And he did offer readers a detailed catalog of Caribbean roots, shrubs, plants, and so on, but he seemed also to be fascinated by natural phenomena that do not fit into this category. Hughes began the treatise by describing objects that he called "rarities," or "remarkable things which were exposed to my consideration on when I first visited the shore; which indeed, although they grow, yet cannot properly be called Herbs, Roots, &c."[18] From the first pages of the treatise then, Hughes's attempt to present to readers the useful applications of tropical flora and the "Vertues and Uses of them, either for Diet, Physick, &c." is disrupted by a class of things that "grow" but do not qualify as herbs and roots.[19] Thus while he aimed to characterize the Caribbean as a place with plants that have specific uses and benefits for English colonists' health, he also admitted that the tropics contain unique and astonishing objects, those which have unknown effects on colonists and which cannot be grouped in familiar categories.

Despite his departure from his stated focus, Hughes was careful to ensure that his readers did not engage tropical rarities immoderately (or in ways that would threaten their bodily and cultural identities). Most entries on a rarity contain a section of introduction, followed by a description, the places the object could be found, and how to use it. Interestingly, the instructions for "use" convert the rarities into objects that readers in England could collect and appreciate in decidedly non-tropical spaces, spaces in which rarities are transformed into objects of knowledge. For example, Hughes noted that he discovered what he calls "sea eggs" are sea urchins, when he and other travelers went "into the water to wash and solace ourselves in that hot Climate."[20] Wading in the water, he "hapned to tread on them, there being very many in the shallows, near unto the shore."[21] The "prickles" of these "sea eggs" "made such an entrance into my bare feet, that startled me, fearing a worse event might follow there-upon."[22] Even though Hughes's discovery of the sea eggs was intimately connected to his experience of the "hot Climate," and thus to the medical dangers of the Caribbean, he imagined readers experiencing the sea eggs in a radically different way. He wrote that the sea eggs "are very pretty Rarities for your Ladies Closets and cannot but please the Eye and Fancy very much in beholding them."[23] Similarly, Hughes noted that another rarity, "sea star fish," was often found on rocks that "Mariners most fear."[24] The sea star fish travels "always in boystrous weather," in which mariners hold onto coral, fearing that they "should be cast on shore, and lost, as it were, by shipwreck."[25] Yet Hughes went on to cast the sea star fish as an object of pleasure and acquisition, writing, "I know not the use of this kinde of Fish; but doubtless it is good for something, there being nothing made in vain: as for the shell, it is a very pretty Toy."[26] Hughes recontextualized tropical rarities by imagining them in European collections, removed from the contexts in which they prick one's foot without warning and from the rocks that threaten to shipwreck mariners. In his treatise, the rarities do not challenge or threaten British identities or disease their bodies but instead have the potential to enhance his readers' status. The ability to own and observe a "sea egg" in one's closet, or cabinet of curiosities, could suggest one's status and learning while also demonstrating one's "control over the natural world."[27] Importantly, in the collections, the rarities are distanced from their connection to dangerous climatological phenomena; they instead are valued and useful, "pretty Toy[s]" that bring pleasure when observed. The rarities may be safely consumed once they are converted into objects for collecting, displaying, and viewing.[28]

After an apology for his digression, Hughes returned to the stated focus of his text by describing tropical plants, herbs, and roots, their uses, and their effects on English bodies. In this section, he more overtly considered how colonists' bodies responded to the tropical climate and offered guidance for how to use plants' properties to maintain health. Hughes described tropical foods as good for British bodies and argued that they were easier to digest than their English counterparts. Yet, he also insisted that such foods must be consumed in moderation to benefit from their qualities. For example, he noted that peas and bonavis are both good foods, and "easier of digestion" or "more pleasant" than "ours are."[29] He warned readers that these peas and bonavis, among other foods, should not be "eaten too freely,"[30] must "be moderately eaten;"[31] or "be taken moderately,"[32] or they will "oppress the head" and stomach, causing "wind."[33] Hughes's warnings point not only to the qualities of the food but also to the ways that colonists' bodies had been weakened by the heat. His instructions work to limit the dangers of tropical plants and food by pointing to their medical value even while ensuring that improper or immoderate use does not harm colonists' bodies.

The material form of *The American Physitian* promotes moderation as a literary and readerly practice, one that should ideally parallel the moderate forms of consumption that Hughes recommended within the text. The body of the text is preceded by an alphabetic "table," which organizes the profusion of "Plants, and rarer things" in a familiar, orderly form and provides page numbers for each entry.[34] Thus, if Hughes encountered sea eggs and sea star fishes as he sought relief from the tropical sun, readers first encounter these objects as entries in an alphabetic list that allows them to choose which objects they wish to encounter and to go directly to the corresponding page in the text. The table allows readers to moderate their use of the text and thus to practice controlling how they encounter and use Caribbean objects. The body of the text and its form also support this material moderation, for Hughes organized each entry into categories of place, time, name, and use. These sections, like the alphabetic table, incorporate even unfamiliar foods and plants into familiar categories, ones that render Caribbean flora and fauna in terms of their medical and dietary functions, not their potential danger to English bodies. The material form of the text allowed Hughes to represent the botanical and medical fecundity of the Caribbean even while ensuring that its hazardous elements did not overwhelm or harm colonists.

Finally, Hughes's material and rhetorical forms of moderation efface immoderate labor from the text. The enslaved Africans who plant, harvest, and process the plants discussed in the treatise are absent, even though Hughes described sugar cane and offered a detailed account of how it is harvested and processed. As he detailed each stage of cultivation and management, Hughes named the planter as the primary actor providing the labor required for each stage. When discussing processes that required multiple laborers, Hughes used the passive voice or a non-specific "they" to refer to the myriad people involved in these processes. For example, he wrote that "When they [sugar cane plants] come to maturity (which the Planters know by several signs, as well as we know when our Harvest is ready) they do cut them down at or above the first joint from the ground."[35] The "Planters" are the only antecedents for the pronoun "they," despite the fact that readers in the West Indies and in Europe would have known that it was African slaves who were cutting the plants. The closest Hughes came to recognizing the effects of slave labor on Africans is when he wrote—again without using specific nouns—that "Those who work very much in the Sugar-houses are very subject to the *Scurvie,* by reason of excess in the use thereof: not that Sugar is apt to breed the *Scurvie,* (for Salt will do the same, being immoderately used, as we see among Seamen) but rather the contrary in both; for they are both Preservatives to the body, as well as to fruit or flesh, being used accordingly."[36] Hughes seemed to suggest that Africans get scurvy because they use—or consume—too much sugar, not because the excessive, forced contact they have with sugar in the course of its processing and production is unhealthy.

Yet, the trope of the Caribbean as a site of excessive consumption effaced the connection between Africans' illness and their forced labor, leaving readers to assume that African workers, not the system of plantation slavery and colonists' own desires for sugar, are to blame for their illnesses. Hughes's text exposes the ways that arguments for moderation as a means of maintaining health rested upon an accompanying erasure of the immoderate labor—slavery—required to extract foods like sugar and transport it to England, where it could be consumed in moderation. Representing slavery would show that English colonization could not be extricated from immoderation, both colonists' own desire for profits from sugar and other crops and the conditions of enslaved Africans (and indentured servants). The continued focus on the dangers of tropical climates and diseases thus allowed colonists to avoid the question of how immoderate labor practices were connected to cases of colonial disease and debauchery. As the next section shows, Africans' illnesses and medical knowledge could bring these connections into plain sight in ways that challenged colonists' interpretation of the Caribbean, its wealth, and its dangers.

AFRICAN BODIES AND ILLNESSES OF IMMODERATION

In *Voyage to Jamaica*, Hans Sloane presented the diseases of Jamaica in a catalog of case studies that transformed the illnesses from entities that endangered colonists into objects to be observed. In a section of his introduction titled "*[Of] the Diseases I observed in* Jamaica, *and the Method by which I used to Cure them*," Sloane delineated the symptoms, diagnoses, and outcome of various maladies.[37] He had collected these examples in the course of his work as the physician to Christopher Monck, second Duke of Albemarle and Governor of Jamaica, during which time he was also called upon to treat other colonists and, sometimes, enslaved Africans. To organize his case studies, Sloane drew upon the *historia*, a narrative form with classical origins. The form of the *historia* paralleled the temporal progress of disease: both proceeded from a beginning to a middle and end, even if, in the case of disease, some of these elements might be invisible to observers or patients. *Historia* endowed case studies with authority by providing a familiar framework in which to describe symptoms, diagnose an illness, and discuss its outcome.[38] In Sloane's case, the *historia* represented disease as a chain of causes and effects that he and his patients could manipulate: Sloane by identifying and diagnosing the disease and his patients by taking proper actions to moderate their exposure to the conditions causing illness, thus eradicating the cause of disease. As Sloane discovered, however, not only did his British patients consistently fail to follow his advice, but the ill Africans whom he encountered also disrupted the narrative form of the *historia*. Thus, while Sloane, like Hughes, attempted to advance moderation as a path to colonial health in the tropics, his focus on bodies rather than plants exposes the ways in which African bodies and knowledge challenged colonial theories of tropical fecundity and mortality. His case studies exposed the limits of British medical advice, even as he attempted to demonstrate the efficacy and transportability of European medical knowledge.

Sloane's case studies begin with an identification of the patient, usually his or her name, age, and state of body. Next, he identified the patient's symptoms, documented the remedy or course of action he recommended, then described the body's response to the remedy before stating the outcome of the case. The *historia* link the patient's symptoms with Sloane's remedies and the patient's gradual recovery, so that by the conclusion of each case, Sloane's instructions and expertise are positioned as the cause of the patient's recovery. In this way, the *historia* support Sloane's argument, made at the beginning of the section, that, despite conventional wisdom, "any person who has seen many sick People, will find the same Diseases here [in Jamaica] as in *Europe*, and the same Method of Cure."[39] The outcome of the case studies as well as the familiar form of the *historia* support the argument that even if British colonists traveled to a new climate, their bodies would be afflicted by the same diseases and healed by the same forms of treatment as in Europe. In the context of medical philosophies and popular beliefs that colonists' bodies adapted to new climates and required different medical advice from their counterparts in Europe, Sloane offered reassurance that colonists' health and illness would continue to reflect their British identities. This argument thus also implicitly assured readers that any changes colonists' bodies underwent in the tropics were not permanent.

Significantly, in the cases in which a patient did not recover, Sloane suggests that it was usually due to his or her failure to follow Sloane's instructions to moderate his or her diet, drinking, or regimen. The case studies that end with the patients' death include incidents in which the patient disobeys Sloane by engaging in immoderate consumption. They usually slip back into drinking or were "much given to drinking and sitting up late, which I supposed had been the original cause of his present

Indisposition."⁴⁰ One man found relief in drinking "*Madera*-wine and water for the present, [but] he made use of it too often, whereby he became usually, the more he drank, the more dry, so that after a small time he was necessitated to drink again."⁴¹ Finally, another man, "Not being able to abstain from Company, he sate up late, drinking too much, whereby he not only had a return of his first Symptoms, but complain'd he could not make water freely."⁴² These examples of immoderate behaviors that undercut Sloane's medical advice form a pattern in which immoderate consumption of the Caribbean's wealth—namely, sugar, or more specifically, rum—stands as the primary cause of English colonists' deaths.

Just as Hughes converted rarities into objects of collection and pleasure, so Sloane's case studies transform acts of immoderate consumption into objects of knowledge that support Sloane's authority. He argued at the beginning of the case studies that British bodies could maintain their health if they followed his advice and controlled their consumption of food and drink. When considered alongside his statement that British bodies are afflicted by the same diseases in the Caribbean as in Europe, the cases in which patients die suggest that they are killed not by some lethal tropical illness but by a failure to follow medical advice (that is, death by drinking can happen in England just as easily as in the Caribbean). These instances become specimens of Caribbean illness and debauchery that, when examined by readers, expose the fact that the failure to follow Sloane's advice for moderation results in death.

Yet Sloane's account of diseases does highlight the limits of British medical advice when it comes to healing Africans' illnesses. Significantly, these cases do not involve familiar, European diseases nor are they cured by a regimen of moderation. Instead, the cases of two enslaved Africans, whose names Sloane gave as Rose and Emmanuel, present symptoms that Sloane struggled to classify and to cure and that consequently disrupt the form of the *historia*. Sloane explained that a woman named Rose became "Melancholy, Morose, Taciturn, and by degrees fell into a perfect Morishness [an uncivilized, barbarous state] or stupidity"; she refused to work and would sometimes stand for long periods of time holding a broom and staring into space.⁴³ Sloane recommended that Rose be "cupt and scarified"—a process that drew blood from the body through suction, but he also noted that this procedure did nothing for her. Next, he gave her several doses of an emetic and an herbal remedy, which, he noted, "sometimes wrought none at all, and at other times would work pretty well."⁴⁴ While Rose eventually and slowly improved through this circular process, Sloane acknowledged the presence of conflicting interpretations of her condition, and these interpretations, as well as Rose's resistance to his remedies, obstructed his narrative of diagnosis and recovery. He noted that after Rose recovered, she "was concluded not to be bewitched by her own Country people, which was the Opinion of most [who] saw her. This happens very often in Diseases of the Head, Nerves or Spirits, when the Symptoms of them are extraordinary, or not understood, to be attributed by the common People to Witchcraft, or the Power of the Devil."[45] Sloane did not make clear who "concluded" that Rose was not bewitched by her own people, suggesting only that her "country people" changed their views of her illness but also leaving open the question of whether he or other colonists came to this conclusion as well. Indeed, Sloane's own diagnosis of Rose's condition as a perfect "Morishness or stupidity" connected her symptoms not to a natural cause but to the barbarous nature that presumably derived from her African origins; he thus suggested that Rose's condition was not a physical malady but an interior condition. However, Rose's symptoms—her tendency to stand staring into space holding a broom—highlight the role that her status as a slave played in her malady— the disease rendered her unable to work, even as she was unable to change her enslaved position.

Emmanuel's case likewise highlighted labor as a cause of disease. Sloane explained that the African man suddenly became ill when told that he was ordered to guide a group on a hundred mile journey to confront some pirates. Sloane concluded that Emmanuel "pretended himself to be extraordinary sick, he lay straight along, would not speak, and dissembled himself in a great Agony, by groaning, &c."[46] And, as he had done in Rose's case study, Sloane included multiple opinions about Emmanuel, writing that Europeans "who stood by thought him dead, Blacks thought him bewitch'd, and others were of opinion that he was poyson'd."[47] Yet if in Rose's case Sloane decided that the enslaved Africans misinterpreted her illness as bewitchment and insisted that she had a malady with a physical cause, in Emmanuel's case he decided that the man did not have a malady at all but was faking illness. Sloane prescribed a "cure" of punishment and torture: Emmanuel was to have coals thrown on his head and candles applied to his hands and feet.[48] Sloane thus departed from his usual practice of diagnosing all diseases as having physical causes in order to suggest that Emmanuel's malady—similar to Rose's—was not an illness at all. He commented shortly after his discussion of Emmanuel's case that it was common for servants, both Black and White, to "pretend, or dissemble sickness of several sorts, but they are very easily with attention found out by Physicians, who are used to converse with Diseases, for the Symptoms do not answer one another, and they may, by proper questions be discovered as Forgeries, Perjuries, or Lyes."[49] Here, Sloane again attempted to recover the narrative order of the case study: he noted that if physicians ask "proper questions," they may discover the forgeries with which African and British servants fake their illnesses. Yet, he also noted that the symptoms in these cases "do not answer one another," and his description of disease as a rhetorical performance—a forgery, a perjury, or a lie—suggested that Africans' illnesses posed alternate conceptions of disease, symptoms, and cures as well as alternate, non-narrative strategies of communicating about and healing disease.

Keith Sandiford writes that Creole—or colonial—desire was always problematized by Caribs and Africans, by the "bodies linked to [sugar's] production" and by the ways in which those bodies "collude to infiltrate and defy" colonists' efforts to erase them.[50] It is because Africans and Caribs are "always elusive, never attaining total presence, and therefore never accommodating themselves to full apprehension" that they disrupt and contest Creole desire.[51] Rose's and Emmanuel's cases suggest that what I would propose calling "excessive presence" could also disrupt colonial desire. Their bodies refused to be contained in the form of the *historia*, but stand still, like Rose, exhibiting symptoms of the system on which colonists' production of knowledge, wealth, and moderation stands. Significantly, their symptoms cannot be entirely reduced to "Morishness"— that is, to their African origins in a tropical climate that, colonists argued, suited Africans for labor in the Caribbean.[52] While Sloane did write that Rose exhibits "Morishness," he observed that her illness also manifested itself as an inability or unwillingness to work and that she was cured not when he offered a treatment for nerves but after a secret medical practice conducted by Rose's own people. Her illness cannot be diagnosed and explained within Sloane's case study and its focus on natural causes and remedies, for it exceeded his medical philosophy and his modes of diagnosing and treating disease. Similarly, Emmanuel's illness rendered him unable to work, so that he also performed the effects of the immoderate labor that supported the colonial system and British colonists' ability to consume sugar, rum, and knowledge from the West Indies. While Sloane attempted to position Rose's and Emmanuel's diseases (and bodies) as objects of knowledge within his case studies, both Africans refused to occupy that position: their diseases slip out of Sloane's category for "illness," and their bodies respond not to his diagnoses and treatment but to medical practices that originated in their own communities. Their illnesses, bodies, and knowledge were not converted into specimens or objects of knowledge for readers to consume; instead they remained unobservable and unknowable, while also fully present and problematic in the text. Rose and Emmanuel represent "consuming practices as embodied material relations," thus offering a glimpse into the connections among slave labor, the production of knowledge, and colonial consumption, a glimpse that stands as a critique of colonial practices of consumption and of the erasure of slavery as an immoderate practice contributing to disease in the Caribbean.[53]

Systems and Fictions of Moderation

Finally, we can trace the influence of eighteenth-century medical caribbeana and tropes of immoderate consumption in two additional genres: first, in nineteenth-century medical treatises, planters modeled themselves on the ideal of the moderate colonist in order to support pro-slave trade interests. Second, fictional accounts convert colonists' concerns about immoderation and illness into a trope, in which the cruel immoderate planter is contrasted with the kind, benevolent master whose slaves save him from rebellion. In each of these cases, writers appear to critique the immoderate consumption of African bodies even as they support the continuation of slavery and the slave trade.

In the nineteenth century, medical practitioners began to urge planters to provide medical care for their slaves in order to lengthen their lifespans, thus shifting prior practices of maintaining slave populations by purchasing more slaves from Africa.[54] As movements to abolish slavery gained force and after England outlawed the slave trade in 1807, planters sought to maintain sugar production by replenishing slave populations with Africans born in the Caribbean. Key to this strategy were plantation medical treatises, which argued that planters should moderate Africans' labor and provide medical care for newly arrived slaves as well as for those born in the West Indies. Medical practitioners such as James Grainger, James Thomson, David Collins, and John Williamson produced such treatises, in which they offered practical instructions for healing the various maladies that afflicted enslaved Africans, from yaws and burns to worms and cholera. In addition, each physician presented his treatise and its information as a testament to the "humanity" of planters and overseers.[55] In the treatises, concern for Africans' well-being stands as a testament to planters' "distinguished humanity," and their medical care likewise ensured that Africans would be less likely to die from tropical diseases or immoderate labor.[56] For example, Grainger dedicated his treatise to planter Daniel Mathew (who was related to Grainger's wife), in order to "recommend [...] to others that distinguished humanity wherewith your Negroes have ever been treated."[57] The medical treatises presented an image of planters and overseers as moderate, humane, and industrious men who ensured their slaves' well-being and "manag[ed]" their slaves with "steadiness, judgment, and humanity."[58]

A number of nineteenth-century novels support this emphasis on moderation and "humanity" by constructing a dichotomy between good masters, identified with reason and kindness, and cruel ones, identified with excessive consumption and greed. For example, in William Earle's *Obi; or the History of Three-Fingered Jack,* Mr. Harrop (the father of the book's villain) is a kind master whose slaves mourn his death.[59] However, his son is of a "cruel and vindictive temper."[60] Captain Harrop sold his father's property, "converted it into money," and then purchased two slave ships, with which he quickly made back his investment.[61] Harrop uses cunning to acquire property and wealth, to convert property into money and relationships into wealth. When he is rescued and cared for by two Africans, he is still "running his own interest; trade was his idol, and there was no relief to his busy mind."[62] Harrop enslaves his African rescuers and ships them to his Jamaica plantation, thus converting them into assets on his plantation. Finally, Harrop is captured by Jack, the son of his African rescuers, who takes Harrop to his mountain hideaway where he dies, "starved to death in Jack's cave."[63] Harrop's death by starvation is ironic, given his extreme desire for advancement and wealth; he cannot survive when he cannot consume bodies, people, and things, and his death seems an apt punishment for his cruelty.

Similarly, Maria Edgeworth's 1804 "The Grateful Negro" describes two plantation owners: Mr. Jefferies has a "cruel and barbarous" overseer (Durant), but even when his slaves' complaints reach him, "Mr. Jefferies was moved to momentary compassion, he shut his heart against conviction: he hurried away to the jovial banquet, and drowned all painful reflections in wine."[64] Jefferies's desire for consumption of food and drink drives his unfeeling consumption of Africans' labor and bodies. By contrast, the planter Edwards gave his slaves "reasonable and fixed daily tasks; and when these were finished, they were permitted to employ their time for their own advantage or amusement. If they chose to employ themselves longer for their master, they were paid regular wages for their extra work."[65] When the slaves rebel against Durant's and Jefferies's cruelty, Edwards is saved by Caesar, the story's eponymous "grateful negro," who warns his master of the rebellion, thus allowing him to defend his house against the rebels. By contrast, Durant dies when his house is set on fire, and Jefferies loses so much in the fire that "he and his lady returned to England, where they were obliged to live in obscurity and indigence."[66] Like Harrop, Jefferies is punished for his acquisitiveness and over-reaching consumption with starvation and hunger, while the benevolent master is rewarded with an intact plantation and no threats to his wealth.

Both fictional and nonfictional accounts of moderate colonists and their humane treatment of Africans might seem to suggest that colonists could change their behavior to counteract the degenerative effects of the climate and the lure of the Caribbean's medical, natural, and commercial wealth. By treating Africans with moderation and caring for their maladies, colonists could hone their ability to, like Edwards, engage in sugar cultivation and production without falling prey to immoderate desires or consumption. Moreover, figures such as Caesar suggest that enslaved Africans would reward moderate, humane behavior with loyalty. Plantation medical treatises and West Indian novels alike worked to preserve the plantation system and slavery at a time when slavery was under fire in England, by suggesting that it was feasible to continue planation slavery as long as it was moderated. As planter David Collins noted in his medical treatise, "It may be laid down as a principle, susceptible of the clearest demonstration, that every benefit conferred on the slaves, whether in food, or clothing, or rest, must ultimately terminate in the interest of the owner."[67] As these two genres show, ongoing concerns with consumption and moderation continued to be marshaled in the defense of slavery, in an effacement of Africans' labor, and in arguments that colonists could withstand tropical degeneration. Even as medical treatises and novels ostensibly addressed the question of how to care for Africans and to ensure that their labor did not endanger their lives, they did so precisely in order to argue that planters could continue to consume slaves' labor and the botanical and medical wealth of the Caribbean.

NOTES

1. Hans Sloane, *A Voyage to the Islands Madera, Barbados, Nieves, S. Christophers and Jamaica, with the Natural History of the Herbs and Trees, Four-footed Beasts, Fishes, Birds, Insects, Reptiles, &c. of the Last of Those Islands,* vol. 1 (London, 1707), xviii.
2. Ibid., lxxiii.
3. Ibid., xlviii.
4. For a biography of Sloane and excellent reading of his botanical and medical writings on Jamaica, see James Delbourgo, *Collecting the World: Hans Sloane and the Origins of the British Museum* (Cambridge: Harvard University Press, 2017). On British physicians who were also writers, see Steven Thomas, "Doctoring Ideology: James Grainger's *The Sugar-Cane* and the Bodies of Empire," *Early American Studies* 4, no. 1 (2006): 78–111 and Kelly Wisecup, "All Apollo's Arts": Divine Cures, Afro-Caribbean Knowledge, and Healing Poetry in the British West Indies," *Literature and Medicine* 32, no. 2 (Fall 2014): 299–324. Richard B. Sheridan likewise discusses British physicians in the West Indies, although he focuses on medical practice and philosophy rather than writing. See Sheridan, *Doctors and Slaves: A Medical and Demographic History of Slavery in the British West Indies, 1680–1834* (Cambridge: Cambridge University Press, 1985).
5. Richard Eden, "The first voyage to Guinea," in *The First Three Books on America,* ed. Edward Arber (Birmingham, 1885), 376.
6. Nicolás Wey Gómez, *The Tropics of Empire: Why Columbus Sailed South to the Indies* (Cambridge: MIT Press, 2008), 53.
7. Mimi Sheller, *Consuming the Caribbean: From Arawaks to Zombies* (London: Routledge, 2003), 13.
8. Ibid., 14.
9. Ibid., 14. See also Sheller's discussion in *Consuming the Caribbean* 21.
10. Ibid., 13.
11. See Keith Sandiford, *The Cultural Politics of Sugar: Caribbean Slavery and Narratives of Colonialism* (Cambridge: Cambridge University Press, 2004), 3.
12. Ibid., 9.
13. Ibid., 16.
14. For previous studies see, for example, Susan Scott Parrish, *American Curiosity: Cultures of Natural History in the Colonial British Atlantic World* (Chapel Hill: University of North Carolina Press, 2006), James H. Sweet, *Domingos Álvares, African Healing, and the Intellectual History of the Atlantic World* (Chapel Hill: University of North Carolina Press, 2011), Christopher P. Iannini, *Fatal Revolutions: Natural History, West*

Indian Slavery, and the Routes of American Literature (Chapel Hill: University of North Carolina Press, 2012), and David Buissieret, "Studying the Natural Sciences in Seventeenth-Century Jamaica," *Caribbean Quarterly* 55, no. 3 (2009): 71–86.

15. Christopher Iannini argues that colonial writers such as Sloane employed "emblematic techniques" to address the problem of producing knowledge about natural specimens in the West Indies, a problem directly related to the fact that plantation slavery transformed humans into objects of knowledge, objects who sometimes also served as valuable sources of medicinal and botanical knowledge. Emblematic representations allowed writers to include the histories of objects in their accounts and thus to attempt to resolve the complicated relation between things, commodities, and people in the West Indies. While Iannini's focus on the emblem usefully elucidates particular problems in the production of knowledge about natural specimens, I focus here on the relations between bodies and texts, that is, on the ways in which the material and rhetorical forms of medical writing attempted to manipulate the consumption of tropical medicinal plants, food and drink, and African labor. Moreover, while Iannini suggests that planters' natural historical representations of slavery were created with the threat of slave rebellion in mind, I consider how specific African bodies disrupt these forms, not, in these cases, with the threat of a rebellion but with subtle yet powerful performances of the effects of colonial immoderation. See Christopher P. Iannini, *Fatal Revolutions*, 25.

16. William Hughes, *The American Physitian* (London: 1672), title page.

17. Sloane, *Voyage to the Islands*, xc.

18. Hughes, *American Physitian*, 2.

19. Ibid., title page.

20. Ibid., 6.

21. Ibid.

22. Ibid.

23. Ibid., 8.

24. Ibid., 11.

25. Ibid.

26. Ibid.

27. Paula Findlen, *Possessing Nature: Museums, Collecting, and Scientific Culture in Early Modern Italy* (Berkeley: University of California Press, 1994), 4. As Findlen argues of collecting in early modern Europe, "Through the possession of objects, on physically acquired knowledge, and through their display, one symbolically acquired the honor and reputation that all men of learning cultivated" (3).

28. As Sheller notes, the mobilization and movement of objects from the Caribbean was a key facet of Europeans' practices of consumption. See Sheller, *Consuming the Caribbean*, chap. 1.

29. On peas, see Hughes, *American Physitian*, 18 and on bonavis, 20.
30. Ibid., 20.
31. Ibid., 21.
32. Ibid., 80.
33. Ibid., 20.
34. Ibid., D1r–D2r.
35. Ibid., 30.
36. Ibid., 35.
37. Sloane, xc.
38. See *Historia: Empiricism and Erudition in Early Modern Europe*, eds. Gianna Pomata and Nancy G. Siraisi (Cambridge: MIT Press, 2005).
39. Sloane, *Voyage to the Islands*, xc.
40. Ibid., xcviii.
41. Ibid., xcv.
42. Ibid., xcviii.
43. Ibid., cxiv.
44. Ibid.
45. Ibid.
46. Ibid., cxli.
47. Ibid., cxlii.
48. Ibid.
49. Ibid.
50. Sandiford, *Cultural Politics*, 16. While the term "Creole" was historically used to refer to people of European and African descent who had been born in the Americas, I follow Sandiford here by using "Creole" to refer to people of European descent.
51. Ibid., 16–17.
52. Sloane, *Voyage to the Islands*, cxiv.
53. Sheller, *Consuming the Caribbean*, 14.
54. On such proposals, see Elsa V. Goveia, *Slave Society in the British Leeward Islands at the End of the Eighteenth Century* (New Haven: Yale University Press, 1969), 32–38, 144, 190–202 and J. R. Ward, *British West Indian Slavery, 1750–1834: The Process of Amelioration* (Oxford: Clarendon Press, 1988).
55. John Williamson, *Medical and Miscellaneous Observations, Relative to the West India Islands*, (Edinburgh, 1817), 55.
56. James Grainger, *An Essay on the More Common West-India Diseases*, ed. J. Edward Huston, (Jamaica, Barbados: University of the West Indies Press, 2005), 5.
57. Ibid., 5.
58. Williamson, *Medical and Miscellaneous Observations*, 93.
59. See William Earle, *Obi; or the History of Three-Fingered Jack* (Worcester, 1804), 111.

60. Ibid., 127.
61. Ibid., 111.
62. Ibid., 113.
63. Ibid., 168.
64. Maria Edgeworth, *Popular Tales,* vol. III (London, 1804), 194.
65. Ibid., 195–96.
66. Ibid., 239.
67. David Collins, *Practical Rules for the Management and Medical Treatment of Negro Slaves, in the Sugar Colonies. By a Professional Planter* (London, 1811), 22.

CHAPTER 5

Order, Disorder, and Reorder: The Paradox of Creole Representations in *Caribbeana* (*1741*)

Jo Anne Harris

From the moment of their first settlement, West Indian colonies were points of contact for diverse groups of peoples occupying spaces "in between" those of conqueror, conquered, indigenous or immigrant, master or slave. As a group, the original creoles, descendants of white European settlers, or long-term residents of the islands, defied social, legal, and economic theories argued in Europe. This, combined with the economic realities of maintaining an obsolete plantation system on the periphery of the imperial social structure, relegated early West Indian colonists to second class status; for England, their primary purpose was to ensure a steady supply of money and goods to fund other colonial projects. Despite this, those settlers who persevered and adapted told stories, sang songs, argued cases, and created laws that documented the process of societies being and becoming something new. This literary output, in combination with other colonial discourses, challenged notions of not only who was English, but also what constituted English literature on islands far from the center of power and literary exchange. In retrospect, these artifacts may be viewed

J. A. Harris (✉)
Georgia Gwinnett College, Lawrenceville, GA, USA

© The Author(s) 2018
N. N. Aljoe et al. (eds.), *Literary Histories of the Early Anglophone Caribbean*, New Caribbean Studies,
https://doi.org/10.1007/978-3-319-71592-6_5

as foundational elements of a literary tapestry representing the early Caribbean (Fig. 5.1).

This raises the question, when did early Caribbean literary history begin? Why have some argued that Caribbean literature as a genre begins with the postcolonial? What pulls academics to focus primarily on the binary master/slave relationships intrinsic to an obsolete plantation project that failed miserably? Any attempt to answer these questions becomes paradoxical. For instance: If one focuses on the construction of Whiteness, is one a racist? If modern West Indians are a hybrid of many cultures, why are some cultures more prevalent in the literature than others? For that matter, is Caribbean literature really literature at all? The answers are complicated by a conundrum that derives more from the writings that have not been carefully examined, than those that have. In other words, how do scholars deal with an unknown body of artifacts that are not necessarily considered part of the region's literary history, or which may be buried in restrictive archives elsewhere? One approach might be to engage in a remedial study of accessible literary artifacts using rhetorical tools typically used for postcolonial analyses of race, power, and ethnicity in Caribbean writing today. Through this approach, remediation can indirectly lead to uncovering texts that, much like their authors, have been omitted or "othered" in literary canons. Taking this type of archaeological approach to engage in a retrospective study of early quotidian texts seems crucial if we are to untangle historical relationships that evolved within an unequally shared colonial space.

In order to illustrate how remediation and an archaeological approach might operate, this essay focuses on *Caribbeana* (1741), a collection of works originally printed in the *Barbados Gazette* (1732–38). Few physical copies of either work are in existence, although an electronic version of *Caribbeana* may be accessed through subscription to the ECCO online repository. This, combined with the fact that *Caribbeana* pioneers as the first anthology of English language West Indian poetry, essays, and letters written and published in the West Indies, offers a unique opportunity to uncover artifacts representing the evolution of writing in the West Indies during the settlement period. Although the colonies were economically as important to the expanding British Empire as those on the North American mainland, until recently, their literary output has been conspicuously absent from anthologies of seventeenth- and eighteenth-century literature.

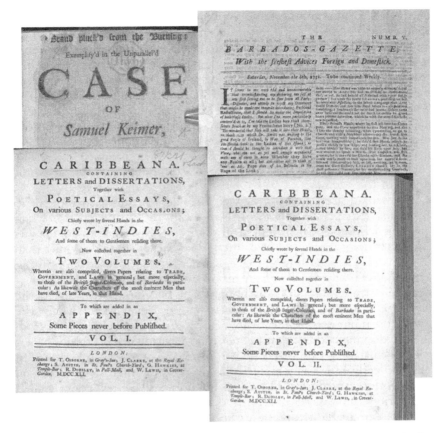

Fig. 5.1 Labeled 'An Odd Fish', Samuel Keimer provided readers in Barbados with entertainment and a public forum that records both their becoming and being West Indians (Images of *Caribbeana* (1741) ©British Library Board, 87.k.21)

Started in 1731 by David Harry and Samuel Keimer, the *Barbados Gazette* is historically important as Barbados' first newspaper and the first bi-weekly newspaper in the Americas. As the only periodical on the island, the *Gazette* quickly became a medium of literary exchange between Barbados and London, in part due to the literary aspirations of Keimer who served as its editor. A rather odd character with literary ambitions of his own, evidence in Isaiah Thomas' *History of Printing in America* informs us that, despite his newspaper's popularity, Keimer had trouble collecting payment from his customers. In 1734, on the verge of bankruptcy, the paper printed a poem in the May 4 edition, "The Sorrowful Lamentation of Samuel Keimer: Printer of the Barbados Gazette." He addressed the poem to "Those wou'd be thought gentlemen, who have long taken this paper, and never paid for it, and seem never to design to pay for it." Apparently, the poem produced no results and although it is included in Thomas' *History of Printing*,[1] it is not found in *Caribbeana*.

Financial distress was not new to Keimer, who prior to moving to Barbados had operated the *Pennsylvania Gazette*[2] during a period when printing in America was limited primarily to government documents and other items that could be printed more cheaply in the colonies than in England. Disregarding this fact, Keimer instead focused on printing English literary works, especially his own creations. As a result, his business failed miserably and was bought out by Harry who moved the press to Barbados. Ironically, it was on this small island where the Barbados public was intellectually near to, but geographically far from the London metropolis, that Keimer found a ready market for his paper, which he patterned after the popular *Tatler* and *Spectator* in London. In this vein early editorial commentaries reflect local interests interspersed with reprints of works published in London. As the newspaper gained popularity, the essays, poetry, and articles written by residents of Barbados circulated throughout the British Atlantic colonies. Many of the published "dissertations" discussed current issues in the islands, but many also challenged the authority of the King and Parliament to control the colonies, especially imposing high tax rates on sugar. After Keimer stopped publishing the *Gazette* in 1738, other newspapers in Barbados began to print locally written essays and commentaries, but none with the literary scope or unique style of the *Barbados Gazette*. Fortunately for scholars today, many of the most popular entries were compiled into a two-volume anthology printed in 1741, shortly after Keimer's death in 1739.[3] For a hundred years, this volume provided the only collection of original English language poetry and essays written and published in the West Indies by creoles.[4] Interestingly, although

London remained the stylistic model for this literature, its discourse reflects an increasingly Caribbean mode of thought that foreshadows today's West Indian cultural identity. However, to fully appreciate the nuances of the writings in *Caribbeana*, one must first understand both the historical contexts and eccentricities of both its editor and the period.

A Paradox of Disorder

> The Subjects of those islands [in the West Indies] must at all times depend upon the Parent State for Protection, & for every Essential resourse[sic]. The mart of their Produce will ever be at home; & the Public credit is security for their acquired Wealth if established in our Bank or Funds. Their aim is only to get Fortunes & return to their native Land. Such is the consequence of an Empire over Islands to Britain.[5]

Benedict Anderson argues, "Indirectly, the Enlightenment also influenced the crystallization of a fatal distinction between metropolitans and creoles."[6] Although Anderson was writing of Spanish America, the same may be said of West Indian settlers and their discourse in the British West Indies during the period of early Caribbean literary history. Geographically relocated within the empire, their growing numbers made these creoles increasingly rooted to remote islands they called "home," with "each succeeding generation presenting a historically unique political situation."[7] Increasingly, this distinction between metropolitans and creoles created enormous tensions in the British West Indies—especially in Barbados. Consequently, as West Indian settlements acquired an increased sense of community, their societies constituted a paradox of stability and instability within the British Empire that played out in contentious written exchanges.

On the one hand, as the frontier settlements evolved into stable societies, the empire was guaranteed an uninterrupted supply of labor and goods. On the other hand, as West Indian settlers acquired the legal, political, and cultural means to act as agents for their own economic interests, the hegemony of imperial control became threatened. Therefore, it became important for the metropolitan Englishman to depict West Indian creoles as corrupt, un-English inferiors, in order to justify trade policies designed to maintain control over plantation production. Operating within this paradox, British governance formulated and constructed its colonial creole subjects as cultural commodities to administer English agricultural interests.

Ironically, while England was busy de-Anglicizing the English creole, these same West Indian subjects focused on constructing and romantically glorifying their image as "English" within the landscape of a tropical island and culture built on a slave economy. Implicit in this bi-directional project was the understanding that being "English," also meant being "White," with the implications extending far beyond the phenotype to encompass Enlightenment notions of Englishness as a line of demarcation between "civilized" and "uncivilized." In this complicated process of constructing a West Indian Englishness, "white" became a qualifier for English, or civilized; conversely, "black" or non-white signified un-English, or uncivilized. From the imperial perspective, any acts of miscegenation and abuses of power were dismissed as products of disruption and disorder in places where "others" had somehow confused the boundaries. Yet, paradoxically, the West Indian colonies provided the English with sugar, tobacco, cotton, rum, and other commodities that enhanced their wealth and created signs of Englishness and order back home. Thus the notion of being creole, being from the Caribbean, became the center of a war of representations that continues to plague studies of Caribbean history with conflicting notions of who or what was English in the eighteenth century, and who or what is Caribbean in the twenty-first century. In that sense, this essay approaches the works first published in Keimer's newspaper, and later compiled and reordered in *Caribbeana*, as cultural artifacts through which we can engage in a literary archaeology to uncover ways in which the creoles in Barbados resisted imperial control during the 1730s.

Until recently, literary scholarship seems to have viewed this period of Caribbean history as a general notion of historical events, rather than a particular perception of how those events evolved into popular representations of the Caribbean that European powers used for political purposes. With this in mind, engaging in a literary archaeology of events surrounding periodical texts can be enlightening and challenging to the more Euro-centric view of history presented in textbooks. On the surface, these relics project an imperial style of writing and social constructs. However, careful study reveals that British residents in the West Indies were much less submissive than the image they conveyed to Parliament. As outliers in the empire, creoles reflect the premise expressed by Michel Foucault, who argues in *The Order of Things: An Archaeology of the Human Sciences* that all periods of history have possessed certain underlying conditions of truth that constituted what was acceptable, and history reflects a chronology of events that may be reorganized so that one event may lead to many representations and many temporalities.[8] That notion of fluidity of historical perceptions underpins current perceptions that little "real" or significant literary output was produced prior to Emancipation. The problem with that view stems not so much from a fragmented and sparse literary output, but in teasing out the particular Caribbean discourses buried inside the larger European discourses. In the 1730s, the West Indian islands and colonies were not independent, they were objects of colonization and production; therefore, most writing was tagged and archived as part of its colonial power. This makes discovery and retrieval problematic.

Another piece of the puzzle relates to the issue of public opinion over the years prior to the abolition of slavery. Somewhat akin to the proverbial elephant in the room, slavery was the engine that drove the colonies, but the fact that human beings were treated as chattel did not become a topic of controversy or writing until the late eighteenth century, when issues with the slave trade came under the lens of public opinion. In a study on slavery in Sierra Leone, David Lambert echoes Catherine Hall's arguments in *Civilising Subjects: Metropole and Colony in the English Imagination*,[9] as he argues that controversies over the Atlantic slave trade meant that "both supporters and opponents of slavery 'were interested in mobilizing public opinion, that increasingly powerful phenomenon.'"[10] From this perspective, writers on all sides felt justified in reordering or reorganizing events to reflect a specific idea or ideology. Although slavery is not a topic of public discourse until later issues of the *Gazette,* the organizer of *Caribbeana* may have used the same reordering tactic to reinforce perceptions that the relationship between Parliament and Barbados were without problems. Supporting this argument is a note in the Preface to the first volume, informing the reader that some of the entries "are removed from the Places they originally held, for the Sake of lengthening some Papers which might otherwise look too short; a Method we were led to by the Poverty of some of the Barbados Prints ... from whence we could pick but very little fit for our Purpose, and we did not care to lose what was" (I: ix).

Although the writer of these words has been presumed to be Keimer, Phyllis Guskin, who has written extensively on *Caribbeana*'s background, argues that Keimer died in 1739 it is more likely Jonathan Blenham, Attorney General for Barbados and a Whig activist, who wrote the introduction.[11] Writing in *Caribbeana* also projects local perspectives foregrounded in such a manner that reinforces the island's autonomy. Thus, Foucault's argument becomes plausible. Entries that had originally appeared chronologically in the *Gazette* over a period of six to seven years were reorganized into a thematic anthology intended to project a certain image favoring the interests of the planters in Barbados over imperial policies dictated by London. As a result, writing in the *Gazette* reflected a narrative quality that seems to foreshadow Hayden White's modern theory of historical narratives as "verbal fictions and narrative representations."[12] In the case of *Caribbeana*, this also foreshadows his *emplotment* theory that the way we tell things creates a plot; a process that transforms journalistic chronicles into literary fiction.

REORDERING THE PARADOX

> Every history, every series of events has a metahistory and deep grammar that allows our minds to make connections.[13]

In *Metahistory: The Historical Imagination in Nineteenth Century Europe*, Hayden White discusses the problem of converting "knowing" into 'telling.' In the case at hand, the individual writings in the newspaper take on a metonymic element. Thus, the entries that began as popular periodical expressions of real historical events, now appear as literary works of fiction that "tell" stories from a particular perspective. While this may or may not be true for the individual poems and miscellaneous literary works originally printed in the *Gazette*, the theory can explain their subsequent reorganization in *Caribbeana*. Once the texts were purposely taken out of their chronological sequence and reordered, the compilation reads as a Creolized literary representation asserting Barbadians' equal status within the empire. Based on that premise, we can then examine the poetry and essays in *Caribbeana* as relics of a literary archaeology. This opens the possibility to revisit, reexamine, and reinterpret the paradoxes of imperial and creole thought and relationships with arguments expressed in their original public forum matched to their socio-historical context. And, finally, remediation allows for the *Barbados Gazette* and *Caribbeana* to be considered emblematic of the evolution of Anglophone West Indian writing. Unwittingly, the *Gazette* and its editor may have provided artifacts documenting the responses of both colonial America and colonial Barbados to events radiating from the imperial center in London. If this is true, then as in any

archaeological endeavor, remediation necessitates digging through accompanying layers of historical deposit surrounding the artifacts in search of evidence to make interpretations about the people and their lives. However, unlike the physical excavations of places, literary archaeologies are not destructive, they are rather instructive and require a different set of tools to be effective. Although the scope of this chapter does not allow for an exhaustive study of *Caribbeana* as a case study, a snapshot look at the symbiotic relationship between politics and print in Britain, along with select entries written by the editor, hint at the promise of uncovering many more literary relics.

As stated previously, in eighteenth-century London, West Indian society with its mixture of races and ethnicities were frequently stereotyped as lacking culture or cultural reason because they fell outside the boundaries of the recognized English social parameters due to their geographic location, physical, socio-political, and economic positioning. Thus, emerging West Indian creole cultures, living in hot "un-English" climates were often portrayed in the media as social anomalies, ruled by passions that philosopher John Locke had labeled in *An Essay on Human Understanding* as the products of "warmed [and] over-weening Brain[s]."[14] While Locke may not have been referring to the creoles specifically, the fact that he had served as the Secretary of the Board of Trade and Plantations makes one suspect that the West Indies may have had some influence on his theories. Regardless, the outcome was that as colonists in Barbados struggled to cope with the realities of life in frontier settlements and the expectations of commercial interests in London, their cultural syncretism made them suspect Englishmen. English society perceived them as corrupted by the societies in which they lived, thus displaced and "othered,"—a fact seemingly unresolved to this date. Isolated both culturally and geographically, the colonists were also marginalized politically. In this sense, they came to view printing and print texts as more than a means of communicating news and gossip. The printing press was a weapon both at home and in the colonies. Letters and newspapers were the link with "home" and provided a forum for colonists to reassert their "Englishness."[15]

POLITICS AND PRINT

"Upon what system," one day inquired that unwearied political student, the Fantaisian Ambassador, of his old friend Skindeep, "does your Government surround a small rock in the middle of the sea with fortifications, and cram it full of clerks, soldiers, lawyers, and priests?" "Why, really, your Excellency, I am the last man in the world to answer questions, but, I believe, we call it 'THE COLONIAL SYSTEM!'"[16]

In the eighteenth century, politics and print were no longer just for the wealthy; everyone had access. The Glorious Revolution in 1689 had marked the end of an era in the English monarchy and the beginnings of popular government. As the new monarchy and the new century began, the British monarch no longer ruled by royal prerogative, but by Parliamentary policies and an English law shaped by arguments on what constituted natural law and reason. Thus, while the previous hundred years had seen kings beheaded, exiled, or overthrown in bloody battles, future monarchs would inherit, negotiate, or assert their right to rule, with wars often fought by proxy, on the seas, or in the faraway colonies of the Empire. At home, reasonable English people would sip tea imported by the East India Company and sweetened with sugar produced by West Indian plantations as they read letters bringing news from Pennsylvania or Jamaica or Barbados. In the new transatlantic context of politics and economics, print text was becoming a powerful political weapon and the most effective means to manipulate public opinion in a rapidly expanding empire. Improvements in the printing process, combined with an evolving print culture, opened new possibilities for print media and encouraged public commentary. This in turn spawned a flurry of journalistic news-sheets and broadsides that had evolved into the daily newspaper by 1702. Both in England and in the colonies, the newspaper became a cultural barometer for "Englishness."[17] If examined from the cultural perspective of signs, semiotics then becomes an important instrument in our archaeological toolset (Fig. 5.2).

In *Semiotics: The Basics*, David Chandler discusses the role of cultural signs and defines the term "text" as "an assemblage of signs (such as words, images, sounds and/or gestures) constructed (and interpreted) with reference to the conventions associated with a genre and in a particular medium of communication."[18] Thus, when the *Barbados Gazette* premiered in 1731 it served as the medium of literary exchange between Barbados and London. Taking advantage of the island's distance from London, Keimer was not especially careful about how or where he gleaned the news; sources included snippets of gossip, parts of letters, and material from unpublished manuscripts attributed to untraceable anonymous London sources. Although these early texts reflected a decidedly imperial

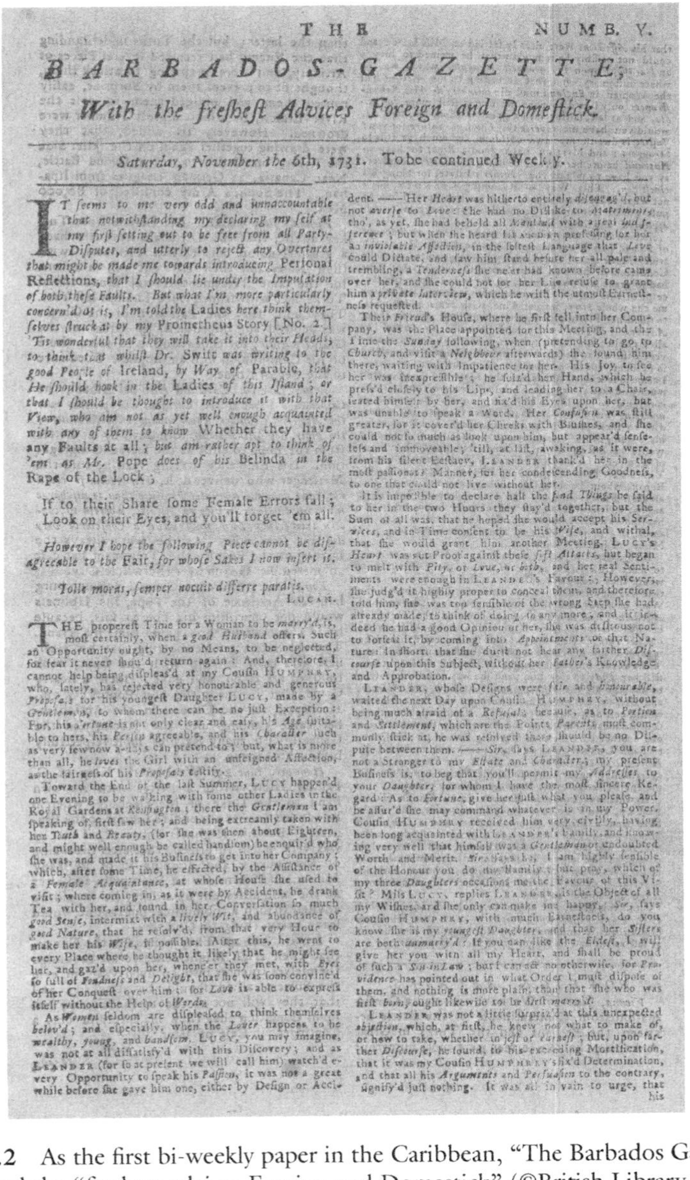

Fig. 5.2 As the first bi-weekly paper in the Caribbean, "The Barbados Gazette" promised the "freshest advices Foreign and Domestick" (©British Library Board, Burney 289B)

perspective of the Caribbean, as the newspaper gained popularity, it became a forum for essays, poetry, and articles written by residents of Barbados advocating local viewpoints on current issues. The fact that many contributors to the periodical were also from the surrounding islands supports the premise that the *Barbados Gazette* provided fertile soil for the seeds of Anglophone West Indian literature. In this sense, both *Caribbeana* and the *Barbados Gazette* were crucial as collections of various textual signs reinforcing the creoles' sense of Englishness. Later issues would demonstrate signs of a growing sense of identity that reflected the islands' diversity of peoples.

Through analyzing these various signs, readers today are afforded an opportunity to examine how the early texts first represented an imperial imaginary in the colonies that later transformed within the colonial setting. Jerome McGann's study of the history of English and American literature and culture provide one example of this type of thought through his examination of minor poetry by women in *Sense and Sensibility*.[19] In his study, McGann deconstructs the liminality of gender roles, including the poetry of an anonymous woman published in the *Barbados Gazette*; he includes a discussion of her arguments on the proper way of writing for a woman. McGann and other scholars have agreed that the "Anonymous Lady's" poetical arguments challenged not only the views of women as writers in English society but also the normalization of masculine domination in society. Furthermore, the fact that her poetry was published anonymously in Barbados by a printer who had once been a member of the French Prophets, a radical and noisy religious sect that maintained a communistic spirit that frequently landed them in jail for either debt or sedition, hints at an interesting comparison. This theory is especially intriguing if viewed from the perspective that Keimer often signed his commentaries with descriptive *noms de plume* such as "Christopher Creole," "John Planter," or "Anglo-Americanus." If naming is a sign of power, then the editor obviously matched his names to his purposes.

A more political view of writing that supports this theory appears in *White Creole Culture, Politics and Identity during the Age of Abolition*, where David Lambert discusses a cultural "war of representation" that engages with "the field of 'whiteness studies,' [influenced by] approaches to British imperial history informed by post colonialism, and work on white identities in the Caribbean region itself."[20] He justifies this as resulting from "Tensions between the British metropolis and its West Indian colonies [that] stemmed from questions of whether white slaveholders could be classed as fully 'English' and whether slavery was compatible with 'English' conceptions of liberty and morality."[21] This particular debate continued well into the nineteenth century as abolitionists and slaveholders shaped their arguments. Lambert also posits that the tensions in Barbados were particularly acute and problematic due to the white colonists' self-portrayal as England's most loyal subjects. These Barbadians described their island as a "Little England," yet historical, legal, and literary records depict them as recalcitrant in adhering to English law and reluctant to adopt social changes already underway in England.

For instance, in 1700, a complaint by Thomas Hodges, "The Present State of Justice in the American Plantations and particularly in the Barbados with some thoughts how the same be amended" was brought before the Board of Trade in London. Hodges' complaint described "the procedures in the courts, their organization in that island, and some of the many defects arising mainly from the lack of qualified judges."[22] Later, this was published in London as *Plantation Justice* (1702), which is an unflattering description of colonial courts and the power they wielded in the American colonies. Subsequently, in 1721, the Barbados legislature officially disenfranchised "free blacks" from the legal system and added the word "white Christian male" to define the term "free-holder." Since only free-holders were eligible to vote, this move effectively ended any possibility of non-whites participating in the legislature or testifying in court. The ramifications of this legislation were far-reaching and fatal since it eliminated any possibility of non-whites participating in local government. This act also racialized the law according to skin color and phenotype, leaving non-whites without legal protection (Fig. 5.3).

While this predates the *Barbados Gazette,* the Barbados planters' legacy of local corruption, defiance of imperial policies, dissatisfaction with imperial taxes, and slavery were the underpinnings of the newspaper. Consequently, one might argue that periodical literature in Barbados had a crucial role—it was not just entertainment or a means of public communication, it was sign of the Barbadians' desire to assert themselves as literary equals with writers in London, a means to voice their arguments and claim political status as fully English. In that sense, print media acquired greater importance, not just as a medium of communication between the metropolitan center and the colonial outposts, but also as a public forum to reinforce the illusion of Englishness by copying the styles and formats of popular literature in London.

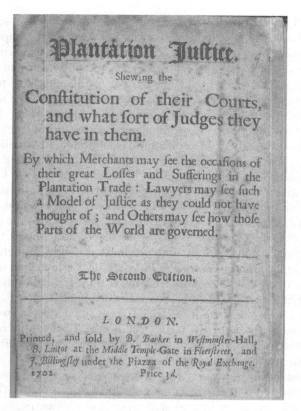

Fig. 5.3 "Plantation Justice" paints an unflattering description of colonial courts and the power they wielded (©British Library Board, 1419.b.46.(1))

Unfortunately, the West Indian colonies were not fully English. Despite a mental cartography that was intentionally imperial, West Indian colonists lived in a society based on enslaved African labor and influenced by African cultural traditions. Therefore, they responded to London's metropolitan discourse with voices that could not be fully English in tone or content. This was the crux of the West Indian paradox.

Earlier in the settlement period, as the British Empire expanded and colonies moved from frontier outposts to stable societies, newspapers in the colonies had served as intellectual arenas in which the English public debated global issues in a format modeled after popular English periodicals. In London, Addison and Steele's *Tatler* (1709–11) and *Spectator* (1711–14) were early print forums for London's debates, while twenty years later the *Gentleman's Magazine* (1731–1922) served as a digest of 'Publick Affairs, Foreign and Domestick.' Started in 1731, the same year as the *Gentleman's Magazine,* Samuel Keimer's *Barbados Gazette* became its West Indian equivalent, with entries reflecting a decidedly English perception of colonial society in Barbados. This intentionality was rather obvious through references to "received from London," or "sent by an English visitor to the island." These comments appear staged to lend credibility that his publication followed the cultural norms of London society.

Much like its London counterpart, the *Barbados Gazette* included poetry, occasional verse, social vignettes, open letters and essays, and a variety of political gossip about governors, judges, and recent cases. However, a close reading of these entries hints that legal relationships on the island might have been less than perfect. One such letter printed in the Saturday, December 18, 1731 edition of the *Barbados Gazette* addressed the Chief Justice of Barbados as follows:

> We have the Satisfaction, however, to be assur'd that there are many Magistrates in the Island, who, like your HONOUR, are neither afraid, nor ashamed to do their Duty; and whilst that is the Case, we hope, it will never be in the Power of any, to bring about that Disturbance and Confusion which the Conduct of *some* amongst us would seem to portend; and, that it never may be the hearty Prayer of Your Honour;[sic]s Most Obedient, Humble Servants.[23]

The editor appears to be alluding to the fact that twenty-nine years after the publication of *Plantation Justice*, a complaint to Parliament about legal nepotism in Barbados, justice in the West Indies was still somewhat arbitrary and the topic of public debate. This type of allegation might have landed him in jail in London. However, in Bridgetown, Barbados, he had a much greater level of freedom to print his opinions and therein lies much of his newspaper's value. Unlike continental papers, or editors, Keimer seemed to have had the freedom to speak and write unfettered by any particular higher authority, therefore providing modern scholars with uncensored slices of colonial life in Barbados.

An Unorthodox Printer

An Odd Fish, ignorant of common Life, fond of rudely opposing reciv'd
Opinions, slovenly to extream dirtiness, enthusiastic in some Points of
Religion, and a little Knavish whithal[24]

Regardless of how one views the historical and literary importance of
the *Barbados Gazette* and *Caribbeana*, one cannot separate the two from
their creator, a colorful eccentric man maligned throughout Benjamin
Franklin's autobiography.[25] Samuel Keimer began his career as a printer
in London, continued it in Philadelphia, and ended it in Barbados. In this
sense, the entries in his paper represent a triangular and transatlantic
focus of the West Indian colonies and their relationship with the American
colonies. Throughout his professional career Keimer's eclectic style
reflected the best and the worst of journalistic practices. Evidence suggests he may have stolen manuscripts in London, only to print them in
Barbados. Franklin described him as less than meticulous in his attribu-
tion of work, and his financial entanglements kept him embroiled in
costly and unproductive conflicts. However, his London experience,
combined with his influence on Franklin, makes him a particularly interesting character and an integral factor in development of periodical literature in the Caribbean.

In order to understand Keimer and how his peculiar brand of journalism fits into the larger scheme of journalism of the period, one must
engage in a brief historiography of journalism leading up to 1731.[26] On
Wednesday, March 11, 1702, three days after King William's death, and
seven months before the *Proceedings of the Old Bailey* printed an advertisement for *Plantation Justice,* Edward Mallet published the first daily English
newspaper, the *Daily Courant,* promising greater coverage of foreign
news. To the contemporary reader with a broadband internet connection
and CNN, it is difficult to imagine the angst of wives, children, mothers,
and fathers eagerly awaiting word of the latest conquest or defeat in foreign wars, or news that ships carrying relatives and friends to or from the
colonies had arrived safely. In this sense, the *Daily Courant* became the
1702 equivalent of the *New York Times* and quickly became a lucrative
endeavor. In spite of its almost instant popularity, Mallet sold the *Courant*
within months to Samuel Buckley, who later printed Addison's and Steele's
famous publication, the *Spectator.* A somewhat controversial and outspo-
ken publisher, Buckley was notorious for printing Parliamentary gossip

and in 1712 was arrested and fined for leaking confidential government information. Nevertheless, the *Daily Courant* remained in print until 1735.

In 1704, two years after the *Daily Courant*'s debut in London, the New England colonists followed suit with John Campbell's *Boston News-Letter*, the first daily newspaper in the North American Colonies. It was not a true newspaper in the modern sense, but a half-sheet, primarily containing news of London's political intrigues and European wars, as well as local announcements and some advertisements. Unlike Buckley and the *Daily Courant*, Campbell's editorial policy was "to give no offence, not meddling with things out of his Province."[27] This earned his newspaper the reputation for being mundane and boring, but kept him out of prison. Several years later, a livelier weekly newspaper debuted in Philadelphia in 1728. Edited by Keimer, this newspaper represented a religious zealousness that was the antithesis of Enlightenment notions of reason and the proper role of religion. Its bombastic title of the *Universal Instructor in All Arts and Sciences; And Pennsylvania Gazette* reflected the ambitions of a newspaper as eccentric as its "enthusiastic" printer who had once written poetry from jail.[28] Abandoned by the French Prophets after publishing a number of their tracts and pamphlets containing libelous remarks about both the King and the English ministry, he languished several times in London prisons. He retaliated by writing vivid accounts of the Prophets and their "very violent and strange Agitation of Shakings of Body, loud and terrifying Hiccups and throbs" in his autobiography, *A Brand Pluck'd from the Burning: Exemplify'd in the Unparallel'd Case of Samuel Keimer*. In the same year, he wrote "The Platonick Courtship: A Poem," a work that also appears to be autobiographical. Perhaps the most interesting part of the poem is an analogy in its preface that "A Book without a Preface, (like a Man without a Nose) makes but an awkward figure at best, I have therefore clapt an Ornament[sic]to such a Face, which otherwise might look very frightful."[29] Apparently, the poem was not well received since he was subsequently jailed several more times for non-payment of debts, before finding his way to Philadelphia where he expected to find an audience more sympathetic to his literary endeavors (Fig. 5.4).

Keimer's *Universal Instructor* displayed his usual disinterest in propriety, a personality trait that would later be foregrounded in the *Barbados Gazette*. His paper's style also departed from the generally accepted English news standards and ignored formatting standards used for British newspapers. Instead, Keimer placed literary items on the front page in lieu

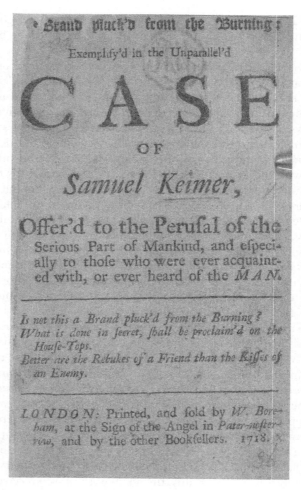

• Brand pluck'd from the Burning •

Exemplify'd in the Unparallel'd

CASE

OF

Samuel Keimer,

Offer'd to the Perufal of the
Serious Part of Mankind, and efpeci-
ally to thofe who were ever acquainted with, or ever heard of the *MAN*.

*Is not this a Brand pluck'd from the Burning?
What is done in fecret, fhall be proclaim'd on the
Houfe-Tops.
Better are the Rebukes of a Friend than the Kiffes of
an Enemy.*

LONDON: Printed, and fold by *W. Bore-
ham*, at the Sign of the Angel in *Pater-nofter-
row*, and by the other Bookfellers. 1718.

Fig. 5.4 Keimer penned his autobiographical poem from jail as retaliation against the French Prophets who he felt had abandoned him when he was accused of sedition for printing their religious tracts (©British Library Board, 1117.f.18.(2))

of the royal proclamations, official transcripts, and foreign news that normally preceded any literary content.[30] Keimer's unorthodox inversion of news and literary items, combined with his flamboyant vision and lack of business skills, were undoubtedly the main reasons for his failure. Two examples in particular reveal his propensity to ignore or disregard established social norms and the fundamentals of economics. First, he placed a notice in the *American Weekly Mercury* in Philadelphia in 1722, shortly after his arrival from London. In this advertisement, he "Freely offers his Services, to teach his poor Bretheren, the Male Negroes, to read the Holy Scriptures, etc., in a very uncommon, expeditious and delightful Manner, without any Manner of expense to their respective Masters or Mistresses."[31] It is unclear how Keimer expected to profit by his charitable offer, since there is no evidence that his advertisement produced any students. Nonetheless, his intentions appear to be honorable, and as modern readers we can only speculate on his motives.

Several years after his reading experiment, Keimer made another ambitious attempt to educate the public in Philadelphia by proposing a new almanac that would teach classical languages in serialized form. His advertisement for this scheme promised to teach first Hebrew, then Latin, Greek, and "Syriack" by printing the characters of each alphabet along with the corresponding rules for pronunciation. Unfortunately, for both the project and Keimer, he printed the first issues of the almanac under the name of a prominent almanac writer, Jacob Taylor—forgetting to inform Mr. Taylor, who was already under contract to a competing almanac printer. The resulting furor over the incident effectively rang the death knell for Keimer's scholarly proposal, as the ensuing public and legal debate surrounding the scandal ended any chance of success.[32] Undaunted, our intrepid editor next proposed publishing Ephraim Chambers' *Cyclopaedia* for the sciences, and Daniel Defoe's *Religious Courtship* in serial form. However, Keimer's grandiose project became bogged down by the fifth issue when he reached the *Ab* section of Chambers' work and printed the article on *Abortion* exactly as it had been written, in full anatomical detail.[33] In conservative Boston, the public was scandalized at such a graphic description of abortion; Benjamin Franklin, a former apprentice to Keimer but now a competing printer, took advantage of the situation to attack his old rival. With full malice, Franklin wrote a number of unflattering anonymous articles that lured Keimer into writing a series of ineffective rebuttals. Unfortunately, this only provided more ammunition for Franklin's cruel attacks and the result of Franklin's campaign against Keimer was devastating. After only nine months of printing the *Universal Instructor,* Keimer was bankrupt; his epistemological failures a joke later immortalized by Franklin in his autobiography. Thus, Franklin, Keimer's onetime apprentice, purchased the newspaper, shortening its title to the *Pennsylvania Gazette* in a brilliant piece of marketing strategy that was highly successful and lucrative. His reputation ruined by imprisonment, religious persecution, bankruptcy, public derision, and general incompetence, Keimer fled to Barbados in 1729. It is perhaps fitting, that in Barbados Keimer ended his triangular transatlantic odyssey in a place with others who like himself were fleeing their own ignoble pasts to make new beginnings. In a sense, the man and the printer had come full circle.

Years later, in his autobiography, Franklin continued his merciless attack on Keimer by describing him as "An Odd Fish, ignorant of common Life, fond of rudely opposing receiv'd Opinions, slovenly to extream dirtiness, enthusiastic in some Points of Religion, and a little Knavish withal."[34] Ironically, the old animosity between Franklin and Keimer, which had led to the demise of Keimer's *Universal Instructor* and an attempt to establish himself as a newspaper publisher and a man of letters in Philadelphia, was resurrected in 1737–38 in several issues of the *Barbados Gazette*. How or why this old vendetta resurrected itself makes for interesting speculation, but Keimer reprinted a long essay that had appeared earlier in the *Pennsylvania Gazette*, undoubtedly authored by his old nemesis, Franklin. Prefaced by a short note signed "Anglo-Americanus," the sender purports to have received the essay from a "friend in Philadelphia." The exchange included here hints at their jealousy as Franklin alludes to the *Barbados Gazette* as a "Curiositie" and Keimer accuses Franklin of printing one of his (Keimer's) pieces without authorization. At the end of the exchange, a note from "Anglo-Americanus" reveals that Keimer is savoring a measure of revenge:

> To the Printer of the Barbados Gazette
> Sir,
> I am oblig'd to you for sending me the Pennsylvania Paper of the 8th of December last, and readily consent to the Publication of it in your next Gazette, as one of the prettiest Curiosities I ever yet saw, of the Kind … I do hereby promise never to encounter him again in the polemical Way; but … sincerely hope he will, in due Time, receive (what I am persuaded he has not hitherto met with) the just and adequate Rewards of his acknowledg'd Merit.
>
> Bridge-Town, Jan. 18, 1737
> Indus Britannicus.[35]

Saturday, January 21, 1737-8
Bridge-town, January 16, 1737-8
Sir,
The inclosed [sic] News-Paper was sent me by a Friend in Philadelphia and seems to have Relation to some "Remarks on Zenger's Trial," which you lately publish'd; as well those of Indus Britannicus, as my own. The Northern Production is so curious that I thought it a Pity to keep it confined to a single Copy, and therefore resolved to put it into your Hands, in order to be multiply'd for the Entertainment of your Readers. But whether it was designed as a Confutation of the "Remarks" just mentioned, is too difficult for me to determine, who am able to collect no more from the Contents, than that the Author was angry, and that his Performance is unanswerable – by any Gentleman.

I am
Your humble Servant
Anglo-Americanus.[36]

Apparently, neither time nor geography had erased the animosity between Keimer and Franklin. The literary warfare continued between them, but it seems appropriate to end our discussion with Keimer's voice as "Anglo-Americanus." Whatever his literary and epistemological flaws, Franklin's "Odd Fish" had provided readers in Barbados with entertainment and a public forum to record both their becoming and being West Indians. In spite of his economic failures and Franklin's descriptions of him as an "Odd Fish" and overweight unkempt idiot, Samuel Keimer's innovative attempts at educating the public, the two newspapers he pioneered, and the anthology he compiled, have preserved literary artifacts representing the foundations of West Indian literature. That alone has earned him more than a footnote to greater men.

NOTES

1. Thomas, Isaiah. *The History of Printing in America with a Biography of Printers, and an Account of Newspapers.* Worcester: Isaiah Thomas 1810. There are no existing copies of this particular edition of the *Gazette*. Notes in Jerome Handler's *Guide to Source Materials for the Study of Barbados History 1627–1834* lists the locations and dates of the few issues of Keimer's newspaper available for study.

2. Charles E. Clark, Charles Wetherell. "The Measure of Maturity: *The Pennsylvania Gazette*, 1728–1765." *William and Mary Quarterly* 46.2

(April 1989): 279–303.This is the same *Pennsylvania Gazette* where Benjamin Franklin apprenticed as a young man under Keimer. Franklin's *Autobiography* also provides details of a bitter rivalry that continued until Keimer's death in 1738.

3. E. M. Shilstone, "Some Notes on Early Printing Presses and Newspapers in Barbados." *Journal of the Barbados Museum & Historical Society* 26.1 (Nov 1958): 19–33.

4. The term "creole" in its strict eighteenth-century English usage denoted a white European born in or residing permanently in the West Indies.

5. John Drummond to Lord George Germain, March 24, 1778, quoted in O'Sullivan frontpage to Benedict Anderson's *In Imagined Communities: Reflections on the Origin and Spread of Nationalism.*

6. Benedict Anderson. *Imagined Communities: Reflections on the Origin and Spread of Nationalism.* London: Verso, 1983. 61.

7. Ibid., 59.

8. Michel Foucault. *The Order of Things: An Archaeology of the Human Sciences.* New York: Routledge, 1970.

9. Catherine Hall. "Civilising Subjects: Metropole and Colony in the English Imagination, 1830–1867." *Journal of British Studies* no. 4 (2003).

10. David Lambert. *White Creole Culture, Politics and Identity During the Age of Abolition.* Cambridge: Cambridge University Press, 2005b.

11. Phyllis J. Guskin. ""Not Originally Intended for the Press": Martha Fowke Sansom's Poems in the Barbados Gazette." *Eighteenth-Century Studies* 34.1 (2000): 61–91.

12. Hayden White. *The Content of the Form: Narrative Discourse and Historical Representation.* Baltimore: Johns Hopkins University Press, 1987.

13. Hayden White. *Metahistory: The Historical Imagination in Nineteenth-Century Europe.* Baltimore: Johns Hopkins University Press, 1974.

14. John Locke. "An Essay on Human Understanding" (IV: XIX.2) 1969. Rpt. in. Ed. Geoffery Tillotson et al. New York: Harcourt and Brace, 1690. 188–204.

15. Charles E. Clark, Charles Wetherell. "The Measure of Maturity: The *Pennsylvania Gazette*, 1728–1765." *William and Mary Quarterly* 46.2 (April 1989): 279–303.

16. Disraeli, Pompanilla, qtd. in Semmel, 100.

17. Ibid.

18. David Chandler. "Semiotics for Beginners." *Semiotics: The Basics.* 2001. April 2005. *Routledge.*

19. Jerome J. McGann. *The Poetics of Sensibility.* Oxford: Clarendon Press, 1996.

20. David Lambert. *White Creole Culture, Politics and Identity During the Age of Abolition.* Cambridge: Cambridge University Press, 2005b.

21. Ibid.
22. Thomas Hodges. *Calendar for State Papers for the American West Indies.* B. Barker, B. Lintot, and J. Billingsley. British Library, London. 1702.
23. *Caribbeana Containing Letters and Dissertations, Together with Poetical Essays on Various Subjects and Occasions in Two Volumes.* Ed. Samuel Keimer. London: T. Osborne, 1741. Millwood: Kraus, 1978. Vol I. 13.
24. Benjamin Franklin. Ed. Leonard W. Labaree. *The Autobiography of Benjamin Franklin.* New Haven: Yale University Press, 1964.
25. Ibid.
26. Clarke, Bob. From Grub Street to Fleet Street: An Illustrated History of English Newspapers to 1899 Aldershot: Ashgate, 2004.
27. David Sloan. "John Campbell and the Boston News-Letter." Early America Review Winter/Spring 2005 (2004). Archiving Early America. 26 Oct 2007.
28. Robert T. Sidwell. "'An Odd Fish,' Samuel Keimer and a Footnote to American Educational History." *History of Education Quarterly* 6.1 (Spring 1966): 16–30.
29. Samuel Keimer. "*A Brand Pluck'd from the Burning: Exemplify'd in the Unparallel'd Case of Samuel Keimer.*" London: Borsham, 1718.
30. Charles E. Clark, Charles Wetherell. "The Measure of Maturity: *The Pennsylvania Gazette,* 1728–1765." *William and Mary Quarterly* 46.2 (April 1989): 286.
31. Robert T. Sidwell. ""An Odd Fish," Samuel Keimer and a Footnote to American Educational History." *History of Education Quarterly* 6.1 (Spring 1966): 21.
32. Ibid., 24.
33. Ibid., 26.
34. Benjamin Franklin. Ed. Leonard W. Labaree. *The Autobiography of Benjamin Franklin.* New Haven: Yale University Press, 1964.
35. *Caribbeana Containing Letters and Dissertations, Together with Poetical Essays on Various Subjects and Occasions in Two Volumes.* Ed. Samuel Keimer. London: T. Osborne, 1741. Millwood: Kraus, 1978. Vol II. 264–271.
36. Ibid.

BIBLIOGRAPHY

Anderson, Benedict. *Imagined Communities: Reflections on the Origin and Spread of Nationalism.* London: Verso, 1983.
Blenman, William, Hart Street, Bloomsburg, to Duke of Newcastle. "Letter to Duke of Newcastle by William Blenman on Behalf of His Father Jonathan Blenman, Attorney General of Barbados." March 23 1761. British Library:

additional manuscripts 32, 921, 27. Large Bound volume of papers for the Duke of Newcastle.

Chandler, Daniel. "Semiotics for Beginners." *Semiotics: The Basics*. Routledge, 2001. April 2005.

Clark, Charles E. and Charles Wetherell. "The Measure of Maturity: The Pennsylvania Gazette, 1728–1765." William and Mary Quarterly 46.2 (April 1989): 279–303.

Foucault, Michel. "The Discourse on Language." N.p: n.p., 1970a.

Foucault, Michel. *The Order of Things: An Archaeology of the Human Sciences*. New York: Routledge, 1970b.

Franklin, Benjamin, and Leonard W. Labaree. *The Autobiography of Benjamin Franklin*. New Haven: Yale University Press, 1964

Guskin, Phyllis. ""Not Originally Intended For The Press": Martha Fowke Sansom's Poems in the Barbados Gazette." *Eighteenth Century Studies* 34; Part 1 (2000): 61–92.

Hall, Catherine. "Civilising Subjects: Metropole and Colony in the English Imagination, 1830–1867." *Journal of British Studies* 4 (2003).

Harris Fiveash, Jo Anne. "Uncovering Creole Representations of Empire in Eighteenth-Century Barbados: From Caribbeana (1741) to Creoleana (1842)." *Dissertation Abstracts International, Section A: The Humanities and Social Sciences* 69.5 (November 2008): 1791.

Handler, Jerome. *A Guide to Source Materials for the Study of Barbados History 1627–1834*. New Castle: Oak Knoll Press, 2002.

Handler, Jerome. *Supplement to A Guide to Source Materials for the Study of Barbados History, 1627–1834*. Providence: The John Carter Brown Library and The Barbados Museum and Historical Society, 1991.

Hodges, Thomas. *Calendar for State Papers for the American West Indies*. B. Barker, B. Lintot, and J. Billingsley. London: British Library, 1702.

Keimer, Samuel. *A Brand Pluck's from the Burning: Exemplify'd in the Unparallel'd Case of Samuel Keimer*. London: Borsham, 1718.

Keimer, Samuel. Editor. *Caribbeana Containing Letters and Dissertations, Together with Poetical Essays on Various Subjects and Occasions in Two Volumes*. Ed. Samuel Keimer. London: T. Osborne, 1741. Millwood: Kraus, 1978. Two volumes.

Keimer, Samuel. *The Platonick Courtship: A Poem*. London: Bettenham, 1718.

Krise, Thomas. *Caribbeana*. Chicago: University of Chicago Press, 1999.

Lambert, David. "Liminal Figures: Poor Whites, Freedmen, and Racial Reinscription in Colonial Barbados." *Environment & Planning D: Society & Space* 19.3/4 (June 2001): 335–342.

Lambert, David. "Producing/Contesting Whiteness: Rebellion, Anti-Slavery and Enslavement in Barbados, 1816." *Geoforum* 36.2005 9 September 2003: 29–43. WWW.Sciencedirect.Com. 2005a. Science Direct. 6/9/05 www.sciencedirect.com.

Lambert, David. *White Creole Culture, Politics and Identity During the Age of Abolition.* Cambridge: Cambridge University Press, 2005b.

Locke, John. "An Essay on Human Understanding." 1969. Rpt. in. Ed. Geoffery Tillotson et al. New York: Harcourt and Brace, 1690. 188–204.

Mc Gann, Jerome J. *The Poetics of Sensibility.* Oxford: Clarendon Press, 1996.

Overton, Bill. *A Letter to My Love: Love Poems by Women First Published in the Barbados Gazette, 1731–1737.* Newark: University of Delaware Press, 2001.

Proceedings of the Old Bailey. 2007. Proceedings of the Old Bailey 1674–1834.

Semmel, Bernard. *The Rise of Free Trade Imperialism: Classical Political Economy the Empire of Free Trade and Imperialism 1750–1850.* Cambridge: Cambridge University Press, 1970.

Shilstone, E.M. "Some Notes on Early Printing Presses and Newspapers in Barbados." *Journal of the Barbados Museum & Historical Society* 26.1 (Nov 1958): 19–33.

Sidwell, Robert T. ""An Odd Fish," Samuel Keimer and a Footnote to American Educational History." *History of Education Quarterly* 6.1 (Spring 1966): 16–30.

Sloan, David. "John Campbell and the Boston News-Letter." *Early America Review* Winter/Spring 2005 (2004). Archiving Early America. 26 Oct 2007.

Thomas, Isaiah. *The History of Printing in America with a Biography of Printers, and an Account of Newspapers.* Worcester: Isaiah Thomas, 1810.

White, Hayden. *The Content of the Form: Narrative Discourse and Historical Representation.* Baltimore: Johns Hopkins University Press, 1987.

White, Hayden. *Metahistory: The Historical Imagination in Nineteenth Century Europe.* Baltimore: Johns Hopkins University Press, 1974.

White, Hayden. *Tropics of Discourse.* Baltimore: Johns Hopkins University Press, 1978.

CHAPTER 6

Testimonies of the Enslaved in the Caribbean Literary History

Nicole N. Aljoe

Representations of slave voices show up repeatedly throughout early Caribbean texts. Although the appearance of the slave voice or slave voices is unique in and of itself, what is especially intriguing is the variety of types of voices represented, as well as the number of places in which those voices appear. For example, in *Friendly Advice to the Gentleman Planters of the East and West Indies* (1684), Thomas Tryon represents a dialog between a master and his slave; James Grainger represents slave knowledge of sugar cane cultivation and the medicinal arts in his Georgic poem; in *An Essay on the Treatment and Conversion of African Slaves in the British Sugar Colonies* (1764), James Ramsay narrates the tale of a loyal slave, Quashie. In addition, there are various dictated slave narratives, by both abolitionists and pro-slavery activists, some of which are written in dialect, as well as narratives of slave lives and representations of slave voices embedded in the travel narratives and memoirs of visitors to the Caribbean, such as that of Edward Lewis in Thomas Gage's *Travels in the New World* (1648) and Joanna in John Gabriel Stedman's *Narrative of an Expedition Against the Revolted Negroes of Surinam* (1796). The different ways and varying

N. N. Aljoe (✉)
Department of English, Northeastern University, Boston, MA, USA

N. N. Aljoe et al. (eds.), *Literary Histories of the Early Anglophone Caribbean*, New Caribbean Studies,
https://doi.org/10.1007/978-3-319-71592-6_6

107

contexts in which the slave voice appears seems to suggest that this thing that we understand or call "the slave voice" may be a more complex entity.

Consequently, this essay is an attempt to begin to grapple with the question: What is the role of the notion of slave voice or slave voices in the early literary history of the Caribbean? What does focusing on representations of slave voices help us to understand about Caribbean literary history or early Caribbean literary texts? To consider this question begs another question, what is it that we mean by "the slave voice?" Do we mean writings by slaves, textual representations of slaves, representations of speaking slave voices? Do we only mean textual reproduction? What about other forms of expression and reproduction?

Attention to notions of slave voice are particularly important right now because so many recent Caribbean writers have sought to represent slave voices in their works, such as M. NourbeSe Philips' poetry collection *Zong!*, and novels such Marlon James' *The Book of the Night Women*, Isabel Allende's *The Island Beneath the Sea*, and Andrea Levy's *The Long Song*.

The traditional understanding of representations of slave voices is exemplified in an essay by Andrea Levy about the writing of her novel, *The Long Song*. She explains,

> There is an excellent body of scholarship, both in Britain and in the Caribbean, on the history of slavery. But there are very few surviving documents and artefacts that I could find where enslaved people speak of and for themselves. Little writing or testimony has emerged that was not filtered at the time through a white understanding or serving a white narrative – whether it be the apologists for slavery and the West Indian planter classes, or their opponents, the abolitionists.
>
> This is where I believe that fiction comes in to its own. Writing fiction is a way of putting back the voices that were left out. Not just the wails of anguish and victimhood that we are used to, although that is very much part of the story, but the chatter and clatter of people building their lives, families and communities, ducking, diving and conducting the businesses of life in appallingly difficult circumstances. Now THERE is a story. (Levy 2014; 5)

Implicit in Levy's understanding of the slave voice is a notion of authenticity—that an authentic slave voice would be written in the slave's hand and therefore "unfiltered" by white concerns. This prevailing understanding of voice is that it is connected to a physical body. Such an understanding of the slave voice is confirmed in Charles Davis and Henry Louis Gates Jr.'s introduction to the edited collection *The Slave's Narrative*, in which they assert that eighteenth- and nineteenth-century readers sought to imagine the face of the race through the voice in the text, directly implicating voice and body. Or as Joan Anim-addo explains, slaves were allowed voice in order to speak their condition (37). Voice in this case seems a simple affair. Yet, if we consider the second paragraph of Levy's essay, the simplicity of voice that she assumes in the first paragraph becomes more complicated. Fiction offers the opportunity, she claims, to recuperate and re-insert voices, as well as to represent the multiplicity of those voices, "not only the wails of anguish but the chatter and clatter of everyday life." Indeed, her comments resonate with the fact that these voices show up in a variety of places and for a variety of reasons.

And while I can understand the desire to insist that the only authentic representations of slave voices should be written in the slave's hand, to do so is to accept that the only significance of slave voices in the archives is to provide testimony of their life experiences. And while this might have been the primary reason why many of their voices were initially sought and recorded, this does not mean that we, as twenty-first-century scholars in a completely different context and reading these narratives for different reasons must understand the voices in these narratives in that same way. As Abdul Jan Mohammed explains, "there are differences between the conditions that attend production of subaltern's speech and those that attend its reception. The former are historically unalterable whereas the latter are amenable to change" (140).

*   *   *

Generally speaking, at its most basic level, voice is understood as an utterance or a set of linguistic markers. Most narratological definitions, since Gerard Genette, draw explicit connections between notions of narrative voice, sound, and bodies. Voice has been described as a metonymic designation for the human presence we hear or imagine we hear (Fludernik 1993), as well as a "linguistically generated illusion of a speaking voice" (257). Voice has also been defined as a metaphor, which suggests individual and perceptible speech (Mieke Bal 2009). It is also understood as the guiding sensibility or consciousness through which we view a story, very similar to perspective and point of view. Finally, voice is often attached to notions of authenticity, authority, and authorship—"an authentic and identifiable thing, a representation of empowered and unfettered autonomy" (Simmons 77).

However, cultural or contextual narratologists, following the work of Walter Ong, argue that rather than grounded in notions of sound and body, the notion of voice is a position, a set of relationships. From this perspective then, to speak of the slave voice is not to speak of slave identity but rather to speak of constellations and representations of power.

This understanding of voice has much in common with Gayatri Spivak's articulation of the "the varied and complex conditions of possibility that attend the production of the subaltern's speech." (Mohammed 2010: 139) Subaltern voice, as Spivak argues, is often a construction invented for a First World readership. It sets the criteria for recognition rather than focusing on the texts as they exist or as they are asking to be read. From this perspective then, rather than an identifiable thing, a sound connected to a body, voice becomes much more complex entity. One that is "fluid and multiply located" (Visweswaran 99). This articulation of voice seems much more useful and flexible enough to encompass the myriad ways in which the slave voice appears in the early Caribbean archive. Such a definition also would force us to acknowledge that slave voices may communicate or speak to more than the lived experiences of historical individuals.

Thus, the question of voice in slave narrative becomes rather more complex. This ambiguity is highlighted in my discussion in *So Much Things to Say: The Creole Testimony of British West Indian Slaves* (2012), which focuses on a close examination of slave narratives of the Anglophone Caribbean. In that text, I argued that while not as numerous as in the United States, a significant number of slave narratives from the Caribbean have survived. Caribbean slave narratives are those texts that focus on describing the experience of Caribbean slavery from the slave's perspective or are "by" Caribbean slaves. When one goes into the archives to look for Caribbean slave narratives or the voices of Caribbean slaves, one encounters not the neat, tidy, self-written, separately published slave narratives such as those by William Wells Brown, Frederick Douglass and Harriet Jacobs, with which we are most familiar, but more complex manifestations: dictated, unsigned and undated testimonies, portraits embedded in other texts, court depositions, medical documents, trial records, newspaper articles, spiritual conversion narratives, letters, interviews, brief narrative and ethnographic portraits, representations of conversations, and so on. By my conservative count there are at least 20 separate and many other embedded narratives from the Caribbean and Latin America that satisfy this general criteria, beginning with Father Arturo Sandoval's interviews with recently arrived African slaves in Colombia in 1627, and including the 1709 "Speech by a Black at the funeral of a slave of Guadeloupe"; the "Memoir of Florence Hall"; James Williams' 1836 narrative of the apprenticeship period in Jamaica; the 1848 biography of the Brazilian slave, Mahommah Gardo Baquaqua; the narrative of the enslaved poet, Juan Francisco Manzano; the Moravian spiritual narrative of Archibald Monteith; the excision of Old Doll's narrative from Thomas Thistlewood's journals; and the 1963 *testimonio* of the Cuban Maroon Esteban Montejo.[1] Although these ephemeral, fragmentary, explicitly mediated documents may seem so different from the more familiar slave narratives, in fact, they are very similar in that they, too, endeavor to describe the experience of enslavement. And while, to date, no one has found a "Caribbean" Douglass or Jacobs (though he/she may exist), it is nonetheless still important to consider these texts on their own terms as they exist, rather than viewing them as contaminated or poor imitations of their US counterparts. These seemingly simple texts not only provide an important resource for understanding the complexities of the experiences of slavery, but they also communicate the inherent diversity of the slave narrative genre, and illuminate its historical and continuing effects across the Atlantic African Diaspora.

One primary distinction is that the Caribbean slave narrative tradition was probably not a totally self-conscious one during the eighteenth and nineteenth centuries. Unlike many of their US counterparts, Caribbean slaves probably did not construe themselves as explicitly creating similar types of texts. And yet the similarities across the Caribbean slave narratives are compelling. In addition to exhibiting creole formats that are frequently elusive and fragmentary, the Caribbean narratives are also not necessarily organized as progressive narratives of fugitiveness moving toward salvation and redemption. Some of the narratives begin in Africa and instead exhibit a circular arrangement, emphasizing a return to the original state of freedom. Moreover, others of the Caribbean slave narratives were not explicitly associated with abolitionist discourses.

The most significant distinction is that every Caribbean slave narrative is explicitly mediated in some way, by a white transcriber, editor, or translator. Only two of the narratives are self-written and both of these, one written in Spanish the other in Arabic, were translated into English before publication. This particular distinction is emblematic of the manner in which the slave narratives from the Caribbean confound the prevailing paradigms for understanding the slave narrative.

It is for these reasons that the concept of creole testimony feels particularly useful for thinking about the slave voice in Caribbean literary history and for acknowledging the generic complexity inherent to the slave narrative form, particularly those from the Caribbean. The possibility of creole testimony as a useful paradigm for understanding and reading Caribbean slave narratives is suggested by Derek Walcott's narration of a performance of the *Ramleela* in Trinidad. Described in his Nobel speech, "The Antilles: Fragments of Epic Memory," Walcott reads the vivid creole performance of the *Ramleela*— itself a fragment of the Hindu epic *Ramayana*—in Trinidad as the cultural embodiment of the fragmentary memories haunting all descendants of nineteenth-century Indian indentured servants. Castigating those "purists" and "grammarians" who would read the celebration as parody or poor mimicry of the "original" celebration in India, Walcott asks why not read the performance on its own terms as "a real 'presence'?" (505). In other words, we should not assume that the only way to read the *Ramleela* in Trinidad is as a derivative reflection of a pure and more authentic original. Walcott argues that the fragments of the *Ramleela*, lovingly performed on the Caroni Plain, are symbolic of the creole culture and art in the Caribbean, "a shipwreck of fragments ... echoes, shards of a huge tribal vocabulary" (507), in which the experiences of the new world creates new forms from the global fragments. Reading these narratives on their own terms, as creole testimony, requires one to focus on the texts as they exist, rather than trying to insert them into a pre-established framework or viewing them as contaminated or poor imitations of their more singular US counterparts.

In addition to acknowledging the collaboration necessary for producing the textual voice in these slave narratives, the notion of "creole testimony" also communicates the syncretic structures and thematic engagements of many early Caribbean texts. Among other things, the term creole speaks to the fact that these narratives exhibit elements from both oral and written traditions. Grounded in the combinatory social culture of the Caribbean, the term is intended to signify that it is a "different" kind of testimony, a "version" or "dub" in the same way that creole names the "different" language that developed in the contact zone of the Caribbean. Finally, the notion of "creole testimony" suggests the necessity for employing more than the usual critical tools and for moving outside classic paradigms, especially in regards to trying to understand texts produced by subaltern groups.

More specifically, the notion of "creole testimony" is anchored by one of the most distinctive characteristics of the West Indian region—the cultural hyper-syncretism commonly referred to as "creolization." Numerous scholars have linked the structures and textual format of West Indian or Caribbean texts to the supersyncretic culture that formed them. As Antonio Benítez-Rojo explains, "Caribbean literature cannot free itself of the multi-ethnic society upon which it floats, and it tells us of its fragmentation and instability" (27).

The culture of the Caribbean archipelago draws influences from a variety of components, including indigenous peoples, as well as groups from the Eastern Mediterranean, Europe, Africa, East and South Asia, and the various permutations across and between these communities. While, as Edouard Glissant acknowledges, "indeed no peoples have been spared the cross-cultural process" (140), creolization has often been interpreted as the cultural interaction and synthesis that grew out of the specific conditions engendered by imperialism and slavery in the 'artificially created communities' of the British West Indies.

Instead of a simple imposition or creation of a new culture based on a collage of the old, creolization includes elements of resistance as well as acceptance and emphasizes the plural, constantly changing nature of culture. More specifically, creolization is defined as

> a syncretic process of transverse dynamics that endlessly reworks and transforms the cultural patterns of varied social and historical experiences and identities. The cultural patterns that result from this "crossbreeding" (or crossweaving) undermine any academic or political aspiration for unitary origins or authenticity. (Balutansky and Sourieau 3)

The structures of creolization in the Caribbean emphasizes the interactions of *all* cultural influences. Glissant explains, "if we speak of creolized cultures (like Caribbean culture, for example) it is not to define a category that will by its very nature be opposed to other categories ('pure' cultures)" (140). Rather, creolization accepts the fact that categories such as "authentic" or "slave voice" can never be absolute, but are always produced by a process of connections and tensions along a continuum of other possibilities that grew out of the Caribbean's colonial history.

The slave narratives of the Caribbean provide key testimony, no matter how tenuous, and give textual "voice" to the aforementioned possibilities of Caribbean colonial history. In regards to the term "testimony," obviously it suggests the act of testifying or bearing witness in a legal or religious sense. Furthermore, I want the notion of "creole testimony" to acknowledge not only the legal and religious associations of the word "testimony" but also to highlight the vital role of collaboration in these associations, whereby the scribe, amanuensis, lawyer, or minister/priest are necessary mediators. I also want to assert connections to the Latin American genre of *testimonio* because it draws on similar cultural, formal, and thematic features to the Caribbean slave narratives.

Testimonio is often defined as a novel or novella-length narrative, told in the first person by a narrator who is the actual protagonist or witness of the events she or he recounts. Since in many cases the narrator is someone who is either functionally illiterate, or if literate not a professional writer or academic, the production of the testimonio generally involves the recording and/or transcription and editing of an oral account by an interlocutor who is often a journalist, writer, or social activist. Publication of the testimonio is usually intended to change or draw attention to an oppressive political situation (Beverly and Zimmerman 173).

Some critics have argued rather forcefully for the connection between testimonio and place. These critics perceive testimonio as a genre tied to the landscape, social, and historical context of Latin America, especially in the 1960s, beginning with Miguel Barnet's *Biography of a Runaway Slave*, a narrative of the life of the 105-year-old Cuban ex-slave Esteban Montejo.[2] Although Barnet may have invented the term testimonio with the publication of Montejo's narrative, in fact this format existed long before the 1960s. Indeed, as Raymond Williams has argued, there is a long history of oral autobiography by oppressed people that is not limited to Latin America (Beverly 71). Furthermore, the fact that the first testimonio is a slave narrative undermines such an argument and supports my association of the two.

Apart from the distinctions of length (the definitions of testimonio often mention "novel-length"), one of the most important similarities between Caribbean slave narratives and Latin American testimonios is that both exhibit a marked syncretism of form and voice. In addition, both require collaboration in the creation of the narrating subject, are polyvocal, exhibit heteroglossia, and are double voiced. Finally, like testimonios, Caribbean slave narratives transgress the boundaries between the public and the private, they are also, "placed at the intersection of multiple roads: oral and literary; authored/authoritarian discourse and edited discourse; literature and anthropology; autobiography and demography" (Gugelberger 10). And as Doris Sommer, John Beverly, and others have argued, the more complex rhetorical strategies of the testimonio require different reading strategies than those employed with single-authored texts.

"The Speech of John Talbot Campo-bell"

The necessity of more nuanced understandings of slave voice is particularly important for considering "problematic" articulations of the slave voice such as "The Speech of John Talbot Campo-bell" (1736). I call Campo-bell's speech problematic because it is probably a fictional creation by a white West Indian pro-slavery writer (Krise). And while, on the one hand the fact that pro-slavery activists would appropriate a slave voice to "speak" pro-slavery ideology seems an obvious case of propagandistic ventriloquism, close analysis of the speech offers a more complex picture that highlights this notion of creole testimony that complexifies notions of voice within Caribbean colonial literary history.

Campo-bell's "speech" appeared in 1736, as a response to the publication of "The Speech of Moses Bon Sa'am," published in 1735. Bon Sa'am's speech was reported to be that of a Maroon leader exhorting a crowd that included slaves to rebel against Jamaican plantation owners. It was recorded anonymously in a letter sent to a London merchant, who gave the letter to Aaron Hill, editor of the *Prompter*. To briefly summarize Bon Sa'am's narrative, in addition to detailing the various abuses inherent under the slave system, the speaker calls upon the members of his Maroon audience to take pride in themselves and their abilities. Because, he claims, these will be key in the eventual overthrow of slavery. On the whole, the speech offers a series of concrete steps intended to facilitate a successful rebellion, and encourages his fellow Maroons, escaped and former slaves, to join him in refusing the oppression instituted by plantation owners and white Jamaican colonists.

The speech also helps to illuminate the high level of anxiety the Maroon attacks caused for white colonists and plantation owners. Not only in terms of the constant threat of physical violence but in the way that the speaker stakes out an alternative worldview, explicitly rejecting the very premises of colonial ideology, and in so doing directly challenging that ideology. For example, the speaker revels in the strength of his body, not his rhetoric (as the European-educated Solomon or Williams might have done): "Let a white Man expose his feeble face to the Winds; let him climb Hills against Rains; Let him go burn his uncover'd Temples in the Heat of the High-Noon, as we do .... The Variations of his changeable Countenance will make manifest the Faintness he was born to" (Krise 2000: 103). In so doing, Bon Sa'am offers a detailed and coherent ideology of resistance against colonial enslavement. On the whole, the speech offered a series of concrete steps intended to facilitate a successful rebellion, and encouraged his fellow Maroons, escaped and former slaves, to join him in refusing the oppression instituted by plantation owners and white Jamaican colonists. Of course, pro-slavery ideologues were compelled to respond.

Like Bon Sa'am's speech, Campo-bell's speech appeared in print anonymously. However, in a 2001 article on Campo-bell's speech, Thomas Krise asserted that the speech was in fact written by a white man, Reverend Robert Robertson of Nevis. Robertson was a staunch defender of slavery and had previously contributed written pieces and letters to support that cause. Drawing on a mix of coincidental timing and Robertson's prior history of inflammatory writing, Krise mounts a persuasive argument that Robertson might have authored the speech.

To briefly summarize, the speech consists of two parts. Part I begins by explaining how Campo-bell was captured in Africa and made prisoner, along with his father, other family members, and about 350 neighbors, by a party of "enemies" in a war between the kings of Angola and Congo. He describes how they were chained on the slave ships as well as a failed shipboard slave rebellion. Upon arriving in Jamaica, Campo-bell, his father, and other members of their community, are purchased by the same master. After his master takes a liking to him, he decides to teach Campo-bell to read and write. He then tells us that his father died after three years of enslavement and his last words to Campo-bell, spoken in their African language were: "Not to forget my Mother-Tongue, but rather to study to improve in it," so that Campo-bell could then "bring over some of our Countrymen to the Ways and Religion of the English, which was his Heart's Desire" (111). Following his father's deathbed commandment, Campo-bell tells us that he has since learned "three of the most current Languages in our Parts of Africa" (111), and as a result he becomes a translator for his master and others in Jamaica. Soon after his father's death, he is sent to England along with his master's son, and in addition to waiting on him while he was studying, he spends several years on a Grand Tour of Europe. Campo-bell tells us that while with his master's son in England and Europe, he was never treated like a slave, but rather like a "companion." After returning to Jamaica, his master dies and leaves him his freedom, a house, and two slaves "of [his] own Colour to wait upon him" (111).

At this point the narrative leaves behind Campo-bell's biography and begins to offer arguments in support of the slave trade and the institution of enslavement on the British Caribbean islands. The speaker begins by asserting that the institution of slavery in Africa was much worse than that in the Caribbean. He also argues that it was unscrupulous independent interlopers who were engaging in the unlawful kidnapping of African slaves, not employees of the Royal African Company. Asserting that "man-stealing" was in actuality considered "so black among all the nations of Europe, that could it be legally proved on any of their people, no Punishment would be thought too severe for them" (112). He then explains the history of European involvement with the slave trade and Africa. This history lesson serves as the springboard for his assertion that England continues to participate in the slave trade because it has to in order to earn money and if it did not, other nations might step in. He brings the first part of his speech to a close when his audience begins to start eating the meal that has been provided for them. After the meal, he presumably resumes his speech and he explains that because the British are more powerful, militarily speaking, to try to rebel as Bon Sa'am suggests would be futile because "the fleets and armies of England would destroy you" (136). He then explains that it is not the plantation owners who should be their objects of revenge, but the financial interests in London. This section also includes several tirades against creole slaves, calling them "Monsters in Wickedness, Devils incarnate, Murders, Ravishers, Robbers, such as have willfully set fire to houses or the growing of Sugar Canes ... they lie with your wives, and ravish your daughters before your eyes and how in their wrath or their rum they will plunge their knives in your bosoms or bellies" (121). This section also includes a point-by-point refutation of many of the arguments raised in Bon Sa'am's speech. Campo-bell concludes by saying, "Your Part is exceedingly plain, even to make yourselves, and all you are concerned with as easy as possible" (140) by turning away from Bon Sa'am's rebellious suggestions and instead to turn over to the British, those "black Creole tyrants" who have been such a "handful."

While language and rhetoric such as "black creole tyrants" seems a straightforward pro-slavery attack, there are also elements of the speech that seem to contradict the intended purpose of the speech. First, the speech seems to consist of several distinct voices. On the one hand, there is the personal, first-person voice of the biographical sections of the speech. The sentences in the biographical sections are pretty simple and relatively straightforward, with few subordinate clauses. The sections on the history of the slave trade and the macroeconomic foundations of the slave trade contain much longer sentences consisting of many more clauses. This section also seems more readerly than speakerly, with its inclusion of numbers, lists, and references to specific places and maps.

Although Campo-bell voices some of the most horrifying arguments in support of slavery—that Africans were used to slavery, that slavery is not illegal, that slavery brings Africans within the realm of civilization, and so on—the speech also includes many incisive critiques of the British. He highlights the hypocrisy of Britons claiming to love liberty but being willing to enslave others. He illuminates the disunion among the British by explaining that not only are there pro-and anti-slavery advocates but that since the British had recently engaged in a civil war they are not as unified as they seem. He also asserts that Britain is in fact enslaved to capitalism and money, arguing that the British could not give up the slave trade even if it was wrong. He makes the claim that without slave labor, Britain would not be as powerful as it is. Intriguingly, toward the conclusion of Part II he asserts that God will probably punish him for engaging in slavery and yet rather than explain this away he says he has written to scholars in England and is awaiting their reply in regards to this question (138). Finally, he asserts that if God is against the slave trade, he will "inspire" the hearts and heads of the European nation to conspire to end it: "He has many Ways of setting Things that are wrong to rights, which the wisest of his Creatures are ignorant of, and must not presume to dive into" (140).

Moreover, despite its pro-slavery rhetoric, heavy mediation, as well the possibility that it might be an invention, like other Caribbean slave narratives Campo-bell's speech conveys important elements about Caribbean slave culture: that in the Caribbean, slaves from the same nation were not always separated; that as in the US, some Caribbean blacks owned slaves; that some blacks might have been invested in continued British rule because they had accumulated some power. The narrative also reveals the fluidity of early Caribbean society; for example, it tracks slaves moving across and between the Maroon–slave divide, and the fact that Campo-bell, a former slave, could become almost "like a member of white society," as he says. It seems incredibly odd that a pro-slavery advocate would want to make these assertions, which seem rather more to complicate pro-slavery ideology than to confirm it.

So, if this speech is an invention by a white pro-slavery writer, why would he appropriate a slave voice in this manner? An answer may lie in considering the context in which the speech appeared.

In 1734, a British Captain led a successful attack on Nanny Town (named for the Maroon Chieftainess of the Leeward Maroon Band).

Aided by Mosquito Coast Indians and tracking dogs, the town was completely leveled. In response, Jamaican Maroon leaders, Quao and Nanny, launched a series of brutal raids against the British. Here again, though Quao and Nanny were supposedly African-born slaves, the most violent activities of the Maroon raids were said to have been caused by creole slaves. The escalation of the war against the Jamaican Maroons and the tremendous losses of British colonial life and property made for extremely high levels of anxiety among plantation owners across the entire Anglophone Caribbean during the 1730s and 1740s.

Even more close to home for Robertson on Nevis, was the 1733 slave rebellion on the island of St. John. That year, the island was lashed first by severe economic problems brought on by continuing fallout from the 1720s' South Sea Bubble, hurricanes, drought, and finally, slave rebels began burning plantations. They managed to take control of the entire island and remained in control for ten months. On two separate occasions, British ships containing militias were launched from nearby Tortola and Anguilla, and in both instances the smaller slave rebel forces routed the much larger and better-armed British forces. The island was only finally wrested from the slave rebels' control when a massive French force from Martinique finally and brutally subdued them. Although many of the leaders of the rebellion were African-born, they received crucial support from creole slaves. The creole slaves were also supposedly responsible for some of the more violent attacks against whites on the island. Living in such close proximity to St. John, Robertson, on Nevis, would have been horrified at the revolt and its duration.

The speech seems to voice the high level of anxiety the Maroon attacks caused for white colonists and plantation owners. Not only in terms of the constant threat of physical violence but in the way that Bon Sa'am stakes out an alternative worldview, explicitly rejecting the very premises of colonial ideology, and in so doing directly challenging that ideology, as well as that of colonial enslavement. Consequently, though Campo-bell's speech communicates strong pro-slavery ideologies, its primary purpose might have been to persuade the Maroons not to engage in the rebellious behavior Bon Sa'am had encouraged. Seen from this perspective then, Campo-bell's narrative seems to have been constructed as an attempt to persuade Jamaican Maroons not to take up arms against the British, but rather, as he repeats over and over again throughout Part II, to "rest easy" and turn in the creole rebels to the British authorities.

Campo-bell's narrative, regardless of whether it is fiction or not, has much in common with other Caribbean narratives. It is highly mediated. Campo-bell is not figured as the writer of the speech. It is also polyvocal, and combines oral and written cultures. The way the narrative undercuts itself at several points also speaks to the impossibility of turning another's voice to your own purposes. I'd like to suggest that if Robertson is the author, he probably based it, like the earlier Bon Sa'am narrative, on an actual speech—probably of one of the several British African translators who were used as intermediaries with the Maroons. It is also creole in form: the narrative appeared anonymously as well as alongside Bon Sa'am's narrative. Moreover, the narrative also reveals what would become an increasingly important tool in the British arsenal against slave rebellion: they relied on a translator, Campo-bell, to communicate their message.

In a 1740 letter to the *Gentleman's Magazine*, in which Robertson claims authorship of Campo-bell's speech, Robertson gloats that he must have been successful because, though he had invited him to do so, Bon Sa'am never replied to his speech. However, I would argue that Bon Sa'am's reply was the 1738 peace treaty that the British were forced to sign with the Maroons. While the treaty curtailed some of the movement, and required that they return any escaped slaves, it also gave them sovereignty, which was what Bon Sa'am had been asking for—in effect a form of freedom from colonial enslavement.

The appearance and proliferation of varieties of first-person narratives of Caribbean slavery throughout the eighteenth and nineteenth centuries suggests that both sides realized the importance of the slave voice, or to quote Ephraim Peabody from his 1849 analysis of the new genre slave narrative, providing "pictures of slavery by slaves." Narratives such as Campo-bell's also contribute to the creation of the textual paradigms constructed for carrying the slave voice.[3] Moreover, to talk of an inherently static, unified slave voice, speaking from a particular liberal oppositional perspective, is to misunderstand the complexity of the slave voice.

When one looks at the variety of places in which the slave voice appears, as well as the variety of types of voices, one begins to consider that these voices may have more to say—speaking not only of direct or observed experiences but also of power relationships, articulations of the subject, and so on. The appropriation of the slave voice by pro-abolitionists not only suggests the importance of notions of the slave voice to conceptions of early Caribbean literary history but also reveals the complexity of that voice and its important significance to the understanding of the early literary history of the Caribbean.

NOTES

1. See Bibliography.
2. See Beverly.
3. And, of course, as many others have argued, all texts are mediated. So, we can talk of degrees of mediation with the understanding that notions of "purity" and "authenticity" are inherently unstable. In other words, "authenticity" is a function of history and reading, not something that is textually inherent.

BIBLIOGRAPHY

Aljoe, Nicole N. *Creole Testimonies: Slave Narratives from the British West Indies, 1709–1838.* New York: Palgrave Macmillan, 2012.

Anim-Addo, Joan. "Sister Goose's Sisters: African-Caribbean Women's Nineteenth Century Testimony." *Women: A Cultural Review* 15.1 (Spring 2004): 35–56.

Bal, Mieke. *Narratology: Introduction to the Theory of Narrative.* Toronto: University of Toronto Press, 2009.

Balutansky, Kathleen M. and Marie-Agnès Sourieau. *Caribbean Creolization: Reflections on the Cultural Dynamics of Language, Literature, and Identity.* Gainesville: University Press of Florida, 1998.

Baquaqua, Mahommah Gardo., Robin Law, and Paul E. Lovejoy. *The Biography of Mahommah Gardo Baquaqua: His Passage from Slavery to Freedom in Africa and America.* Princeton: Markus Wiener Publishers, 2001.

Benítez-Rojo, Antonio. *The Repeating Island: The Caribbean and the Postmodern Perspective.* Trans. James E. Maraniss. 2ne ed. Durham: Duke University Press, 1996.

Beverley, John. *Subalternity and Representation: Arguments in Cultural Theory.* Durham: Duke University Press, 1999.

Beverley, John, and Marc Zimmerman. *Literature and Politics in the Central American Revolutions.* Austin: University of Texas Press, 1990.

Brown, William Wells. *Narrative of William W. Brown, an American Slave: Written by Himself.* Chapel Hill: University of North Carolina Press, 2011.

Costanzo, Angelo. "African-Caribbean Narratives of British America." *American Literary Study* 19.2 (1993): 260–74.

Costanzo, Angelo. "Methods, Elements and Effects of Early Black Biography." *A/b: Auto/Biography Studies* 2.3 (2014): 5–20.

Davis, Charles T. and Henry Louis Gates, Jr., ed. *The Slave's Narrative.* New York: Oxford University Press, 1985.

Douglass, Frederick. *Narrative of the Life of Frederick Douglass.* 1845. Norton Critical Edition. Eds. Andrews & McFeely. New York: W.W. Norton, 1996.

Fludernik, Monika. *The Fictions of Language and the Languages of Fiction.* London: Routledge, 1993.

Gage, Thomas. *The English-American His Travail by Sea and Land: Or, A New Survey of the West-Indias.* London: EEBO, 1648.

Glissant, Edouard. *Caribbean Discourse: Selected Essays.* Trans. J. Michael Dash. Charlottesville: University of Virginia Press, 1989.

Grainger, James. *The Sugar-Cane: A Poem. In Four Books.* With Notes. London: R. and J. Dodsley, 1764. ECDA. ecda.org

Jacobs, Harriet. *Incidents in the Life of a Slave Girl: Written by Herself.* 1861. Ed. Jean Fagan Yellin. Cambridge, MA: Harvard University Press, 2009.

Krise, Thomas W. "True Novel, False History: Robert Robertson's Ventriloquized Ex-Slave in the 'The Speech of Mr. John Talbot Campo Bell' (1736)." *Early American Literature* 30 (1995): 153–166

Krise, Thomas W., ed. *Caribbeana: An Anthology of British Literature of the West Indies.* Chicago: University of Chicago Press, 2000.

Levy, Andrea. "Writing the Long Song." www.andrealevy.co.uk/content/ WritingTheLongSong 2014.

Manzano, Juan Francisco. *The Autobiography of a Slave.* 1839. Trans. Evelyn Picon Garfield. Ed. Ivan Schulman. Detroit: Wayne State University Press, 1996.

Mohammed, Abdul Jan. "Between Speaking and Dying: Some Imperatives in the Emergence of the Subaltern in the Context of U.S. Slavery," in *Can the Subaltern Speak? Reflections on the History of an Idea,* Ed. Rosalind Morris. Columbia University Press, 2010: 139–55.

Monteith, Archibald. "Archibald John Monteith: Native Helper and Assistant in the Jamaica Mission at New Carmel." (1854) *Callaloo* 13.1 (1996): 102–14.

Montejo, Esteban. *The Autobiography of a Runaway Slave.* 1963. Trans. Jocasta Innes. Ed. Miguel Barnet. New York: Random House, 1968.

Prince, Mary. *The History of Mary Prince, a West Indian Slave, Related by Herself.* 1831 (Thomas Pringle ed.). Ed. Moira Ferguson. 2nd ed. Ann Arbor: University of Michigan Press, 1997.

Ramsay, James. *An Essay on the Treatment and Conversion of African Slaves in the British Sugar Colonies.* London: Printed and Sold by James Phillips, George-Yard, Lombard-Street, 1784.

Sa'am, Bon. "The Speech of Moses Bon Sa`am." (1735) in *Caribbeana,* Ed. Thomas W. Krise. Chicago: University of Chicago Press, 1999: 101–107.

Sandoval, Fr. Arturo. *Sandoval: Treatise on Slavery.* (Selections from *De Instauranda Aethiopum Salute* by Alonso de Sandoval, S.J., 1627). Edited and Translated by Nicole von Germeten. Indianapolis: Hackett Publishing Company, 2008.

Simmons, K. Merinda. "Beyond 'Authenticity': Migration and the Epistemology of 'Voice' in Mary Prince's *The History of Mary Prince* and Maryse Condé's *I, Tituba. College Literature* 36.4 (Fall 2009): 75–99.

Spivak, Gayatri C. "Can the Subaltern Speak?" In *Marxism and the Interpretation of Culture,* Eds. G. Nelson, and L. Grossberg. Chicago: University of Illinois Press, 1988.

Starling, Marion Wilson. *The Slave Narrative: Its Place in American History.* 1946. 2nd ed. Washington, DC: Howard University Press, 1988.

Stedman, John Gabriel. *Narrative of an Expedition Against the Revolted Negroes of Surinam.* 1796. ECDA. ecda.org

Thistlewood, Thomas. *In Miserable Slavery: The Diaries of Thomas Thistlewood in Jamaica 1750–1786.* Ed. Douglass Hall. London: Macmillan, 1989.

Tryon, Thomas. *Friendly Advice to Planters[…].*[London]: Printed by Andrew Sowle, 1684. ECDA. ecda.org.

Visweswaran, Kamala. *Fictions of Feminist Ethnography.* Minneapolis: University of Minnesota Press, 1994.

Walcott, Derek. "The Antilles, Fragments of Epic Memory: The 1992 Nobel Lecture." *World Literature Today* 67.2 (1993): 261–67.

Williams, James. *A Narrative of Events Since the First of August, 1834, by James Williams, an Apprenticed Labourer in Jamaica.* 1837 (London: Printed for J. Rider, 14, Bartholomew Close). Ed. Diana Paton. Raleigh: Duke University Press, 2001.

CHAPTER 7

Beyond Bonny and Read: Blackbeard's Bride and Other Women in Caribbean Piracy Narratives

Richard Frohock

Pirates of the late seventeenth and early eighteenth centuries have often been credited with establishing progressive societies built on notions of equality and liberty for all members.[1] Many texts from the period critically examine these notions, confirming or satirizing the thesis in their representation of pirate communities on ships and settlements in the Caribbean and beyond. But what place did these purportedly egalitarian brotherhoods provide for women? The question has perhaps most frequently been addressed by turning to the well known stories of Anne Bonny and Mary Read, the notorious female pirates who were apprehended with Captain Jack Rackham and who were immortalized in Charles Johnson's *A General History of the Pyrates* (1724) for their cross-dressing and masculine behavior and bravado. The emphasis on these two exceptional characters tends to obscure, however, the way women appear in pirate narratives more broadly. While there are few female characters as prominent as Bonny and Read in this literature, there are consistent references to female captives and their treatment at the hands of pirates. How men treat women

R. Frohock (✉)
Oklahoma State University, Stillwater, OK, USA

N. N. Aljoe et al. (eds.), *Literary Histories of the Early
Anglophone Caribbean*, New Caribbean Studies,
https://doi.org/10.1007/978-3-319-71592-6_7

who are under their power functions as a prominent trope in Caribbean voyage narratives; rather than playing the role of transgressive and empowered individuals, women most often serve as passive touchstones of male virtue and vice. In this essay, I consider how stories of female captives are used as reference points in articulating the attributes of male captors, beginning with privateer Captain Woodes Rogers's account of the women captives of Guayaquil in his *Cruising Voyage Round the World* (1712), then examining the images of sexual violence directed against women in Exquemelin's *Buccaneers of America* (1678) and Johnson's *General History*. Looking beyond Bonny and Read generates new insights about the role of women and the limits of egalitarian qualities of piratical societies as represented in key eighteenth-century piracy narratives.

WOODES ROGERS

To provide some context for its appearance in Caribbean piracy narratives, I want first to consider a striking instance of the trope of the captive woman from Captain Woodes Rogers's *A Cruising Voyage Round the World* (1712), one of the most important privateering narratives of the early eighteenth century. Although the incident Rogers describes occurs while he was cruising on the Pacific coast of the Americas, his privateering outlook provides a valuable contrast for understanding transformations of the trope of the captive woman in Caribbean piracy narratives. Commissioned during the War of the Spanish Succession, Rogers sailed to the Americas, where he preyed upon Spanish ships and settlements, and he succeeded in capturing a rich Spanish galleon off the coast of Mexico. After circumnavigating the globe, Rogers was appointed governor of the Bahamas with a particular charge to eradicate piracy in the region. Several decades after his privateering venture, an unknown artist prepared several engravings of key scenes from Rogers's narrative to illustrate Edward Cavendish Drake's *A New and Universal Collection of Authentic and Entertaining Voyages and Travels* (1768). One of the engravings, titled "Captain Rogers's People stripping some Ladies of their Jewels in the Neighbourhood of Guiaquil," depicts a party of Rogers's men who, after the capture of Guayaquil (in present day Ecuador), were sent out to search the countryside for townspeople and treasure. In the illustration, the privateers have discovered a group of genteel Spanish women in a country home and are searching their persons for valuables, particularly gold chains, which the women concealed under their clothes by wrapping them around their torsos and thighs. The men grouped at the right of the engraving are gesturing and leering, seemingly taking pleasure in the spectacle of the women being searched in an intimate way; the men patting down the women smile as well. The engraving makes clear, however, that the search is a controlled one; the group of men, however prurient their expressions may be, are held at a distance, while a man in charge, presumably one of the leaders of this search party—Lieutenant Connely or Alexander Selkirk, who was recently retrieved from his castaway condition on the island of Juan Fernandez—directs the search and serves as a visual barrier between the sexes (except for the men doing the searching). His hand gestures indicate that what is at issue is the transfer of goods—the acquisition of the plunder, the gold chains that the distressed women produce. The scene is charged with the possibility of sexual assault, but the engraving depicts the search party as resisting desire and opportunity and remaining focused on sanctioned plundering (Fig. 7.1).[2]

This same tension is evident in Rogers's narrative account of this scene. Rogers eroticizes the incident, stressing the attractiveness of the "handsom genteel young Women well dress'd," and he notes that due to the hot climate they were "very thin clad with Silk and fine Linnen, and their Hair dressed with Ribbons very neatly." Rogers equally underscores the restraint of the searchers and the propriety of the search, specifying that his men felt for the chains "with their Hands on the Out-side of the Lady's Apparel"; and, when they discovered hidden valuables, they "modestly desired the Gentlewomen to take 'em off and surrender 'em."[3] Rogers claims that his men treated their captives with so much civility that the women afterwards offered to cook them a meal and serve them liquor. Like the engraving, the narrative sets up the moment as an example of temptation resisted. Although the women are alluring, the mariners stay within the boundaries of their commission, and Rogers touts the incident as evidence of his sailors' virtue. The ordinarily indecorous act of men touching female strangers' torsos and thighs through thin clothing is here narratively and visually transformed into something sanctioned, even modest. By remaining chaste when confronted with temptation and opportunity to commit sexual violence in a remote river settlement in South America, the men preserve their reputations, their civil English identity, and thereby their eligibility as good matches for the "fair sex" back home. Because they resist desire, Rogers proclaims that his men should be rewarded with the esteem of women in Great Britain after their return. Like the engraving, Rogers depicts the moment of the search as sexually charged, but he turns

Fig. 7.1 "Captain Rogers's People stripping some Ladies of their Jewels in the Neighbourhood of Guiaquil," in Edward Cavendish Drake's *A New and Universal Collection of Authentic and Entertaining Voyages and Travels, from the Earliest Accounts to the Present Time* (London, 1771), following p. 94. At the bottom of the engraving appears the caption "engraved for Drake's Voyages." (Courtesy of the John Carter Brown Library at Brown University)

that eroticized description of the women's bodies and their vulnerability into a "Proof" of the male privateers' personal and national merits.

Other editions of Rogers's *Cruising Voyage*, including a French edition *Voyage Autour du Monde* (Amsterdam 1716) and the travel compendium *The World Displayed* (London, 1760), elected to illustrate more typical scenes from the military assault on Guayaquil.[4] The choice to illustrate the searching of the women of Guayaquil for Drake's *New and Universal Collection* instead of a defining moment on the battlefield raises the issue of this scene's particular appeal. The scene may have been selected for the voyeuristic pleasure it afforded readers who are also positioned as spectators of the intimate searching of the women. Beyond its titillating value, however, the scene is connected to one of Rogers's most important narrative purposes, which is to define English privateering identity as lawful and socially respectable.[5] Temptations appear frequently, and Rogers constantly battles forces that threaten to pull his men out of good order and identity, away from privateering and into piracy. Over the course of the voyage, Rogers and his imposition of order prevails, and he continually trumpets the fact that privateer identity is not compromised in the course of his journeys into the American wilderness; his privateers do not succumb to lawlessness in places where the reach of law is tenuous (Figs. 7.2 and 7.3).

Rogers expands on the particularity of English privateering identity also by means of contrasts between his crew and the buccaneers who preceded and who undertook many of the same military actions in which he engages. The town of Guayaquil had formerly been raided by French pirates, Rogers notes, but those men "committed a great deal of Brutishness and Murther after they had the Place in their Power" (150). The details of the atrocities are missing but the contrast is clear—English privateers are not French, are not pirates, and they are not brutes, and a signal way he illustrates this difference is in terms of the English sailors' treatment of captive women. The discreet searching of the ladies of Guayaquil powerfully dramatizes English privateer commitments to preserving familiar civil order and identity when traveling to the colonial periphery.

Rogers further reinforces his characterization of English privateering respectability by means of overdetermined contrasts with the Spanish. Not long after leaving Guayaquil, Rogers and his men capture a ship from Panama that has on board a newlywed "pretty young Woman of about 18" and her husband. The threat of sexual assault once again charges the scene; Rogers reassures readers, however, that although her husband feared for her safety, the young bride was well treated by the English privateers. Rogers explains that Mr. Connely, who was also a leader of the party at Guayaquil, took precautions to guard the woman and her family, although they were never under threat; as Rogers put it, "all our young Men have hitherto appear'd modest beyond Example among Privateers; yet we thought it improper to expose them to Temptations." Rogers takes modesty a step further, ordering a "female Negro" to conduct the search of the Spanish daughter and mother who were suspected of concealing jewels under their clothing. The same tension evident in Guayaquil appears here as well, and the attractiveness and vulnerability of the women allows Rogers to make a case for the moral rectitude of the English privateers. After their ordeal and eventual release, the young couple express their

Fig. 7.2 The attack on Guayaquil was illustrated for a French edition of Rogers *Cruising Voyage Round the World* (*Voyage Autour du Monde*), (Amsterdam, 1716), vol. 1, following p. 254 (Courtesy of the John Carter Brown Library at Brown University)

Fig. 7.3 The engraving captioned "The Town of Guaiaquil Plundered by Capt. Rogers" appeared in the travel compendium *The World Displayed; or, A curious collection of Voyages and Travels, Selected from the Writers of all Nations* (London, 1760), vol. VI, following p. 146 (Courtesy of the John Carter Brown Library at Brown University)

surprise at having been treated so well, stating that the English "had been much civiller than they did expect, or believe their own Countrymen would have been in the like case" (243). In Rogers's narrative, English privateers are as different from Spanish colonials as they are from French pirates, and that difference is palpably marked in terms of their relation to, and treatment of, captive women's bodies.

ALEXANDRE EXQUEMELIN

As in Rogers's privateering narrative, pirate narratives frequently employ tales about women to illustrate the principal qualities of male voyagers, but with a difference: the trope of civil restraint usually is replaced with one of aggression and reckless excess. Exquemelin's *Buccaneers of America* (first published in Dutch in 1678) was one of the first and most influential accounts of multinational Caribbean piracy, and it openly details the "brutishness" that Rogers references. Exquemelin's *Buccaneers* has no examples of female pirates—no Anne Bonnys or Mary Reads—but it tells several anecdotes about women who are the object of male attention, desire, and violent aggression. Exquemelin depicts himself as above the fray, an observer rather than participant who critiques the men around him for succumbing to immoral desires and behaviors that modern psychologists might describe as sociopathic.[6] Instead of establishing ties to European civil identity, the encounters with women that Exquemelin reports mark the pirates as severing social norms and civil behaviors and turning wild on the Caribbean seas and shores.[7]

In contrast to the privateers who carefully maintain propriety, the buccaneers indulge carnal desires at every opportunity. After taking prizes, the buccaneers spend heedlessly until their wealth is gone. Exquemelin complains that the money goes to "dicing, whoring, and drinking," and exclaims that "I have seen a man in Jamaica give 500 pieces of eight to a whore, just to see her naked. Yes, and many other impieties."[8] The buccaneers reverse the flow of exchange evident in the scene at Guayaquil by trading riches for access to women's bodies. Exquemelin objects to the buccaneers' profligacy, and the word "impieties" suggests further levels of transgression beyond sexual indulgence and a willful distortion of exchange value norms. Impieties are, most literally, offenses against God, and so this indulgence in women's bodies marks the buccaneers not just as lecherous but as fallen men. The figure of the woman as prostitute indexes the buccaneers' break with the laws of society, morality, and divine authority.

Exquemelin complicates matters of gender by overlaying them with his perceptions of race. Exquemelin appears to rank ethnicities in a hierarchical chain of being, and in a few examples he reports the animalistic traits of non-European races, particularly in relation to female sexual and mothering behaviors. He remarks that African mothers carry their babies in a way that resembles monkey behavior, and he tells an anecdote in which Native American women are revealed to copulate with their spiritual animals (216; 111). Because Exquemelin represents non-European women as less than fully human, it is unsurprising that he does not appear to place much value on their lives. His view of them as expendable commodities is made evident when he reports the death of two enslaved African women who are barbarously killed in a Native American attack. Rather than expressing sympathy or shock at their gruesome deaths, he marvels at the craftsmanship of the arrows used to kill them and provides readers with an illustrated diagram of the weapon (217) (Fig. 7.4).

Since Exquemelin holds non-European women in such low regard, it follows consistently with his perspective that European men who have sex with non-European women indulge in unnatural appetites, thereby marking themselves as depraved and threatening to social order. Exquemelin gives the stereotype of the libidinous Spanish a colonial dimension, reporting that "since Spaniards are of such a nature they cannot live without women, he [a trader] took himself an Indian wife, to look after him and for

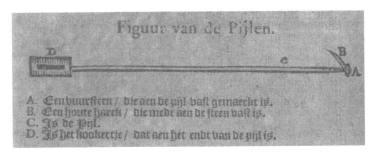

Fig. 7.4 Figure of the arrow, from *De Americaensche Zee-Roovers* (Amsterdam, 1678) (Courtesy of the Library of Congress; digital copy located at http://lccn. loc.gov/02017955)

him to use for his pleasure (if one may call this pleasure)" (111). This is the same woman who purportedly copulates with her spirit animal—a lion— and she is caught in the act by her Spanish husband, who consequently throws her out of his house. He further remarks that the Spanish are "extremely fond of Negro women," and that even Spanish priests force local chieftains to give them their daughters as concubines (36). He additionally states that buccaneers of various nationalities force native women into sexual servitude, either by purchasing them cheaply or by kidnapping them, thereby often creating strife with native communities (209, 219).

A more developed way that Exquemelin uses women to illustrate buccaneer depravity is in terms of their treatment of captive European women. In contrast to Rogers's report of privateer behavior at Guayaquil, Exquemelin describes the buccaneers as routinely neglecting and cruelly abusing women in their power. After the capture of Puerto del Principe, the pirates ignore the pleas of the starving Spanish female prisoners, even those nursing babies, and at Porto Bello, Captain Henry Morgan infamously uses captured monks and nuns as human shields in carrying out his assault on the fort; after the successful capture of the town, he and his men "began making merry, lording it with wine and women" (131, 136).

After the fall of Panama City, abuses abound, and female prisoners discover that they can either submit sexually to their captors for better food and treatment or be beaten and raped. Exquemelin illustrates the plight of these women through the anecdote of one exceptional woman who vows to die resisting Morgan. Rather than force her, Morgan attempts to break her will and have her consent to becoming his sexual partner, an indication that power is more of an issue than desire for Morgan in this contest. In a demonic inversion of Christian injunctions to clothe the naked, feed the hungry, and comfort the distressed, Morgan has the woman stripped, starved, and held in a constant state of terror. Morgan eventually releases her but only because he wants to punish the Spanish monks who tried to misappropriate her ransom money for their own liberation. The anecdote celebrates the steadfast woman for her courage and resolution, but it also is designed to reveal characteristics of the males who determine her fate. Her case exposes the monstrosity of Morgan and the treacherousness of the monks, and it allows Exquemelin to make a case for his own humanity when he secretly aids the woman by bringing her food during her imprisonment. Once again, the captive woman's body serves as a critical reference point for triangulating male civility and morality in the American wilderness.

CAPTAIN CHARLES JOHNSON

Johnson's *General History*, the most prominent compendium of pirate narratives from the early eighteenth century, also provides numerous examples of women among pirates. Most famously, it contains the stories of Anne Bonny and Mary Read, the two women who were captured with Captain Jack Rackham and tried and convicted for piracy in Jamaica in the 1720s. Johnson's *General History* takes the bare elements of their stories as reported in a Jamaican trial narrative and enlarges them into exotic tales of cross-dressing bravado.[9] Since Johnson's *General History*, Bonny and Read have been recast many times in literary works through the centuries, and they have been have been the subject of significant academic interest. Scholars frequently have contextualized these two transgressive figures in historical and narrative traditions of other outlaw women: Bonny and Read of the *General History* have been compared and contrasted to warrior women of medieval balladry, have been juxtaposed with female cross-dressers and criminals in the eighteenth century, and have been discussed in relation to other female pirates through the centuries and around the globe.

Much attention has been directed at their potential subversiveness and narrative containment. Luella Putnam D'Amico has stressed the differences between Anne Bonny and Mary Read, arguing that the former is the "bad" girl who transgresses and the latter is the "good" girl who seeks to have normative, heterosexual relationships and who gravitates toward familiar domestic roles. Sally O'Driscoll has argued that these female pirates have some agency in their ability to pass as men and enter into masculine gender spaces, but that the narrative emphasis on their breasts signals that the women are ultimately contained by their sex and linked to reassuring domestic spheres. Similarly, Rob Canfield argues that in the *General History*, Bonny and Read are subversively masculine but ultimately limited by their sex; their histories are grafted onto romance plots, and their revolts also are terminated at the end of their narratives by their verdicts in court. Marcus Rediker has emphasized their subversion rather than their containment, arguing that as working class women, Bonny and Read are indeed able to create a liberated social space on the pirate ship that contrasts the oppressive environments of a capitalist world that exploits the working class.[10] Bonny and Read have also been analyzed in terms of their legacy of retellings, the many novels and films that their story generated and which have remained popular through the ensuing centuries. For instance, Lizabeth Paravisini-Gebert has considered how various retellings of the Bonny and Read story are used to narrate the Caribbean generally, and Marcus Rediker has discussed connections between Bonny and Read, John Gay's *Polly*, and Delacroix's famous French portrait of liberty.[11]

The critical attention paid to Bonny and Read is understandable, given the rich possibilities in their stories for considering gender identity, female empowerment, and socially progressive outlaw spaces. One essential context has been largely overlooked, however: although Bonny and Read are the only two prominent female pirates in the *General History*, there are numerous other women in the text, and consideration of their understudied stories tells us much about the possibilities and hazards that Johnson imagined for women in the pirate world. The emphasis on Bonny and Read obscures the more representative experience of women, who are most frequently the targets of violent, abusive treatment at the hands of male pirates in this narrative.[12] Instead of discovering agency through transgressive action, most women in the *General History* are forced into passive victimization; and, as in other privateering and piracy narratives, disempowered women in the *General History* serve primarily to define the nature of masculine agency in the territories opened up on the edges of empire.

Like Exquemelin, Johnson uses non-European women to illustrate the depravity of male pirates, but he does so in terms of contrast rather than by asserting corruption through association.[13] Johnson reports that pirates sometimes make non-European women their concubines or wives, but he does not bestialize them or repeat Exquemelin's disdain for interracial sex and marriage. On the contrary, the *General History* tends to portray non-European women as Noble Savages who exemplify virtues, such as loyalty and duty to family, that the pirates lack. For instance, one African woman who trades with Europeans bravely assists Captain North after he is shipwrecked and washed naked onto shore, displaying compassion for a stranger and caring for his needs.[14] The wives of pirate leaders Misson and Caraccioli show their loyalty by insisting on traveling with their husbands on voyages and "never quitted the Decks" during battles, while another African wife of a pirate shows her devotion by committing suicide when her husband dies (415; 413–414). In another instance, one of the pirates' African wives runs twenty miles in the night to warn her husband of a planned insurrection. In contrast to these devotional acts, the pirates generally treat non-European women with contempt and abuse, and they reap the animosity of native populations in return. When pirate Captain Howard retires to India, he marries a local woman, but because he abuses her, her relatives murder him (494). William Davis, who sailed with Captain Roberts, one night sold his African wife "for some Punch to quench his Thirst"; he applied for protection under the Royal African Company, but the company turned him over to the relations and friends and who sold him to a "Christian Black" in retaliation (280). While making a stop on the West African coast, Captain England and his men live "very wantonly for several Weeks, committing such outrageous Acts, that they came to an open Rupture with the Natives" (117). Such accounts illustrate at once the marauders' bad policy and their degeneracy, which is underscored thorough contrasts with the noble traits of their non-European female victims.

European women appear most often in the *General History* as captives who are taken during raids on ships and settlements. The *General History* reports that male pirates customarily banned women from their ships and protected those who were captured in order to prevent the disruptions and quarrels that their presence might create. This does not mean that women were spared from abuse aboard pirate ships, however. A letter included in the second volume of the *General History* reports that Captain Martel's crew captured a ship "that had two Women Passengers on board; how they pass'd their Time I need not say; tho', I fancy, as they had formerly made a Trip or two to the Bay, there was no Rape committed" (69). The letter writer, a ship captain named Evans, who had himself been taken captive by the pirates, seems to imply that these female passengers are prostitutes and therefore cannot be the victims of sexual assault. The pirate articles listed in the Phillips chapter make a similar distinction between the protections afforded chaste and unchaste women: "If at any Time we meet with a prudent Woman, that Man that offers to meddle with her, without her Consent, shall suffer present Death" (343). For these pirates, socially respectable, "prudent" women have exceptional protection, and raping them is a capital crime, whereas impure women have none at all—raping them has no consequence, and is not defined as a crime. More broadly, these statements suggest that from a piratical viewpoint, women who transgress sexual rules of propriety forfeit their rights to their bodies and enter a lawless realm that affords them not new liberties and empowerment but rather new ways of being victimized with impunity.

Even when pirates formulate rules banning women from their ships or prohibiting rape, women's safety was not assured. A major satirical point made in the *General History* is that pirates continually break their own rules for personal advantage. According to the *General History*, many pirates great and small show little or no interest in equality and freedom but instead are driven by a will to power and are prepared to cheat, harm, or kill one another to get it. For example, the Roberts chapter lists among its pirate articles the rule that "no boy or Woman [was] to be allowed amongst them. If any Man were found seducing any of the latter Sex, and carry'd her to Sea, disguised, he was to suffer Death"; furthermore, when a woman was captured "they put a Centinel immediately over her to prevent ill Consequences from so dangerous an Instrument of Division and Quarrel." The rule prohibiting seduction or sexual abuse is only part of the story, however. As Johnson goes on to explain, "here lyes the Roguery; they contend who shall be Centinel, which happens generally to one of the greatest Bullies, who, to secure the Lady's Virtue, will let none lye with her but himself" (212). Systematic victimization of female captives takes place in spite of the rule prohibiting it; instead of affording protection to women, the articles become the occasion for power struggles within the male pirate community.[15]

In other instances reported in the *General History*, pirates make no pretensions about protecting women and instead openly brutalize them. The Captain Vane biography reports that his crew captured a vessel with two women "whom [the pirates] kept for their own Entertainment, contrary to the usual Practice of Pyrates, who generally sent them away, least they should occasion Contention" (620); the Captain Martel biography reports that the pirates "diverted" themselves with enslaved African women (68); the Captain Smith chapter tells how the boatswain kidnapped two women who were then "used in the most inhumane manner" (365); and Captain England's biography reports that his men forced captured women "in a barbarous Manner to their Lusts" (126). The Captain Anstis biography contains an utterly horrifying account of a captive woman who is raped twenty-one times successively, has her back broken, and is then tossed overboard.[16]

These tales of the ultra-violent treatment of women help define the limits of the male pirates' commitment to building progressive alternative societies in the pages of the *General History*. The most fully articulated example of a progressive pirate community is the fictional account of Captain Misson's community on Madagascar, described in the second volume. In this account, the pirates under Misson form a community based on principles of equality and brotherhood; their society is democratic and extends equal rights even to formerly enslaved Africans who join their community. A notable shortcoming of this pirate utopia, however, is the mass exploitation of captured women. When the pirates seize a ship belonging to the great mogul, they discover a hundred women between the ages of twelve and eighteen on board. The women plea desperately for their release, but the pirates force them to join their community on the island of Madagascar, where they face certain abuse (428). The male piratical escape from conventional mores and social authority leads here not to enlightened reforms but rather to lawless exploitation.

Edward Teach, alias Blackbeard, one of the most tyrannical pirates in the *General History*, takes matters a step farther because he, more than other pirates, describes in explicit terms how he exploits women for the purpose of consolidating his power. When Blackbeard visits Carolina planters on shore, he sometimes treats them well and trades with them, but other times he and his men terrorize their families and rape their wives and daughters. An important aspect of Blackbeard's acts of aggression are their seeming randomness; because he is utterly unpredictable, he is a constant threat. Blackbeard himself theorizes the power in random violence when he shoots one of his cronies in the knee one day without warning or cause. When asked why he did this, Blackbeard replied "that if he did not now and then kill one of them, they would forget who he was" (84). Blackbeard's power is generated through a rejection of norms and logical expectations of reciprocal friendship and camaraderie—the arbitrary application of power builds absolute power. The rape of women on the plantations serves Blackbeard's purposes well and dramatizes his transcendence of colonial law and authority. In the same paragraph that reports these rapes, the narrator notes that Blackbeard would sometimes act "in a lordly Manner towards [the planters], and would lay some of them under Contribution; nay, he often proceeded to bully the Governor, not, that I can discover the least Cause of Quarrel betwixt them, but it seemed only to be done, to shew he dared do it" (77). By means of these unpredictable acts of aggression—including, prominently, the sexual assault of women—Blackbeard asserts his power over the colonial elite.

In a particularly perverse extension of the theme, Blackbeard ruthlessly exploits his own young bride. The *General History* reports that Blackbeard married a sixteen-year-old woman from Charleston, making her his fourteenth wife, although he may have had a dozen still living at the time (76). Blackbeard's polygamous wedding demonstrates his contempt for the social conventions of marriage and the power the governor wields in presiding over the ceremony. Whether the governor was aware of the polygamy or not, Blackbeard puts him in a position of blessing an unholy union, and the wedding he conducts is a sham. The governor becomes Blackbeard's pawn or dupe, and Blackbeard effectively strips him of his power to regulate colonial society according to accepted social customs.

Blackbeard's ensuing brutal treatment of his new bride displays even more dramatically his break from social and ethical norms. After lying with her all night, Blackbeard forces her, as "was his Custom," to have sex with five or six of his cronies while he watches. Isabel Karremann has interpreted this scene as an indication of Blackbeard's homoerotic desire, arguing that by ordering his men to rape his bride, Blackbeard takes scopic pleasure in watching males have sex, thereby indirectly fulfilling urges that he cannot gratify directly.[17] I propose that the rape scene can be viewed not in terms of desire but in terms of power. In subjecting his young bride to this horrific brutalization, Blackbeard dramatizes his extreme contempt for social expectations, which put a premium on the male obligation to protect their wives. By becoming a willing cuckold, Blackbeard brings not shame and contempt to himself but instead converts that customary outcome to one of further self-empowerment. Blackbeard transgresses ordinary ethics and social bonds so radically that he arranges and presides over the sexual victimization of his own bride. In doing so, he shows that no one is entitled to his protection, loyalty, or aid, not even those with whom he, conventionally viewed, would have the closest ties. Blackbeard crosses over to a purely transgressive space where he makes all the rules and becomes utterly self-determining. His liberty is unqualified and his power unchecked, and his exploited bride is reduced to a prop in his self-aggrandizing political theater.

As the many stories of women who are the victims of piratical violence illustrate, the *General History*, like *Buccaneers of America*, does not imagine an alternate social sphere that encourages widespread revisions of gender roles or opportunities for women's empowerment. The vast majority of women in these histories become victims with no recourse to protections of law. Even allegedly progressive pirate law fails them because of binary distinctions about chaste and fallen women built into those laws or because many pirates are self-serving villains who follow their articles only as long as it is individually advantageous to do so. Rather than discovering opportunities for self-fashioning new identities, these women become defenseless in the hands of male pirates who brutalize them for their own gratification and empowerment. *Buccaneers of America* and the *General*

History present most women in narrowly defined categories: prostitutes, concubines, servants, slaves, and captives. They represent innocence and helplessness, reproductive and mothering functions, and sexual allure, and their bodies serve as loci for male enactments of morality, depravity, and power.

Some scholars have argued that pirates were exploited men with few or no economic alternatives, who turned to piracy in order to provide for themselves and their families; in breaking away from unjust conditions, they embraced progressive ideas of self-governance and formed compacts that established far-reaching liberties and equalities. In theory, at least, moving beyond the borders of law and authority can be a liberating moment, an opportunity to enter transversal space where one has the freedom to radically revise notions of personal identity and social organization.[18] The narratives of Rogers, Exquemelin, and Johnson, however, evince a wariness of the abyss that confronts one in the colonial periphery. Abandoning oppressive customs can create exhilarating possibilities for self- and social-fashioning, but embracing absolute personal freedom can lead in short order to ethical implosion, the ruthless exploitation of others, and self-destruction. These privateering and piracy narratives present unregulated spaces as holding not only the promise of progressive reform but also the prospect of moral collapse; voyaging the seas can unleash base desires unchecked by law, and the results can be horrifying. Beyond Bonny and Read, these narratives contain a multitude of exploited women who index the threats to civil authority and personal morality when males venture to, and beyond, the edges of empire.

NOTES

1. For example, see Peter Linebaugh and Marcus Rediker, *The Many-Headed Hydra: Sailors, Slaves, Commoners, and the Hidden History of the Revolutionary Atlantic* (Boston, MA: Beacon Press, 2000).
2. For discussion of illustrations in major pirate narratives, see Carolyn Eastman, "'Blood and Lust': Masculinity and Sexuality in Illustrated Print Portrayals of Early Pirates of the Caribbean," in Thomas A. Foster, ed., *New Men: Manliness in Early America* (New York University Press, 2011), 95–115.
3. Woodes Rogers, *A Cruising Voyage Round the World: First to the South-Seas, Thence to the East-Indies, and Homewards by the Cape of Good Hope. Begun in 1708, and Finish'd in 1711* (London, 1712), 131. Eighteenth

Century Collections Online: Range 15133. Subsequent references are to this edition and are given parenthetically in the text.

4. Woodes Rogers, *A Cruising Voyage Round the World* (*Voyage Autour du Monde*), (Amsterdam, 1716), vol. 1, following page 254; *The World Displayed; or, A Curious Collection of Voyages and Travels, Selected from the Writers of all Nations* (London, 1760), vol. 6, following page 146.

5. For a discussion of Rogers's interest in privateer identity, see Richard Frohock, "Consummate Privateers: Edward Cooke and Woodes Rogers," in *Buccaneers and Privateers: The Story of the English Sea Rover, 1675–1725* (Newark: University of Delaware Press, 2012), 77–103.

6. For discussion of Exquemelin's narrative subject position, see Richard Frohock, "Exquemelin's *Buccaneers*: Violence, Authority, and the Word in Early Caribbean History," *Eighteenth-Century Life* 34.1 (2010): 56–72.

7. Jo Stanley, ed., *Bold in Her Breeches: Women Pirates Across the Ages* (London: Pandora, 1995), is one of the only scholars who remarks on the victimization of women in pirate narratives. Stanley notes in particular that "women are seldom referred to in accounts of buccaneers, for instance in the main source, Exquemelin, except as victims of men" (27–8).

8. Alexander O. Exquemelin, *The Buccaneers of America*, trans. Alexis Brown (Mineola, New York: Dover, 1969), 82. Subsequent references are from this edition and are given parenthetically in the text.

9. The original account of Anne Bonny and Mary Read appears in *The Tryals of Captain John Rackam, and Other Pirates, Viz. As Also, The Tryals of Mary Read and Anne Bonny* (Jamaica, 1721). *The Tryals* are included in Joel H. Baer, ed., *British Piracy in the Golden Age: History and Interpretation, 1660–1730*, vol. 3 (London, 2007), 7–66. Julie Wheelwright, "Tars, Tarts and Swashbucklers," in *Bold in Her Breeches*, 176–200, discusses the differences between the trial narrative and the account in the *General History*. David Cordingly, *Women Sailors and Sailors' Women: An Untold Maritime History* (New York: Random House, 2001) 79–87, discusses a few further archival documents that relate to Anne Bonny and Mary Read.

10. Luella Putnam D'Amico, "Disciplining Bad Girls: 300 Years of Trying Anne Bonny and Mary Read," *The Nautilus: A Maritime Journal of Literature, History, and Culture* 5 (2014): 52–70; Sally O'Driscoll, "The Pirate's Breasts: Criminal Women and the Meanings of the Body," *The Eighteenth Century* 53 (2012): 357–379; Rob Canfield, "Something's Mizzen: Anne Bonny, Mary Read, 'Polly,' and Female Counter-Roles on the Imperialist Stage," *South Atlantic Review* 66 (2001), 45–63; Marcus Rediker, "Liberty Beneath the Jolly Roger: The Lives of Anne Bonny and Mary Read, Pirates," in *Iron Men, Wooden Women: Gender and Seafaring in the Atlantic World, 1700–1920*, eds. Margaret. S. Creighton and Lisa

Norling (Baltimore: The Johns Hopkins University Press, 1996), 1–33. Rediker also dedicates a chapter to Anne Bonny and Mary Read in *Villains of All Nations: Atlantic Pirates in the Golden Age* (Boston: Beacon Press, 2004).

11. Lizabeth Paravisini-Gebert, "Cross-Dressing on the Margins of Empire: Women Pirates and the Narrative of the Caribbean," in *Women at Sea: Travel Writing and the Margins of Caribbean Discourse*, ed. Ivette Romero-Cesareo and Paravisini-Gebert (New York: Palgrave, 2001), 59–97; Marcus Rediker, "Liberty Beneath the Jolly Roger." Cross-dressing narratives of female mariners proliferated in the nineteenth century: see Daniel A. Cohen, *The Female Marine and Related Works: Narratives of Cross-Dressing and Urban Vice in America's Early Republic* (Amherst: University of Massachusetts Press, 1997). For more on cross-dressing motifs, see Dianne Dugaw, "Female Sailors Bold: Transvestite Heroines and the Markers of Gender and Class," in *Iron Men, Wooden Women*, 34–54.

12. Stanley, *Bold in Her Breeches*, cites numerous examples of pirate abuse of women in the *General History* (132–4). See also Julie Wheelwright, "Tars, Tarts and Swashbucklers," in *Bold in Her Breeches*, 176–200.

13. See Stanley, *Bold in Her Breeches*, 125–9, for discussion of pirate relations with non-European women.

14. Daniel Defoe [Captain Charles Johnson], *A General History of the Pyrates*, ed. Manuel Schonhorn (Mineola, New York: Dover, 1999), 520. Subsequent references are from this edition and are given parenthetically in the text.

15. Rediker, "Liberty Beneath the Jolly Roger," 9–10, makes the point that pirate policy prohibited the rape of captives, but he does not mention the many examples of rape in the *General History*, which he uses as a principal source. Rediker claims that Roberts was more "straightlaced" than most pirates, and he quotes Roberts's requirement about having a sentinel guard all female captives to prevent their being a cause of dissention, but Rediker ignores the narrator's assertion that the sentinels themselves routinely raped female captives.

16. Johnson, *General History*, 289. Schonhorn, ed., *General History*, 678, notes that this rape was reported in *The Weekly Journal, or Saturday's-Post*, later known as *Mist's Weekly Journal*.

17. Isabel Karremann, "'The Sea Will Make a Man of Him?' Hypervirility, Effeminacy, and the Figure of the Queer Pirate in the Popular Imagination from the Early Eighteenth-Century to Hollywood," *Gender Forum* 32 (2011): np, http://www.genderforum.org/issues/historical-masculinities-as-an-intersectional-problem/the-sea-will-make-a-man-of-him/. Karremann's argument has some connection with Hans Turley, *Rum, Sodomy, and the Lash: Piracy, Sexuality, and Masculine Identity* (New York:

New York University Press,1999), who argues that Bonny and Read are reassuring heterosexual objects of attraction in a world that otherwise can seem to be unsettlingly homosocial.

18. For a discussion of criminality and transversal space, see the introduction to Bryan Reynolds, *Becoming Criminal: Transversal Performance and Cultural Dissidence in Early Modern England* (Baltimore: Johns Hopkins University Press), 2002, 1–22.

BIBLIOGRAPHY

Baer, Joel H., ed. *British Piracy in the Golden Age: History and Interpretation, 1660–1730.* 3 vols. London, 2007.

Canfield, Rob. "Something's Mizzen: Anne Bonny, Mary Read, 'Polly,' and Female Counter-Roles on the Imperialist Stage." *South Atlantic Review* 66 (2001), 45–63.

Cohen, Daniel A. *The Female Marine and Related Works: Narratives of Cross-Dressing and Urban Vice in America's Early Republic.* Amherst: University of Massachusetts Press, 1997.

Cordingly, David. *Women Sailors and Sailors' Women: An Untold Maritime History.* New York: Random House, 2001.

Defoe, Daniel [Captain Charles Johnson]. *A General History of the Pyrates.* Ed. Manuel Schonhorn. Mineola, New York: Dover, 1999.

D'Amico, Luella Putnam. "Disciplining Bad Girls: 300 Years of Trying Anne Bonny and Mary Read." *The Nautilus: A Maritime Journal of Literature, History, and Culture* 5 (2014): 52–70.

Dugaw, Dianne. "Female Sailors Bold: Transvestite Heroines and the Markers of Gender and Class." In *Iron Men, Wooden Women: Gender and Seafaring in the Atlantic World, 1700–1920.* Eds. Margaret S. Creighton and Lisa Norling. 34–54. Baltimore: The Johns Hopkins University Press, 1996.

Eastman, Carolyn. "'Blood and Lust': Masculinity and Sexuality in Illustrated Print Portrayals of Early Pirates of the Caribbean." In *New Men: Manliness in Early America.* Ed. Thomas A. Foster. 95–115. New York: New York University Press, 2011.

Exquemelin, Alexander O. *The Buccaneers of America.* Trans. Alexis Brown. Mineola, NY: Dover, 1969.

Frohock, Richard. *Buccaneers and Privateers: The Story of the English Sea Rover, 1675–1725.* Newark: University of Delaware Press, 2012.

Frohock, Richard. "Exquemelin's *Buccaneers*: Violence, Authority, and the Word in Early Caribbean History." *Eighteenth-Century Life* 34.1 (2010): 56–72.

Karremann, Isabel. "'The Sea Will Make a Man of Him?' Hypervirility, Effeminacy, and the Figure of the Queer Pirate in the Popular Imagination from the Early Eighteenth-Century to Hollywood." *Gender Forum* 32 (2011). http://www.

genderforum.org/issues/historical-masculinities-as-an-intersectional-problem/the-sea-will-make-a-man-of-him/.

Linebaugh, Peter and Marcus Rediker. *The Many-Headed Hydra: Sailors, Slaves, Commoners, and the Hidden History of the Revolutionary Atlantic*. Boston, MA: Beacon Press, 2000.

O'Driscoll, Sally. "The Pirate's Breasts: Criminal Women and the Meanings of the Body." *The Eighteenth Century* 53 (2012): 357–379.

Paravisini-Gebert, Lizabeth. "Cross-Dressing on the Margins of Empire: Women Pirates and the Narrative of the Caribbean." In *Women at Sea: Travel Writing and the Margins of Caribbean Discourse*. Eds. Ivette Romero-Cesareo and L. Paravisini-Gebert. 59–97. New York: Palgrave, 2001.

Rediker, Marcus. "Liberty Beneath the Jolly Roger: The Lives of Anne Bonny and Mary Read, Pirates." In *Iron Men, Wooden Women: Gender and Seafaring in the Atlantic World, 1700–1920*. Eds. Margaret S. Creighton and Lisa Norling. 1–33. Baltimore: The Johns Hopkins University Press, 1996.

Rediker, Marcus. *Villains of All Nations: Atlantic Pirates in the Golden Age*. Boston: Beacon Press, 2004.

Rogers, Woodes. *A Cruising Voyage Round the World: First to the South-Seas, Thence to the East-Indies, and Homewards by the Cape of Good Hope. Begun In 1708, And Finish'd In 1711*. London, 1712.

Rogers, Woodes. *A Cruising Voyage Round the World (Voyage Autour du Monde)*. Amsterdam, 1716.

Reynolds, Bryan. *Becoming Criminal: Transversal Performance and Cultural Dissidence in Early Modern England*. Baltimore: Johns Hopkins University Press, 2002.

Stanley, Jo, ed. *Bold in Her Breeches: Women Pirates Across the Ages*. London: Pandora, 1995.

The Tryals of Captain John Rackam, and Other Pirates, Viz. As Also, The Tryals of Mary Read and Anne Bonny. Jamaica, 1721.

The World Displayed; or, A Curious Collection of Voyages and Travels, Selected from the Writers of All Nations. London, 1760.

Turley, Hans. *Rum, Sodomy, and the Lash: Piracy, Sexuality, and Masculine Identity*. New York: New York University Press, 1999.

Wheelwright, Julie. "Tars, Tarts and Swashbucklers." In *Bold in Her Breeches*. 176–200.

CHAPTER 8

Early Creole Novels in English Before 1850: *Hamel, the Obeah Man* and *Warner Arundell: The Adventures of a Creole*

Candace Ward and Tim Watson

Given the importance of the West Indian colonies in the economic, social, and cultural transformations of early modern England, and given the importance of the early English novel in the representation of those new social, cultural, and economic arrangements, it is not surprising that the Caribbean is a principal focus of the two works most often cited as the first novels in English: Aphra Behn's *Oroonoko* and Daniel Defoe's *Robinson Crusoe*. The Caribbean was the place that most acutely crystallized the modern tension between individual freedom on the one hand—the chance for men and women to travel, transform, and reinvent themselves—and, on the other hand, legally sanctioned unfreedom—the capture and bondage of millions of men and women in the transatlantic slave trade and chattel slavery. For these reasons, the Caribbean continued to be a key fictional component of many novels in English as the genre diversified,

C. Ward (✉)
Florida State University, Tallahassee, FL, USA

T. Watson
University of Miami, Coral Gables, FL, USA

© The Author(s) 2018
N. N. Aljoe et al. (eds.), *Literary Histories of the Early Anglophone Caribbean*, New Caribbean Studies,
https://doi.org/10.1007/978-3-319-71592-6_8

split, and reinvented itself, as recent critical interest in Jane Austen's *Mansfield Park*, Maria Edgeworth's *Belinda*, and other lesser known novels such as *Jonathan Corncob*, *Tom Cringle's Log*, and *The History of Sir George Ellison* attests.[1]

However, with the possible exception of *Tom Cringle's Log* (whose author, Michael Scott, resided in Jamaica for a number of years), this body of work would not readily earn the label "Caribbean fiction." Their West Indian material is certainly central, but the region is clearly represented from a British, or even an imperial, point of view, and most often by authors who themselves knew about the region only from reading or hearing about it. Our interest in this essay lies in those Caribbean novels written from a different perspective, produced by authors resident in, and to a greater or lesser extent themselves the products of, Britain's increasingly far-flung colonial empire. Specifically, our focus is on what we call "creole novels," works written by individuals born in or resident in the British West Indies for long periods, who identified with white creole culture, some in more sustained ways than others. The most representative of these works include *Montgomery; or the West Indian Adventurer* (1812–13), Cynric Williams's *Hamel, the Obeah Man* (1827), *Marly; or a Planter's Life in Jamaica* (1828), E. L. Joseph's *Warner Arundell: The Adventures of a Creole* (1838), and J. W. Orderson's *Creoleana* (1842).[2] Works by authors of color did begin to appear in the period after Emancipation, with the first that we can reliably identify being *Emmanuel Appadocca, or, Blighted Life: A Tale of the Boucaneers*, by the Trinidadian writer Michel Maxwell Philip, which appeared in 1854.[3] Given the economic, cultural, and social hegemony of the white planter class throughout the Anglophone Caribbean, however, it is not surprising that the earliest fiction from the region that we deal with here was written by, and privileged the point of view of, the white creole elite. After a survey of the stakes involved in identifying and analyzing this genre of the early Caribbean creole novel, we focus the bulk of this chapter on the two examples that we take to be the most interesting and significant: *Hamel* and *Warner Arundell*.

Each of these novels foregrounds a local authority rooted in their authors' insider knowledge of life in the Atlantic slave colonies—what one of us has called "eyewitness insiderism."[4] Validating their authorial role in ways that metropolitan writers cannot, these authors demonstrate a self-consciousness about working through and within a "creole realism" that was "novel" by emphasizing New World settings and New World characters.[5] In so doing, they have created fictional narratives that are themselves products of creolization in the sense that they reflect (albeit in limited and self-serving ways) connections between groups that cross the racial spectrum of Caribbean society, including individuals and groups that threatened the local white authority upheld and ostensibly validated by the novels.

The claim to a privileged perspective on the situation in the West Indies, made consistently by the novelists, along with the plantocracy and their British-based supporters, was a crucial component of the pro-slavery arguments during the furious debate over the slave trade and—after its abolition—over the institution of slavery itself in the period between about 1780 and 1838 when slavery finally ended. For example, when the Jamaica-based Anglican minister George Bridges launched a blistering pro-slavery attack on abolitionist leader William Wilberforce, he relied heavily on personal experience as an authenticating proof of his argument: "You, Sir, have never been in the West Indies; you have never viewed the habits of negro life in its indigenous state, nor ever had communication with that people ... Allow then one who has profited by all those opportunities which you want ... to tell you that you are fatally in error throughout."[6] White creole men and women consciously deployed their status as eyewitness observers to convey a particular version of Caribbean life to readers, who were demographically much more likely to be based in Britain than in the region itself.

Early creole novels performed the cultural work of challenging metropolitan constructions of both West Indian subjects and West Indian history, specifically those parts of Caribbean history documenting the institution of slavery and resistance to it by the enslaved—even in the novels produced after the Emancipation Act of 1833 went into effect. In *Montgomery, Hamel, Marly, Warner Arundell,* and *Creoleana* this project is evident in the description of generous and humane, paternal and rational members of the planter class, a clear response to images of the scourge-wielding tyrants described in abolitionist writings. As for the enslaved—with the marked exceptions of the rebel leaders Hamel and Combah in Cynric Williams's novel—they are most often described as either anonymously suffering victims of anomalous cruelty, as in *Montgomery,* or as loyal and faithful retainers who rebel only if they are led astray by outside abolitionists and missionaries. In the case of *Warner Arundell*'s depiction of Julien Fédon, a real-life planter of French and African descent who emancipated his slaves and led a rebellion on the island of Grenada, even that revolutionary action is attributed to the undue influence of French Jacobinism rather than the assertion of political agency on the part of insurrectionaries.

All of these constructions, of course, neatly obscure the inherent and routine violence of chattel slavery and recast the master–slave relationship in romantic terms that celebrate bonds of love and gratitude. In post-Emancipation novels, the tendency to adhere to and persist in the construction of a benign and pastoralized planter past continues the work of overturning metropolitan constructions of white West Indians, even as the urgency of that project is tamped down by the fact of Emancipation. Whereas novels produced before the 1833 Act clearly were engaged in the intense debate, those written afterward respond to the new realities of Emancipation. That response, however, is often a nostalgic look back, as in *Creoleana*, published in 1842 but set sixty years earlier, in "Barbados in Days of Yore," or as in *Warner Arundell*'s mild satire of "creole gentlemen of the old school" like the eponymous narrator's father, who "had high notions with regard to the absolute authority of an owner over his slaves; yet, like most creoles, was an indulgent master and more under the influence of his bond-servants than he himself was aware of, or than the mere European would believe."[7]

Such depictions, of course, make clear that laying claim to first-hand observation did not mean these texts were neutral accounts of local life—far from it. We can say that these novels all explicitly attempted to intervene on behalf of a historiography and natural history that were told from the point of view of the white planter elite. From such a perspective, they tended to be partisan accounts of slave societies, even in cases where, as in *Montgomery* and *Warner Arundell*, there appears a critique of slavery's (occasional) brutality. Even these critiques, however, are validated by the authors' insider perspective. As *Montgomery*'s author explains, it is his intimacy with "West-India scenes and West-India characters" that enables him to encourage his fellow creoles to emulate "whatever was amiable and praiseworthy in human nature."[8]

This is all to say that early creole novels pose an interesting conundrum for scholars now working in early Caribbean studies, who may be keen to see them as part, or even as inaugural texts, of a specifically Caribbean literary tradition, or who are interested in tracing connections between nineteenth- and even eighteenth-century fiction of the Caribbean and the later flourishing of Caribbean literature in English in the twentieth century.[9] Such scholarship, of course, must acknowledge that privileging the insider status of the authors—or imputing it, in the case of anonymously published texts—runs the risk of privileging the point of view of those white creoles who had the most to gain from misrepresenting local society, local cultures, and the local environment. It is unsurprising that creole novels produced before 1850 have not been enthusiastically endorsed by later generations of Caribbean writers, who have inherited a quite different cultural and political perspective on the days of slavery and colonial rule.[10]

Nevertheless, we continue to value and privilege eyewitness accounts—and fiction produced on the basis of experience, even if it was relatively brief. We do not expect to learn much about Africa from the African section of *Oroonoko* (though we might learn a great deal about royalism), but we are willing to learn some interesting things about Surinam from the Caribbean section of that novel because we know that Aphra Behn spent time there. The intensity of the critical debate that has followed from Vincent Carretta's claim that Olaudah Equiano was born in South Carolina, rather than in present-day Nigeria, demonstrates that we are still highly invested in the idea of first-hand, eyewitness experience giving authority to narrative accounts—if *all* of Equiano's account of his African childhood and Igbo customs is borrowed from secondary sources, many readers feel the rest of his *Interesting Narrative* is somehow devalued.[11] The novels that we discuss in this essay illustrate the problematic inclination to privilege the "real" in fiction: grounded in Caribbean reality, even if their vision skews toward one, often insensitive, version of that world, they speak to our historical moment by depicting their own. And, while it may not be possible to draw a satisfactory straight line of literary influence from these early Caribbean texts to the writings of later figures such as Derek Walcott, George Lamming, and Sam Selvon, for example, these texts are nevertheless part of a larger Caribbean history.

From our survey of the early creole novels, we can say that one provocative link between twentieth- and twenty-first-century Caribbean fiction and the pre-1850 novels is their shared attempt to use the power of fictional narrative to reframe historical events in thought-provoking and persuasive ways. In particular, many of these novels turn to narratives of rebellion and revolution to overturn conventional wisdom about the region. Indeed, as in the Caribbean literature of the anti-colonial and independence periods, in the early creole novels "revolution" operates as one of the most powerful tropes through which to assert the rightness of the novel's message. All of the early creole novels we identify above, whether pre-Emancipation or post-Emancipation, whether self-consciously or not, deal with rebellion and resistance in some form, whether in the shape of large-scale anti-slavery revolt, as in *Hamel* and *Warner Arundell*; of assertions of independence by free blacks, like those of the Jamaican Maroons featured in *Montgomery* and *Marly*; or in the more subtle attempts by women of color to assert agency from the margins of white creole domesticity, as in *Hamel* and *Creoleana*.

For this reason, we will devote the rest of this essay to exploring the historiographical and novelistic work of rebellion in the early creole novel. Because it is impossible to discuss all of them, we have chosen the two in which themes of revolt are most extensively developed: *Hamel, the Obeah Man*, published a half-decade before slavery was formally abolished, and *Warner Arundell*, which appeared the first year of full freedom for previously enslaved subjects of the British Caribbean. Both of these novels display their "creole-ness" in ways that are problematic as well as provocative; both represent their authors' response to metropolitan representations of white West Indians and their attempts to overturn metropolitan versions of Caribbean history—even as that history was unfolding in the momentous last decades of British Atlantic slavery. Both novels, and especially *Hamel*, with its pronounced pro-slavery stance, appear to us now to have been written from the wrong side of history. Nevertheless, we argue that their attempts to produce an expansive, even comprehensive, account of Caribbean society (the island of Jamaica in the case of *Hamel*; the whole Caribbean region, in the case of the picaresque *Warner Arundell*) forced them to include a wide array of characters, voices, and points of view, including ones that were ostensibly at odds with their authors' political positions. To that extent, they are among the most interesting of all documents that we possess from this crucial period in Caribbean history and culture, marked as it was by revolutionary ferment and social and political upheaval of all kinds—agitation that is visible in both the form and the content of these intriguing novels.

*   *   *

In our introduction to the 2010 Broadview edition of *Hamel, the Obeah Man* (which had been first published by Hunt and Clarke in London in 1827), we called it "the most important nineteenth-century English novel of the Caribbean."[12] As we argue below, there are good reasons to single out *Hamel* for its complexity and its ambivalence about its own pro-planter perspective. However, in the broader context of this essay, it is helpful to see Williams's novel as part of a significant group of early

Caribbean novels in English, rather than as a *sui generis* text or as a tale belonging mostly in the tradition of the British gothic novel that just happens to have a Caribbean setting. A number of these novels were identified almost fifty years ago now in Kamau Brathwaite's pioneering article "Creative Literature of the British West Indies during the Period of Slavery." Of these, *Hamel* seemed to him the most interesting and the most open to voices of non-white West Indians.[13] What made *Hamel* stand out for Brathwaite? Simply put, it was the expansive way in which the novel includes the perspective of the enslaved, black majority, however problematically, and the way it privileges the eponymous black hero against the white evangelical missionary antihero, Roland: "What this novel does ... is recognize the fact that African slaves, in the New World, despite their transportation, would have continued to be cultured beings ... and that such slaves were not Nature's playthings, but moral sentient beings neither Toms nor Noble Savages."[14] *Hamel*, therefore, is a significant participant in what Brathwaite called "the development of creole society."[15] It would be interesting, however, to think about how creolized Hamel really is, or rather the extent to which his African survivals—his African birth and early memories, his knowledge of spoken and written Arabic and familiarity with the Qur'an, and so forth—contribute to his fictional stature. In particular, Hamel's ethnic origin as a "Coromantee" (a member of what are now called the Akan people from present-day Ghana) signals both his African-ness and his rebelliousness: Coromantees, in the questionable but consistent ethnology constructed by the planter class, were notorious for their fierceness, their proneness to revolt, but also for their bravery. They were the quintessential African noble savages in the white West Indian imagination, in other words, from whom rebellion was always likely to spring. At the end of the novel, in a sign of his desire to return to his African roots, Hamel sails off eastward, toward Africa, his "mother's country," although the white planter Guthrie seems to think Hamel is sailing off to Haiti to "deliver himself up to the rebels" who have fled there.[16]

Hamel, then, is the novel of this group of early Caribbean fictions most committed to the inclusion of black voices (although that is perhaps not saying much in the case of these pro-planter novels); it is a recognition, albeit ambivalent and backhanded, that, as Brathwaite put it in *The Development of Creole Society*, "white and black, master and slave" were not separate units but "contributory parts of a whole."[17] In *Hamel*, the aspect of the novel that best represents this ambivalent commitment to representing black Jamaica is its representation of slave revolt. The rebellion that begins in northeast Jamaica and threatens to spread across the whole island is the central event of *Hamel, the Obeah Man*, one that completely dominates the second half of the novel, and structures all the other plot events surrounding it. It is not surprising that rebellion is a common trope in early creole fiction, since it was obviously the greatest fear of the white creole elite in the eighteenth century and first third of the nineteenth century, as their constant allusions to the dangers of giving enslaved people more autonomy amply demonstrate. Of course, Williams's representation of Hamel's slave revolt could be read as clear evidence of the self-organization and militant activity of the enslaved black majority; to include it, especially in such an expansive way, is to take a risk for a pro-planter novel like *Hamel*.

And so, whether from lack of authorial skill or from a sense of historical necessity, the novel in the second half moves away from its early focus on the malign white instigator of rebellion—the trope that was most common among British and white creole commentators alike, as in the way that John Smith, a white missionary, became the focus of the inquiry and narratives that followed the 1823 uprising in Demerara that inspired the author of *Hamel*.[18] Instead, for most of the second half of the novel, Roland, the evil English Methodist, is off-stage, in prison or hiding in Hamel's cave. In *his* stead, Combah, the rebel king, and Hamel himself come to the fore, along with a cast of more peripheral rebel characters.

So here is the paradox of the novel: when Hamel declares to the representatives of the white plantocracy, "'There is justice upon the earth, though it seems to sleep; and the black men shall, first or last, shed your blood, and toss your bodies into the sea!'",[19] he is expressing the sometimes paranoid, sometimes justified fears of the planter class, the ones embodied in the oft-repeated phrase "San Domingo massacres." At the same time, he is uttering what Brathwaite, albeit hyperbolically, called "probably the first Black Power speech in our literature."[20]

We want to argue that it is only in the creole novel that black self-organization and activity could be so represented at this moment—and this is one of the things that makes these novels historically interesting, even if few would make strong claims for their significance simply on the grounds of their literariness or innovation in terms of genre or narrative technique. In fact, an analysis of the differences between non-fictional and fictional accounts of slave rebellion and revolution during this historical moment shows an intriguing divergence. Four of the authors of these early creole novels also wrote nonfiction works seeking to vindicate the objectivity of the white creole point of view: John Stewart's *A View of the Past and Present State of the Island of Jamaica* (if we agree that Stewart was the author of *Marly*, following Karina Williamson's proposal of him as a "plausible candidate")[21]; E. L. Joseph's *History of Trinidad*; J. W. Orderson's pamphlets and newspaper activities; and Cynric Williams's *Tour through the Island of Jamaica* published in 1826.[22] Williams (probably a pseudonym) was the author of *Hamel*, and as we have seen, an island-wide conspiracy dominates the novel. And yet while his travelogue covers the exact period when the colonial authorities and magistrates in the northeastern parishes (where *Hamel* is set) claimed to have discovered an island-wide plot by rebel slaves, his traveler-narrator in the *Tour* is serenely untroubled by the events in St. Mary and St. George, instead passing his time in flirting with the beautiful mixed-race teenage girl Diana, drinking "sangaree," and testing his mountain-climbing skills, twice attempting to reach the summit of the Blue Mountains. He does comment on white creole anxiety about insurrections: near the beginning of Chapter 8, he says that "considerable apprehensions have been entertained respecting the discontents of the negroes, and a report has arrived here of insurrections in Saint Mary's," and later he meets a Miss Neville and her uncle on the road who are heading for the capital, Spanish Town, out of "apprehension of disturbances in the Island."[23] However, the action remains off-stage, and the effect of Williams's tale in the end is to make the reader skeptical of the planters' "real dread of being murdered by the negroes," to see it as a kind of overblown paranoia (and this despite the travelogue being explicitly sympathetic to the planters).[24] By the time he makes his way around the island to Port Antonio, in the northeast, he has ceased to mention the "insurrection," instead casually referring to the punishments meted out to several slaves suspected of plotting rebellion in the parishes of St. Mary and St. George who were "hanged at Port Maria and Buff Bay."[25]

Why is there such a striking contrast in the way these two texts, by the same author, written at almost the same moment, treat the topic of slave rebellion? Is it because certain historical truths could only be told in fiction? The fear of slave uprisings was part of the common vocabulary of creole whites, an anxiety based on repeated insurrections, from the large-scale uprisings in Barbados (1816), Demerara (1823), and of course the still living memory of the Haitian Revolution, to the small-scale revolts and possible plots in every corner of the region, such as St. George and

St. Mary on the Jamaican north coast, right up until the 1831–32 uprising in northwest Jamaica that hastened the end of slavery itself. Despite the ubiquity of slave revolts, however, there was a curious reticence on the part of white West Indians to speak about them after the fact. This was not specific to the Caribbean, it should be said. In 1835, Alexis de Tocqueville, discussing slave rebellions in *Democracy in America*, wrote that "in the southern states there is a silence; one avoids discussing it with one's friends, each man … hides it from himself."[26] Recently, two books have cast new light on the South Carolina slave revolt at Stono in 1739, one of the most extensive uprisings in the mainland American territories before Nat Turner's rebellion in 1831, one that was little discussed in the 250 years afterward, such that Peter Hoffer, the historian who has most recently written about Stono, emphasizes the amount of imaginative reconstruction required to recover the story in the absence of reliable source material. In discussing his methods for dealing with the Stono sources (or lack thereof), Hoffer ends by saying he "resorted to the inspiration of the historical novel":[27] "Adapting the literary skills of the novelist enables the historian to peer over, if not cross, the 'boundary' between fact-based scholarship and fiction … Novelesque techniques allow us to think about what might have happened at Hutchenson's store that night, what the slaves were thinking in the field alongside Pon Pon Road, and how masters coped with the memory of Stono."[28] As a historian, Hoffer tends to see this formal experimentation as something he "resorted" to. But by peering over the boundary between "fact-based scholarship and fiction," the contemporary historian can establish a concrete connection between his or her storytelling method and the historical truths embedded—sometimes rather deeply embedded—in an implausible gothic melodrama like *Hamel*—at least when it comes to the deeply fraught question of subaltern rebellion. Perhaps the author of *Hamel* felt that black revolt could be safely contained in the fanciful world of the novel, drawing on the powerful, pan-imperial influence of Walter Scott's *Waverley*, in which the Jacobite rebellion similarly dominates half the novel and draws in another hero who is actually fighting for the other side, Edward Waverley, just as Oliver Fairfax in *Hamel* becomes a symbolic rebel in literal blackface.

There is a difference, however. The Jacobite rebellion could be so extensively dramatized—and sympathy elicited for the Highlanders who joined it—precisely to the extent that the iron laws of History had already shown it to be a failure, and that the Highlands had been incorporated into modernizing Britain. In *Hamel,* however, the action is set at a moment that is all but contemporaneous with the novel's composition (the novel takes place in 1822, according to its opening lines, although the author is sometimes careless with the historical timeline, as we document in the footnotes to our edition). The events of *Hamel* cannot be safely consigned to the past; in fact, if anything the winds of History seem to be behind the abolitionist side, so there is a significant risk to the defenders of the plantocracy in dramatizing black agency in this way.

The irony, therefore, is that the plots in St. George and St. Mary in Jamaica, downplayed in Williams's *A Tour through the Island,* instead become the major sources for *Hamel,* starting with the title character himself, a blend of two key figures in the Jamaican plots, obeah Jack and Henry Oliver, the rebel leader.[29] Moreover, there is a further irony: these plots, which were averted in the planning stages and never actually broke out into open rebellion, may not in fact have existed in any meaningful sense. Despite all the eyewitness testimony and trials, it is still possible to see them as products of the magistrates' and whites' paranoia about plots, and then the understandable willingness of enslaved people to testify to the things they knew the whites wanted to hear when it might save their necks.

So this is perhaps one part of the answer to why novels are the most appropriate way to represent slave revolt: because so many of those revolts are themselves driven by, and in some sense actually caused by, the circulation of stories. In many cases throughout the Americas, slaves rebelled when they heard and retold stories about how freedom had been granted to them by the Queen, or the authorities in Paris or Madrid, but that the local authorities were blocking it or denying it. These stories, even though they were often factually inaccurate, played crucial roles in driving the enslaved to take the ultimate risk of rising up. In Stono, for example, slaves heard—correctly, in this case—that Spain, in the build-up to war with England, had offered freedom to any slaves in British territories who could reach the border of Spanish Florida, and so they headed south.

(This dialog between imagination and history, between eyewitness authenticity and literary license, has been given an additional twist by a piece of information that we discovered as this chapter was being prepared for publication. While the identity of "Cynric R. Williams" remains a mystery, our previous speculation that the author may have been the Jamaican creole coffee planter Charles White Williams has been called into question by our further research.[30] The famous library of William Beckford, the wealthy English author of *Vathek* who had inherited a fortune based on Jamaican sugar estates and slavery, contained a copy of Williams's *Tour through the Island of Jamaica*. When portions of Beckford's library were put up for auction later in the nineteenth century, the sale catalog transcribed part of the "MS. notes by Mr. Beckford" added to the Jamaica travelogue: "The name of Williams is merely the *nom de plume* of a Mr. Johnson, who drew upon his imagination for his facts."[31] Our research is ongoing to attempt to identify this Johnson and to confirm, or refute, Beckford's private observation, which may have been based on Beckford's extensive family connections to Jamaica or on his literary network in London. For now, therefore, the *Hamel* author's creole identity must be considered unproven. It should be noted that Kamau Brathwaite, in his early praise of *Hamel*, while generally assuming the author's white West Indian provenance, does suggest parenthetically that a detail like the "South American poncho" that Hamel sometimes wears, "throws doubt on whether the author knew the West Indies" first-hand.)[32]

When it comes to a novel like *Hamel*, we now appreciate its willingness to represent the revolt; apart from anything else, it makes it a good novel to teach. It raises some of these complicated questions about historical knowledge and the representation of the past in narrative form; it also puts the enslaved at the center of history and turns them into ambiguous heroes. The subsequent developments of History have reversed the ostensible meaning of the novel, and students often prefer it to the disappointment they feel when they find out that Olaudah Equiano, for instance, sailed on slaving voyages and helped to set up a settlement on the Mosquito Coast (on the border between modern-day Nicaragua and Honduras) that used slave labor.

Hamel allows us to ask more complicated questions too, such as: to what extent did slaves rebel against slavery itself? It would seem obvious that they did, but some historians, most notably João Pedro Marques, are skeptical of narratives that impute abolitionist motives to rebel slaves, seeing them instead as engaged in local power struggles that were not about Enlightenment concepts of "liberty" or "rights" at all.[33] If we take this point of view, it significantly disrupts our ability to see a transatlantic continuum between slave revolts in the colonies and anti-slavery political campaigns in Britain. *Hamel* represents the slaves rising up for "freedom" for sure; but also for the ability to celebrate religion in the ways they wanted; and for mundane, local reasons too. And Hamel himself, while we want to focus attention on his remarkable status as one of the first fully-drawn black characters in English fiction (which is why Brathwaite was drawn to him), does also represent some of the conflicts between loyalty to friends and community and loyalty to white "masters" that surely played out throughout the region and just as surely spelled the end of many slave revolts.

*   *   *

If *Hamel* is a defensive novel of slavery that anxiously anticipates the coming emancipation of the enslaved in the Caribbean, *Warner Arundell*, published in 1838 (the year that saw the end of the four-year apprenticeship period and the beginning of full freedom for the formerly enslaved), looks back from a vantage point just after Emancipation and tries to take stock of the wider Caribbean world during the period of slavery. It also looks forward, attempting to project a future for a "new" Caribbean plantocracy no longer dependent on the institution it once vigorously justified. But, as one of us has pointed out elsewhere, despite the obvious changes occurring after 1838, in other respects there was no tidy and absolute break between the periods "before" and "after" slavery.[34] Aware of this, Joseph also understands the need to rewrite the story of that institution's past, the need, in effect, to assert a semblance of control over its representation by appropriating actual events from the Caribbean past. In so doing, Joseph dramatizes the push and pull of historicity and fictionality, the promise and limitations of both.[35]

Joseph's attempt to exercise such control is evident in the opening pages of the novel, introduced by a fictitious editor's introductory remarks, which situate History at the forefront of the narrative: "The Adventures of a Creole," we are told, has been extracted from a voluminous manuscript penned by the eponymous hero, abridged and edited by a fellow creole. The value of Arundell's papers, the creole editor tells us, lies in their historical accuracy: Arundell "possessed a most powerful memory. Every thing he had heard, seen, read, or thought, he seemed to recollect …. For example, he opens his journal with an account of the first settlement of his family in the West Indies. This induces him to give a history of the Bucaniers," as well as "an immense number of anecdotes of all the old families in the West Indies" (4). Crucially, Arundell's history of English settlement of the West Indian colonies also includes a history of resistance by the enslaved: "In the progress of his Work he gives the whole history of the two Maroon wars in Jamaica" (i.e., the First ending in the Treaties of

1739–40 and the Second war of 1795–96) and "an account of the rise, progress, and termination of the wars in the West Indies consequent on the French revolution" (4).

Confronted by such a trove of historical documentation—doubly verified by the creole authority of Arundell and his editor, and a West Indian genealogy intended to impress—the editor is persuaded to abandon his own project of writing a history of the South American wars of independence, proposing instead to help Arundell extract his "personal narrative" from the alarmingly large manuscript. Arundell agrees, but only if his fellow creole will undertake the task of extraction. If left to a British publisher, one "so utterly ignorant of West India manners, feeling, and even climate," Arundell insists, "the most egregious blunders would be introduced into every paragraph" (5). Such disdain for metropolitan authority is humorous, but telling as well—the novel, after all, was published in London and favorably reviewed in British periodicals. More importantly for our reading, however, is the suggestion that the historical accuracy of Arundell's (hi)story is blunder-free, that it constitutes an authoritative version of events.

The novel's engagement with history, with its writing and re-writing, is not surprising given Joseph's own role as Caribbean historian. His *History of Trinidad* was published in Port of Spain in 1838, the same year that *Warner Arundell* appeared in London.[36] The blurring of lines between fictional memoirs and non-fictional history, the deployment of literary and non-literary discursive modes, was remarked by the novel's reviewers, one of whom observed that "some portions look like fiction, some like truth, some like novel, some like history, and that the whole is remarkable for its views of men, manners, and places in these regions than for any other quality."[37] In the sense that the novel was received, as the same reviewer put it, as "evidently founded on a basis of fact," it would seem that the novel succeeded in legitimating creole historiography, one that replaces metropolitan corruptions and inaccuracies with a "true" knowledge of and intimacy with creole "reality."[38] Such claims to narrative authority based on "eyewitness insiderism" recall the implicit authority claimed in pre-Emancipation works such as *Marly* and *Hamel*. It also, in the case of *Warner Arundell*, provides the narrative license for Joseph to fill in the gaps of one of the Caribbean's "lost" histories, the history of Julien Fédon.

As mentioned above, Fédon was a Grenadian planter of African-French descent, a member of a large, propertied class of people of color whose role in shaping the region's past has often been ignored.[39] As for

the rebellion led by Fédon, its history was most typically rendered as part of a wave of Jacobin-inspired revolts of 1795–96, the fever of rebellion having spread southeastward from Haiti. Particularly troubling to the British in economic and ideological terms were republican activities in the eastern Caribbean, where Victor Hugues—the "Colonial Robespierre"—had wrested the island of Guadaloupe from British control. From there—aided, as historians note, by the National Convention's proclamation of emancipation, a printing press, and a guillotine— Hugues successfully recruited from, among others, disaffected white and mixed-race Francophone planters in St. Vincent, Martinique, Trinidad, and Grenada, the islands' free black populations, and French slaves.[40] Despite their contemporary significance, however, the events taking place in Grenada over the fifteen months during which Fédon's forces controlled the island are cursorily treated in Joseph's *History of Trinidad*. As for Fédon himself, Joseph describes him only in a footnote: "I have heard from authority which I cannot doubt, that the infamous Fédon, the chief of the Grenada insurrection, escaped to this island [Trinidad], and was here at the time of its capture [from the Spanish in 1797]. The story of his having been drowned, coming from Grenada, was a mere fabrication."[41]

Here Joseph rejects mere anecdotal evidence of Fédon's drowning, repeated in contemporary accounts such as Bryan Edwards's *The History, Civil and Commercial, of the British West Indies*. Despite the general acceptance of this account, predicated on the discovery of "a canoe, with a compass belonging to [Fédon] nailed to the bottom of it … found overset at some distance from the island,"[42] Joseph uses the absence of "facts" about Fédon's fate to construct his own version of the rebel and his cause. In *Warner Arundell*, Julien Fédon is given life in what can be read as a relatively sympathetic treatment, which is surprising given colonial history's vilification of him for killing forty-eight British prisoners, including the lieutenant-governor of Grenada, Ninian Home. This act, which was denounced by Joseph (but not explicitly attributed to Fédon) in his *History* as "one of the most atrocious massacres known in modern history,"[43] does not, however, dissuade the novelist from resurrecting the infamous Fédon. Indeed, the rebellion itself gives birth, quite literally, to Joseph's hero and his "new," post-Emancipation planter class: Warner Arundell is born at the height of Fédon's rebellion in 1795, his life spared by the rebel leader, and, at the novel's end, restored to his patrimony through Fédon's interventions.

The drama of Fédon's first rescue of Warner is heightened by the impassioned speech made to Warner's father, who on an earlier occasion had defended Fédon from racial insults. In gratitude for Bearwell Arundell's act of tolerance, Fédon saves his infant son and returns the child to his father on the night he escapes the island. When accused by Bearwell of seeking revenge and letting himself be used by Victor Hugues and the National Convention, Fédon sets the record straight: "My object was more noble," he insists:

> I fought for liberty and equality—not as these words are, I find, understood by the hollow-hearted French … I aimed at emancipating the slaves, although I myself possessed a valuable gang. I wished to make the negro respected despite his inky skin, to induce the mulatto to consider himself a man, although his brown complexion told him he was the son of the tyrannical white man.[44]

Fictional representations of the "abominable prejudice of the West Indies" against people of color like Fédon are not new to early creole novels, as seen in the lengthy discussion of "mulatto" rights in *Marly*.[45] Nor, as the discussion of Hamel's powerful speeches above demonstrates, is Fédon's rightful condemnation of historical wrongs a new subject. But, we would argue, Fédon's "place" as a man of color—explained in the novel much more fully than in the actual "Declaration" he dispatched to the island's Council in the opening days of the rebellion—becomes central to the novel's re-writing/re-righting of History, suggested by the fictional Fédon's allusion to contested meanings of "liberty and equality" in his speech above.[46]

In other words, even as Joseph runs a risk similar to Cynric Williams in *Hamel*, allowing Fédon to speak of injustice and the immorality of slavery, the rest of his novelized history demonstrates the "wrongness" of Fédon's attempts to emancipate slaves through violent rebellion and the "rightness" of the Anglo-creole position of amelioration and gradual emancipation. Thus, when the adult Warner encounters Fédon, who has spent twenty-five years wandering the Caribbean, exiled from his beloved Grenada, he is unrecognizable as the fiery revolutionary. A "worn skeleton" with skin of "such a pallid hue … that it was not easy to decide from what race or races he was descended" (405, 312), the ardent spokesman for the rights of all people, "of whatever colour,"[47] is so reduced that, when Arundell realizes Fédon's identity, he decides not to turn him over to colonial authorities: "I had no wish to give this unhappy man up to justice. True, he had committed one act which is scarcely to be paralleled in the annals of the crimes of civil war; but ... he possessed one virtue: he was grateful, and to his gratitude I owed my life. His death on the gibbet at this time could have answered no good purpose; and the local government would not have thanked any one who should have forced them to punish a man for crimes committed a quarter of century ago."[48]

Arundell's magnanimity here is crucial, operating much like Oliver Fairfax's munificent offer to let Hamel—despite his role in orchestrating a rebellion intended to kill or expel all the white people of Jamaica—live his days on the island in peace. In both *Hamel* and *Warner Arundell*, the white creole's generosity reasserts plantocratic order over local events and, in effect, over the course of Caribbean history. In the case of *Warner Arundell*, the threat once posed by Fédon has been subdued and his mistaken ideas about liberty and equality corrected through his reinscription as the grateful (and tragic) "spectral Mulatto."[49] As such, Joseph's Fédon functions as a mediator between the old school plantocracy and the new: his gratitude to Arundell's father moving him to preserve the infant's life; his gratitude to the younger Arundell for forgiving his revolutionary crimes prompting him to secure the son's place in the emerging new order. This latter feat is performed when Fédon returns documents stolen during the rebellion that prove Warner's ownership of his father's mortgaged estates.[50] But even though Warner replaces his father as planter and proprietor, his "mastery" is defined in new ways, his creole identity no longer tied to the institution of slavery, but "liberated" from its immorality as he looks ahead to the post-Emancipation Caribbean.

* * *

In the preceding discussion of the early creole novel, *Hamel* and *Warner Arundell* in particular, we have argued for the need to consider these works as a crucial part of Caribbean literary history. We hope, too, that this chapter provokes other questions. To what extent do these works form part of the larger history of the novel in English, with its Caribbean origins, as in the narratives of Defoe, Behn, Edgeworth, and Austen that we mention in the opening of this chapter? To what extent do they form a separate and distinctive branch of that literary history? And to what extent do they belong in a discussion that would link them with other early novels of the colonies, such as Sydney Owenson's *The Missionary*,

Phebe Gibbs's *Hartley House, Calcutta*, or—even more influentially— Walter Scott's Highlands tales, starting with *Waverley*? And finally, in considering these works as distinctly Caribbean literature, to what extent did their constructions of emancipation-era colonial culture shape the rise of the "West Indian novel" of later periods?

Our essay's emphasis on *Hamel*'s and *Warner Arundell*'s revolutionary elements—their representations and (re)configurations of resistance, rebellion, and revolution—provide an opening through which to entertain such questions and to challenge what Alison Donnell has called our sense of the region's history and literature "on offer." The intertwined operations of history- and fiction-making, we believe, provoke a formal expression that we see articulated in early creole novels. As we stated at the outset, these works are problematic in their privileging of white plantocratic dominance. But despite—or rather, because of—that fact, through them we can access many points of revolutionary history that disrupt the textual production of authority during the period, as well as the way the novels are perceived today.

NOTES

1. See, for example, Edward Said's germinal essay, "Jane Austen and Empire," in *Culture and Imperialism* (New York: Vintage: 1993), 80–96, and a recent response by David Bartine and Eileen Maguire, "Contrapuntal Critical Readings of Jane Austen's 'Mansfield Park': Resolving Edward Said's Paradox," *Interdisciplinary Literary Studies* 11.1 (2009): 32–56; Alison Harvey, "West Indian Obeah and English 'Obee': Race, Femininity, and Questions of Colonial Consolidation in Maria Edgeworth's *Belinda*," in *New Essays on Maria Edgeworth* (Aldershot, England: Ashgate, 2006): 1–29; Brycchan Carey, *British Abolitionism and the Rhetoric of Sensibility: Writing, Sentiment, and Slavery, 1760–1807* (Basingstoke, England: Palgrave Macmillan, 2005), esp. 51–7; and Eve W. Stoddard, "A Serious Proposal for Slavery Reform: Sarah Scott's *Sir George Ellison*," *Eighteenth-Century Studies* 28.4 (1995): 379–96.

2. See Candace Ward, *Crossing the Line: Early Creole Novels and Anglophone Caribbean Culture in the Age of Emancipation* (Charlottesville: University of Virginia Press, 2017). Modern editions of most of the major early creole novels of the first half of the nineteenth century have appeared in recent years. New editions of *Marly*, *Creoleana*, and *Warner Arundell* fall into this category most directly; but we should also draw attention to new editions of novels that are Caribbean-focused, and show some knowledge of the region, even if we cannot be sure that their authors had first-hand

experience of the West Indies: William Earle's *Obi; or, The History of Three-Fingered Jack*, and the anonymous *Woman of Colour*. In a separate category, and still waiting for their modern academic moment of attention, are the massively popular *Tom Cringle's Log* (1834), by Michael Scott, and the nautical novels of Frederick Marryat, beginning with *The Naval Officer* (1829) and *Mr. Midshipman Easy* (1836). Scott, in particular, can lay some claim to being a Caribbean author, given that he spent much of his adult life as a merchant in Jamaica. See also Catherine Hall, "Reconfiguring Race: The Stories the Slave-Owners Told." *Legacies of British Slave-ownership: Colonial Slavery and the Formation of Victorian Britain,* edited by Catherine Hall, et al. (Cambridge: Cambridge University Press, 2014), 163–202.

3. *Emmanuel Appadocca* was reissued by the University of Massachusetts Press in 1997, edited by Selwyn Cudjoe.

4. Tim Watson, *Caribbean Culture and British Fiction in the Atlantic World, 1780–1870* (Cambridge: Cambridge University Press, 2008), 20.

5. On "creole realism," see Watson, *Caribbean Culture and British Fiction,* 17–65.

6. George Wilson Bridges, *A Voice from Jamaica; in Reply to William Wilberforce, Esq. M.P.* (London: Longman, Hurst, Rees, 1823), 8–9.

7. E. L. Joseph, *Warner Arundell: The Adventures of a Creole*, ed. Bridget Brereton, Rhonda Cobham, Mary Rimmer, and Lise Winer (Kingston: University of the West Indies Press, 2001), 31. Further references are to this edition, given parenthetically in the body of the essay.

8. Anonymous, *Montgomery*, 1.viii-ix, 1.ix.

9. See, for example, Evelyn O'Callaghan, *Women Writing the West Indies, 1804–1939: "A Hot Place, Belonging to Us"* (London: Routledge, 2004); Raphael P. Dalleo, *Caribbean Literature and the Public Sphere: From the Plantation to the Postcolonial* (Charlottesville: University of Virginia Press, 2011); Leah Rosenberg, *Nationalism and the Formation of Caribbean Literature* (New York: Palgrave, 2007); Carl Plasa, *Slaves to Sweetness: British and Caribbean Literatures of Sugar* (Liverpool: Liverpool University Press, 2009); Tim Watson, "Literature of the British Caribbean," *Oxford Bibliographies Online: Atlantic History*, ed. Trevor Burnard (Oxford University Press, Jan. 2013), http://www.oxfordbibliographies.com/view/document/obo-9780199730414/obo-9780199730414-0117.xml.

10. The most notorious of such reactions is Derek Walcott, "A Frowsty Fragrance," *New York Review of Books*, June 15, 2000, p. 61, a polemical response to Thomas W. Krise's anthology *Caribbeana: An Anthology of English Literature of the West Indies, 1657–1777* (Chicago: University of Chicago Press, 1999). Walcott claims the literature of the early Caribbean is of little value, "provincial," and "pompous."

11. Vincent Carretta, "Olaudah Equiano or Gustavus Vassa? New Light on an Eighteenth-Century Question of Identity," *Slavery and Abolition* 20.3 (December 1999), 96–105; Brycchan Carey, "Olaudah Equiano: African or American?", *1650–1850: Ideas, Aesthetics, and Inquiries in the Early Modern Era* 17 (2010), 229–46; John Bugg, "The Other Interesting Narrative: Olaudah Equiano's Public Book Tour," *PMLA* 121.5 (2006), 1424–42.

12. Candace Ward and Tim Watson, "Introduction," *Hamel, the Obeah Man,* by Cynric R. Williams, ed. Ward and Watson (Peterborough, ON: Broadview Press, 2010), 9.

13. Edward [Kamau] Brathwaite, "Creative Literature of the British West Indies during the Period of Slavery," *Savacou* 1 (1970), 46–73.

14. Brathwaite, "Creative Literature," 72.

15. Edward [Kamau] Brathwaite, *The Development of Creole Society in Jamaica, 1770–1820* (Oxford: Clarendon Press, 1971).

16. Cynric R. Williams, *Hamel, the Obeah Man,* ed. Candace Ward and Tim Watson (Peterborough, ON: Broadview, 2010), 427. Further references are to this edition and will be given parenthetically in the text.

17. Brathwaite, *Development of Creole Society,* 307.

18. Emilia Viotti da Costa, *Crowns of Glory, Tears of Blood: The Demerara Slave Rebellion of 1823* (New York: Oxford University Press, 1994); Watson, *Caribbean Culture and British Fiction,* 74–92.

19. Williams, *Hamel,* 357.

20. Brathwaite, "Creative Literature," 71.

21. J[ohn] Stewart, *A View of the Past and Present State of the Island of Jamaica* (Edinburgh: Oliver & Boyd, 1823). On Stewart's possible authorship of the novel, see Karina Williamson, "Introduction," *Marly; or, A Planter's Life in Jamaica* (Oxford: Macmillan Caribbean, 2005), xiv.

22. E[dward] L[anzer] Joseph, *History of Trinidad* (Port of Spain: Henry James Mills, 1838); Cynric R. Williams, *A Tour through the Island of Jamaica, from the Western to the Eastern End, in the Year 1823* (London: Hunt & Clarke, 1826).

23. Williams, *Tour,* 36–7, 88.

24. Williams, *Tour,* 88.

25. Williams, *Tour,* 302.

26. Qtd. in Peter Charles Hoffer, *Cry Liberty: The Great Stono River Slave Rebellion of 1739* (New York: Oxford University Press, 2010), 136.

27. Hoffer, *Cry Liberty,* 163.

28. Hoffer, *Cry Liberty,* 163–64.

29. On this alleged conspiracy, see Appendix C, "Insurrections," in our edition of *Hamel,* 459–60, 468–72; and Richard Hart, *Slaves Who Abolished Slavery: Blacks in Rebellion* (Mona, Jamaica: University of the West Indies Press, 2002).

30. Watson, *Caribbean Culture and British Fiction,* 70–74.

31. Sotherby, Wilkinson, and Hodge, Auctioneers, *The Hamilton Palace Libraries: Catalogue of the Fourth and Concluding Portion of the Beckford Library, Removed from Hamilton Palace* (London: Dryden Press, 1883), 37.

32. Brathwaite, "Creative Literature," 69, n. 1.

33. Seymour Drescher and Pieter C. Emmer (eds.), *Who Abolished Slavery? Slave Revolts and Abolitionism, a Debate with João Pedro Marques* (New York: Berghahn, 2010).

34. Watson, *Caribbean Culture and British Fiction*, 10.

35. Ward, "'In the Free': The Work of Emancipation in the Anglo-Caribbean Historical Novel," *Journal of American Studies* 49.2 (2015): 359–81.

36. According to its title page, *History of Trinidad* was available in Trinidad from the bookseller Henry James Mills, in London through A. K. Newman and Co., and in Glasgow from F. Orr and Sons. It is interesting to note the contemporaneity of the *History* and *Warner Arundell*, suggested by the date affixed to prefatory material: the brief preface of the *History* is dated Port of Spain, December 20, 1837, and the novel's dedication is dated Port of Spain, August 20, 1837, four months apart.

37. Rev. of *Warner Arundell* in the *Literary Gazette; and Journal of Belles Lettres, Arts, Sciences, &c. for the Year 1838*, 71. The *Monthly Review* conveyed a similar opinion: "[T]he whole [contents], we think, from their verisimilitude, hav[e] facts for a foundation." Vol. I (January–April, 1838): 460. The advertisements and reviews for other creole novels often remarked on their verisimilitude: see, for example, the *Morning Chronicle*'s advertisement for *Montgomery*, which claimed the novel "contains a just picture of the manners and customs of all classes in that Island, and of the present state of the Negroes in slavery" (July 1818); similarly the *Atlas* review of *Hamel* opined that, "whatever may be his [Cynric Williams's] faults, he is thoroughly familiar with the manners he has attempted to describe. It is not from books that he has learned his facts, but from a long and acute observance of the subjects of his story" (April 8, 1827), 218–19.

38. *The Literary Gazette; and Journal of Belles Lettres*, 71.

39. For recent discussions of mixed-race peoples in the English-speaking Caribbean, see Sara Salih, *Representing Mixed Race in Jamaica and England from the Abolition Era to the Present* (New York: Routledge, 2011) and Kit Candlin, *The Last Caribbean Frontier, 1795–1815* (Basingstoke, UK: Palgrave Macmillan, 2012), esp. 1–23.

40. For more on Hugues, see H. J. K. Jenkins, "The Colonial Robespierre: Victor Hugues on Guadaloupe, 1794–98, A Dictator and Liberator in the West Indies under the First French Republic," *History Today* 27.11 (1977): 734–40 and Laurent Dubois, "'The Price of Liberty': Victor Hugues and the Administration of Freedom in Guadeloupe, 1794–1798," *The William and Mary Quarterly* 56. 2 (1999), 363–92.

41. Joseph, *History of Trinidad*, 186n.
42. Bryan Edwards, *History, Civil and Commercial, of the British West Indies*, 5th edn., 5 vols. (London: G. and W. B. Whittaker et al., 1819), 4: 75.
43. Joseph, *History of Trinidad*, 186.
44. Joseph, *Warner Arundell*, 27.
45. Ibid., 130; *Marly*, ed. Williamson, 160–79. For a discussion of *Marly*'s depiction of people of color, see Salih, *Representing Mixed Race*, 43–70.
46. Compare, for example, Fédon's speech in *Warner Arundell* with the Declaration reprinted in Gordon Turnbull's *A Narrative of the Revolt and Insurrection of the French Inhabitants in the Island of Grenada* (Edinburgh, 1795): "Without entering into any detail of our rights, we summon you [i.e., the Council], and all the inhabitants, of every denomination, in this colony, to surrender, within the space of *two hours*, to the republican forces under our command" (35–36). Turnbull's account was published before the rebellion ended, in June 1796.
47. Joseph, *Warner Arundell*, 405, 312; Victor Hugues, "Declaration of the Commissioners delegated by the National Convention of France, to the Commanders in Chief of the British forces" (reprinted in Turnbull, *Narrative* 38–41). A copy of this declaration, which circulated throughout the contested islands of the eastern Caribbean, was delivered to the Grenada Council along with Fédon's declaration, both on March 4, 1794.
48. Joseph, *Warner Arundell*, 356–57.
49. Ibid., 314.
50. For a fuller discussion of Fédon's role in validating Warner's claims, see Ward, "'In the Free': The Work of Emancipation in the Anglo-Caribbean Historical Novel." *Journal of American Studies* 49.2 (2015): 359–81.

Bibliography

Bartine, David, and Eileen Maguire. "Contrapuntal Critical Readings of Jane Austen's 'Mansfield Park': Resolving Edward Said's Paradox." *Interdisciplinary Literary Studies* 11.1 (2009): 32–56.

Brathwaite, Edward [Kamau]. "Creative Literature of the British West Indies during the Period of Slavery." *Savacou* 1 (1970): 46–73.

Brathwaite, Edward [Kamau]. *The Development of Creole Society in Jamaica, 1770–1820*. Oxford: Clarendon Press, 1971.

Bridges, George Wilson. *A Voice from Jamaica; in Reply to William Wilberforce, Esq. M.P.* London: Longman, Hurst, Rees, 1823.

Bugg, John. "The Other Interesting Narrative: Olaudah Equiano's Public Book Tour." *PMLA* 121.5 (2006): 1424–42.

Candlin, Kit. *The Last Caribbean Frontier, 1795–1815*. Basingstoke, UK: Palgrave Macmillan, 2012.

Carey, Brycchan. *British Abolitionism and the Rhetoric of Sensibility: Writing, Sentiment, and Slavery, 1760–1807.* Basingstoke, England: Palgrave Macmillan, 2005.

Carey, Brycchan. "Olaudah Equiano: African or American?" *1650–1850: Ideas, Aesthetics, and Inquiries in the Early Modern Era* 17 (2010): 229–46.

Carretta, Vincent. "Olaudah Equiano or Gustavus Vassa? New Light on an Eighteenth-Century Question of Identity." *Slavery and Abolition* 20.3 (December 1999): 96–105.

da Costa, Emilia Viotti. *Crowns of Glory, Tears of Blood: The Demerara Slave Rebellion of 1823.* New York: Oxford University Press, 1994.

Dalleo, Raphael P. *Caribbean Literature and the Public Sphere: From the Plantation to the Postcolonial.* Charlottesville: University of Virginia Press, 2011.

Drescher, Seymour, and Pieter C. Emmer, eds. *Who Abolished Slavery? Slave Revolts and Abolitionism, a Debate with João Pedro Marques.* New York: Berghahn, 2010.

Dubois, Laurent. "'The Price of Liberty': Victor Hugues and the Administration of Freedom in Guadeloupe, 1794–1798." *The William and Mary Quarterly* 56.2 (1999): 363–392.

Edwards, Bryan. *History, Civil and Commercial, of the British West Indies,* 5th edn., 5 vols. London: G. and W. B. Whittaker et al., 1819.

Hall, Catherine. "Reconfiguring Race: The Stories the Slave-Owners Told." In *Legacies of British Slave-ownership: Colonial Slavery and the Formation of Victorian Britain.* Ed. Catherine Hall, et al. 163–202. Cambridge: Cambridge University Press, 2014.

Hart, Richard. *Slaves Who Abolished Slavery: Blacks in Rebellion,* Mona, Jamaica: University of the West Indies Press, 2002.

Harvey, Alison. "West Indian Obeah and English 'Obee': Race, Femininity, and Questions of Colonial Consolidation in Maria Edgeworth's Belinda." In *New Essays on Maria Edgeworth.* Ed. Julie Nash. 1–29. Aldershot, England: Ashgate, 2006.

Hoffer, Peter Charles. *Cry Liberty: The Great Stono River Slave Rebellion of 1739.* New York: Oxford University Press, 2010.

Jenkins, H. J. K. "The Colonial Robespierre: Victor Hugues on Guadaloupe, 1794–98, A Dictator and Liberator in the West Indies Under the First French Republic." *History Today* 27.11 (1977): 734–40.

Joseph, E[dward] L[anza]. *History of Trinidad.* Port of Spain: Henry James Mills, 1838.

Joseph, E[dward] L[anza]. *Warner Arundell: The Adventures of a Creole.* Ed. Bridget Brereton, Rhonda Cobham, Mary Rimmer, and Lise Winer. Kingston: University of the West Indies Press, 2001.

Krise, Thomas W., ed. *Caribbeana: An Anthology of English Literature of the West Indies, 1657–1777.* Chicago: University of Chicago Press, 1999.

Marly; or, A Planter's Life in Jamaica. 1828. Ed. Karina Williamson. Oxford: Macmillan Caribbean, 2005.

Montgomery; or the West-Indian Adventurer. 3 vols. Kingston, Jamaica, 1812/13.

O'Callaghan, Evelyn. *Women Writing the West Indies, 1804–1939: "A Hot Place, Belonging to Us".* London: Routledge, 2004.

Philip, Michel Maxwell. *Emmanuel Appadocca, or, Blighted Life: A Tale of the Boucaneers.* 1854. Ed. Selwyn Cudjoe. Amherst: University of Massachusetts Press, 1997.

Plasa, Carl. *Slaves to Sweetness: British and Caribbean Literatures of Sugar.* Liverpool: Liverpool University Press, 2009.

Rosenberg, Leah. *Nationalism and the Formation of Caribbean Literature.* New York: Palgrave, 2007.

Said, Edward. "Jane Austen and Empire." In *Culture and Imperialism.* 80–96. New York: Vintage, 1993.

Salih, Sara. *Representing Mixed Race in Jamaica and England from the Abolition Era to the Present.* New York: Routledge, 2011.

Sotherby, Wilkinson, and Hodge, Auctioneers. *The Hamilton Palace Libraries: Catalogue of the Fourth and Concluding Portion of the Beckford Library, Removed from Hamilton Palace.* London: Dryden Press, 1883.

Stewart, J[ohn]. *A View of the Past and Present State of the Island of Jamaica.* Edinburgh: Oliver & Boyd, 1823.

Stoddard, Eve W. "A Serious Proposal for Slavery Reform: Sarah Scott's *Sir George Ellison.*" *Eighteenth-Century Studies* 28.4 (1995): 379–96.

[Turnbull, Gordon]. *A Narrative of the Revolt and Insurrection of the French Inhabitants in the Island of Grenada.* Edinburgh, 1795.

Walcott, Derek. "A Frowsty Fragrance." *New York Review of Books.* June 15, 2000.

Ward, Candace. "'In the Free': The Work of Emancipation in the Anglo-Caribbean Historical Novel." *Journal of American Studies* 49.2 (2015): 359–81.

Ward, Candace. *Crossing the Line: Early Creole Novels and Anglophone Caribbean Culture in the Age of Emancipation.* Charlottesville: University of Virginia Press, 2017.

Ward, Candace, and Tim Watson. "Introduction." In *Hamel, the Obeah Man.* By Cynric R. Williams. Ed. Candace Ward and Tim Watson. 9–46. Peterborough, ON: Broadview Press, 2010.

Watson, Tim. *Caribbean Culture and British Fiction in the Atlantic World, 1780–1870.* Cambridge: Cambridge University Press, 2008.

Watson, Tim. "Literature of the British Caribbean," In *Oxford Bibliographies Online: Atlantic History.* Ed. Trevor Burnard. Oxford: Oxford University Press, Jan. 2013.

Williams, Cynric R. *A Tour Through the Island of Jamaica, from the Western to the Eastern End, in the Year 1823.* London: Hunt & Clarke, 1826.

Williams, Cynric R. *Hamel, the Obeah Man.* 1827. Ed. Candace Ward and Tim Watson. Peterborough, ON: Broadview, 2010.

Williamson, Karina. "Introduction." In *Marly; or, A Planter's Life in Jamaica.* Ed. Karina Williamson. xi–xviii. Oxford: Macmillan Caribbean, 2005.

CHAPTER 9

Colonial Vices and Metropolitan Corrections: Satire and Slavery in the Early Caribbean

Brycchan Carey

Although there has been a proliferation of critical interest in the literature of the early Caribbean—encompassing poems, plays, novels, diaries, voyage narratives, slave narratives, natural histories, political treatises, philosophies, sermons, assembly reports, account books, and newspapers—relatively few scholars have been interested in the treatment of the early Caribbean in satirical literature. This is not because no such literature exists. There is in fact a rich seam of writing that satirizes the people, locations, and institutions of the early Caribbean, ranging from occasional asides to book-length satires. This literature has much to teach us about both colonial life and metropolitan attitudes to the Caribbean, but may have been avoided by colonial and postcolonial literary scholars anxious to move beyond traditional literary histories of the long eighteenth century with their focus on metropolitan elites, court intrigues, and the London book trade. It may also be that much greater attention has been paid to Caribbean literature of the later eighteenth century—the so-called "age of sensibility"—when satirical writing was a less prominent feature of literary discourse. Whatever the reasons, close attention to seventeenth- and eighteenth-century satirical literature reveals that the Caribbean was more significant

B. Carey (✉)
Department of Humanities, Northumbria University, Newcastle upon Tyne, UK

© The Author(s) 2018
N. N. Aljoe et al. (eds.), *Literary Histories of the Early Anglophone Caribbean*, New Caribbean Studies,
https://doi.org/10.1007/978-3-319-71592-6_9

171

to contemporary observers than has sometimes been supposed. This chapter accordingly attempts to bring early Caribbean satire back into critical view. Bearing in mind John Dryden's well-known observation that "the true end of Satire is the amendment of vices by correction," I argue that eighteenth-century satirists who represented the Caribbean increasingly saw the region as a location of vice that stood in need of correction, and that as the eighteenth century progressed, the chief iniquities they calumniated were slavery and the slave trade.[1] Thus, satirists became as much a part of the literary proto-abolitionist movement as did the sentimental poets and novelists whose work has been more intensively studied.

The topics of early Caribbean satire are of course as many and various as the activities of colonists, investors, slave traders, and enslaved people. Nevertheless, some recurring themes and forms can be found. This chapter suggests that early Caribbean satirical literature can provisionally be organized into four categories: "Occasional Asides," "Satirical Voyage Narratives," "London Caribbean Tales," and "Abolitionist Satire." These categories are both tentative and overlapping, while some, such as the occasional aside, can clearly be applied to contexts beyond the Caribbean. Nevertheless, together they offer us a useful tool to begin investigating the range of satirical literature being produced in relation to the early Caribbean world. Indeed, once one begins to populate these categories, one realizes that the range is broader than one might at first suppose. A full survey of early Caribbean satirical literature would fill a monograph at least, and there is not enough space in a short chapter to aim at inclusivity. Instead, this chapter offers two or three examples in each category to establish their chief characteristics, while remaining clear that there are many other examples which might be explored in a more substantial study.

Occasional Asides

Most references to the Caribbean in satirical literature of the seventeenth and eighteenth centuries are occasional asides: brief mentions, short discussions, and passing comparisons. These references should not be dismissed. Collectively, they add up to a considerable body of writing and provide evidence that the Caribbean was increasingly important to the literary imagination of the period, as well as being perceived as the location for many forms of vice that stood in need of amendment. The number of occasional asides is so large that they cannot be fully enumerated here, but examples range from very minor comments to passages of a dozen lines or more. In satirical drama, for example, we encounter many throwaway lines or settings that allude to the Caribbean, or to the New World, in a more or less focused way. For instance, Aphra Behn's *Emperor of the Moon* (1687) contains a scene which includes "eight or ten Negroes upon Pedestals" who shortly after "Dance and mingle in the Chorus" as a visual display of Britain's increasing participation in the transatlantic slave trade.[2] More substantial Caribbean references can be found in Dryden's extensive output. *The Enchanted Island* (1670), for example, is a reworking of Shakespeare's *Tempest*, which is often seen as an early Caribbean text, but there are plenty of Caribbean asides in Dryden's output, not least in the prologue to *Cleomenes* (1692), where the actor hopes that 'none but Men of Wit and Sence' are in the audience. As to the others:

> Let 'em go People Ireland, where there's need
> Of such new Planters to repair the Breed;
> Or to Virginia or Jamaica Steer.
> But have a care of some French Privateer;
> For if they should become the Prize of Battle,
> They'll take 'em Black and White for Irish Cattle.[3]

The passage may have raised a quick laugh in the 1690s, but it reveals clearly enough the low opinion in which both Irish and American colonists were held by the theater-going public in the late seventeenth century. Throughout this period, Caribbean planters were routinely derided by metropolitan authors for their boorish manners, their ignorance, their acquisitiveness, their drunkenness, and, very occasionally, for the shocking manner in which they treated their slaves.[4] On stage, the occasional aside works quickly and effectively because it invokes a satirical stereotype with which the audience were already familiar and which they very probably felt approached the truth.

Occasional asides are regularly found in satirical verse as well, including in poems by some of the best-known poets of the period. We recall Corinna, Jonathan Swift's "beautiful young nymph," who in her dreams "to Jamaica seems transported, / Alone, and by no planter courted."[5] Things are desperate indeed for Corinna if transportation to Jamaica cannot restore her fortune since, as a route to getting money at any cost, the West Indies were routinely satirized. Alexander Pope, for example, remarked that:

> To the world no bugbear is so great
> As want of figure and a small Estate.
> To either India see the merchant fly,

Scared at the spectre of pale Poverty!
See him with pains of body, pangs of soul,
Burn thro' the Tropics, freeze beneath the Pole![6]

As the eighteenth century progresses, one detects an increasing critique of colonial slavery in these brief poetic asides. Depictions of slavery in verse of the period have been carefully anthologized by Marcus Wood and, especially, James Basker, who provides many hundreds of short extracts concerning slavery taken from longer poems.[7] Not all of these are satirical and not all explicitly mention the Caribbean. In *The Reformation of Manners: A Satyr* (1702), for example, Daniel Defoe's treatment of those who "seek out to *Africk*'s Torrid Zone / And search the burning shores of *Serralone*" is noteworthy, argues Basker, because of Defoe's early "criticism of the hypocrisy of Christians owning slaves, a theme that would recur ubiquitously in the antislavery literature of the next 160 years."[8] Defoe's poetic journey passes north of the Caribbean, however, as he is more concerned with Mexico, but other poets more clearly signal a passing satirical concern with Caribbean slavery. Basker argues that the "poor Indian" in Epistle I of Pope's *Essay on Man* (1733) is Caribbean since he seeks "Some happier island in the watry waste, / Where slaves once more their native land behold."[9] At the other end of the era of British colonial slavery, Percy Shelley's comparison of the politicians Sidmouth and Castlereagh to a "shark and dog-fish" who wait "Under an Atlantic isle, / For the negro-ship" is undoubtedly a passing West Indian reference in a celebrated satirical poem.

Prose satires and, later, satirical novels, frequently offer passing references to the Caribbean. These can in some cases be quite lengthy, at least in comparison with poetic asides, but remain "occasional" in the sense that they are not integral to the plot of the novel or main thrust of the satire. For example, before he finds Lilliput and Brobdingnag, Lemuel Gulliver "was Surgeon successively in two Ships, and made several Voyages, for six Years, to the *East* and *West-Indies*; by which I got some Addition to my Fortune." Acquiring money was a plausible enough activity for a voyager to the Caribbean, but Gulliver's claims that his "Hours of Leisure I spent in reading the best Authors, ancient and modern; being always provided with a good Number of Books" must have strained the credulity of readers familiar with West-Indian lifestyles.[10] A more conventional depiction of the Caribbean is offered in the final book, as Gulliver sets out on the voyage that would take him to the land of the Houyhnhnms, only to find many of his crew struck down by a tropical fever:

> I had several Men died in my Ship of Calentures, so that I was forced to get Recruits out of *Barbadoes*, and the *Leeward Islands*, where I touched by the Direction of the Merchants who employed me; which I had soon too much Cause to repent; for I found afterwards that most of them had been Buccaneers. I had fifty Hands on Board; and my Orders were, that I should trade with the *Indians* in the *South-Sea*, and make what Discoveries I could. These Rogues whom I had picked up, debauched my other Men, and they all formed a Conspiracy to seize the Ship, and secure me; which they did one Morning, rushing into my Cabbin, and binding me Hand and Foot, threatening to throw me overboard, if I offered to stir.[11]

The depiction of the Caribbean as a lawless zone where great riches might be made by outsiders remained current throughout the eighteenth century, even as the islands became less piratical and the profits more concentrated in the pockets of elites. Indeed, by the early nineteenth century, the convention could itself be reversed by a clever satirist. Jane Austen's Sir Thomas Bertram in *Mansfield Park* accords with the convention in that his fortune appears to be derived from his plantations in Antigua, but differs from it in that he is the locus of law and order, allowing moral lapses to take place in his extended absence from the metropolis; he is, arguably, a caricature of an absentee landlord.[12] When one reads closely, satirical representations of the Caribbean can be found woven into the fabric of literature throughout the long eighteenth century.

SATIRICAL VOYAGE NARRATIVES

Voyage narratives have an ancient pedigree, and satirical voyage narratives have been around for almost as long. In his spoof *True History*, the Graeco-Roman satirist Lucian of Samosata described an expedition to cross the Atlantic. This got as far as the islands of the Hesperides—probably the Canary Islands or Cape Verde—before ascending heavenwards to the moon and returning to Earth via the zodiac and Cloud Cuckoo Land. Lucian's satires were translated into English early in the seventeenth century and influenced generations of satirists including Jonathan Swift, but clearly the Caribbean was not an intentional reference, even if early-modern readers could, and did, compare new worlds in America and the moon.[13] The discovery of the American continent undoubtedly gave rise to a sharp increase in exploratory and colonial voyaging, as well as a corresponding growth in the numbers of narratives describing those voyages. Many early voyage narratives adopted the form of the natural history: a genre of writing which outlined a location's topography, geology, meteorology, population, flora, fauna, agriculture, and manufactures. Caribbean natural histories appeared at regular intervals throughout this period, sometimes written from personal experience but often put together from notes and other accounts. The growth of this literature was a tremendous opportunity for satirists, and there was accordingly an increase in the number and complexity of satirical voyage narratives, among which Swift's *Gulliver's Travels* is merely the most celebrated. In fact, the satirical voyage narrative is a substantial subgenre of satire, represented by many examples and not necessarily involving the Caribbean. In such parodies, mariners visit every country and ocean known to humankind, and some that could not be found on any map, to expose the conventions and assumptions of colonists, explorers, and sea captains, as well as to correct their vices.

When travel writers combined natural history with personal accounts of shipboard and plantation life, the results could be popular and influential. A celebrated early Caribbean example is Richard Ligon's *True and Exact History of the Island of Barbados* (1657), in which the character of the narrator is as prominent a feature as the nature of the island and in which a personal account of the voyage out forms a substantial opening sequence. The form of Ligon's *History*, though not its breadth, is almost exactly reproduced by Edward ("Ned") Ward in his satirical *A Trip to Jamaica* (1698), which begins with an account of the voyage out before ending with a spoof natural history. Howard Troyer has argued that Ward "borrowed the formal details of his account" from Richard Blome's *Description of the Island of Jamaica* (1672), but those formal details amount to less than a quarter of the book, in the final few pages, where Ward offers his parodic natural history. By contrast, Ligon's structure of voyage narrative followed by natural history is precisely adopted by Ward.[14] In any case, personal experience appears to have played as much a part in the composition of the text as did reading and research, although Ward's satire is also no doubt sending up *en masse* the many protestations of genuine, sober, hard luck and poverty made by those who went to seek their fortune in the colonies, many of whom were in fact the authors of their own misfortune.

Ward's *Trip to Jamaica* begins, as does Ligon's *History*, with a confession of poverty. Whereas Ligon had lost everything in "a Barbarous Riot" that destroyed his careful investments, Ward admits that he had "stragled [...] far from the Paths of *Profit* and *Preferment*, into a Wilderness of *Pleasure* and *Enjoyment*." While Ligon soberly resolves to make a journey to try his luck in the Caribbean, Ward "took up a Resolution to Travel, and Court the Blinking Gipsy *Fortune* in another Country" only "after two or three Gallons of *Derby-Ale* had one day sent my *Wits* a *Woollgathering*."[15] Ward then poses for a moment as that stock figure of satire, the innocent abroad, or soon to be so, who believes the "extravagant Encomiums" he has heard about "that Blessed Paradise *Jamaica*, where *Gold* is more plentiful than *Ice*, *Silver* than *Snow*, *Pearl* than *Hailstones*." The joke is crude, and he himself admits he chose Jamaica because "a *Warm Latitude* would best agree with *Thin Apparel*," but there can be no doubt that, in reality, many made the journey after believing other equally extravagant encomiums.

Ward sets out for Jamaica "in the good Ship the *Andalucia*," which is not an auspicious name for a vessel bound for a British colony seized from the Spanish. On the journey, he is accompanied by passengers as luckless as he, including a "*Cherubimical Lass*, who, I fear, had *Lost her Self*, two more, of the same *Gender*, who had lost their *Husbands*; two *Parsons* who had lost their *Livings*, three *Broken Tradesmen*, who had lost their *Credit*; and several, like me, that had lost their *Wits*."[16] The irony, of course, is that his wits are all that Ward retains, and are what he hopes, with this pamphlet, will make his fortune. Before that, however, he encounters the standard voyagers' alarms of a storm and foreign warship, before taking time to gaze at the wonders of nature in a passage that must surely be a direct parody of Ligon's *History*. Ligon had described at length the birds that followed the ship and the fish that were caught, such as "the *Bonito*, the *Spanish Mackerel*, the *Albacore*, *Dolphin*, &c." Later, while stargazing, Ligon described the great variety of clouds and how the tropical sun "caused such glorious colours to rest upon those clouds as 'tis not possible to be believed by him that hath not seen it."[17] Ward is surely responding to Ligon when he lists the "Curiosities in Nature" such as "*Crampos*, *Sharks*, *Porpus*, *Flying-Fish*, *Albacores*, *Bonettas*, *Dolphin*, *Bottlenoses*, *Turtle*, *Blubber*, *Stingrays*, *Sea-Adders*, and the Devil and all of *Monsters* without Names." He goes on to name almost a dozen bird species before concluding that "that which I thought most worthy of Observation, were the *Clouds*, whose various Forms, and beauteous Colours, were Inimitable by the Pencil of the Greatest Artist in in the Univers."[18] Ward's satirical voyage narrative, like many such satires, seems not merely to be a generic satire but rather a parody of this specific text.

In the final three pages, Ward at last offers a spoof of the kind of natural history offered by Blome and others. Under the heading of "A character of Jamaica," he lays into the physical island itself, excoriating it as "the Dunghill of the Universe, the Refuse of the whole Creation, the Clippings of the Elements, a shapeless pile of Rubbish confus'dly jumbl'd into an Emblem of the Chaos, neglected by the Omnipotence when he form'd the world into its admirable Order."[19] In this apparently indiscriminate broadside, Ward is responding to a broader trend in Caribbean natural history in which what we might term the "dung crisis"—a shortage of nutrient for sugar plantations—was a perennial obsession. Richard Blome had certainly commented on it in his *Description of the Island of Jamaica*, already by 1671 seeing Jamaica as a place to which economic refugees from Antigua, St Kitts, and Barbados might flee because of "Their *Plantations* being worn out, and their *Woods* wasted."[20] As Caribbean soils became increasingly depleted it became a more urgent issue for colonists, their supporters, and their detractors. Sir Hans Sloane, visiting Barbados in the 1680s, noted that the island "has had so great a fruitfulness, though it be fallen off from what it was, through the great labouring and perpetual working of it out, so that they are now forc'd to dung extremely what before was of it self too Rank."[21] Another late seventeenth-century visitor, Thomas Tryon, lamented that the habit of planting "the same Vegetations in the same Ground, must have worn it out extreamly in respect to Virtue and Strength," such that "the whole Island is become a kind of a rock." This led to planters manuring excessively, argues Tryon, so much so "that most Land that is often Till'd and Dung'd produce a great multitude of new and unknown Vegetables, called Weeds."[22] These examples could be joined by many others. Manure anxiety manifests itself in dozens of eighteenth-century Caribbean texts leading to some unintentionally comic moments, such as James Grainger's poetic exhortation to planters to "Never, ah never, be asham'd to tread / Thy dung-heaps" and William Belgrove's reminder that, as a planter, you cannot succeed "unless you are regular in your dung."[23]

We can certainly read Ward's depiction of Jamaica as "the Dunghill of the Universe" in the context of the Caribbean dung crisis, but a more complex story can be drawn from his description of the island as "the Refuse of the whole Creation, the Clippings of the Elements, a shapeless pile of Rubbish confus'dly jumbl'd into an Emblem of the Chaos, neglected by the Omnipotence when he form'd the world into its admirable Order." Ward's depiction of Jamaica may have been influenced by an English translation of a French satire, Cyrano de Bergerac's *L'Autre Monde: ou les États et Empires de la Lune*, in which an erstwhile lunar voyager, finding himself propelled only as far as Canada, has an extended discussion on astronomy and cosmology with the governor in which they agree that the planets "are nothing but the froth or foam of the *Suns* purgations" and that "the vast continent of *America*" had not been found before Columbus because it was dung that had not yet, so to speak, been deposited.[24] While Cyrano de Bergerac's characterization of Canada is little different from Ward's description of Jamaica as "the Refuse of the whole Creation," however, Ward's description is neither merely cosmological nor narrowly agricultural. There are also people here. Ward's assessment of the people of the island as criminal chancers is similarly damning but also conventional: "The generallty of the Men look as if they had just nock'd off their Fetters," he claims, and "are very Civil to Strangers who bring over considerable Effects; and will try a great many ways to Kill him farely, for the lucre of his Cargo."[25] This is a familiar characterization of any frontier society and no doubt exaggerated, but on the whole Ward's *Trip to Jamaica* is neither crude nor unfocused. It is instead a sophisticated intervention in late seventeenth-century colonial discourse, emerging from a detailed and nuanced understanding of both specific texts and broader contemporary debates about the society and geography of the Caribbean islands.

Ward has little enough to say about slavery, other than a few passing references to Jamaica's "negroes," but eighteenth-century imaginary voyagers felt more strongly about the issue. One important example is the pseudonymous Captain Samuel Brunt in *A Voyage to Cacklogallinia* (1727). This Swiftian satire offers an extended critique of the South Sea Company—which, among other activities, dealt in enslaved people—through an imagined voyage to the Caribbean island of Cacklogallinia.[26] This nation bears a remarkable likeness to Britain under the then Prime Minister Robert Walpole, with the key difference that it is inhabited by giant, talking chickens who plan to repay their national debt by launching a mission to mine for gold on the moon. Before that, however, the book contains an extraordinary account of an attack by British soldiers on a Jamaican Maroon community, seen from the perspective of the "run away Negroes" who have saved and taken in the slave trader Captain Brunt after a shipwreck, because of a kindness he once extended to one of the captive Africans on his ship. The author presents the Maroons as a legitimate and peaceable community who are simply asserting the same rights to liberty as their British captors. By contrast, the British soldiers respond with "a cruel Slaughter, for none they could light on were spared, but Women and Children, who were all taken"[27] *A Voyage to Cacklogallinia* offers one of the first extended critiques of Caribbean slavery available to British readers, presented unsparingly and with little disguise in a satire that otherwise seeks to encode its attack on the British government in an imaginary voyage to a fantastical land.

By the middle of the eighteenth century, novels were overtaking satires in popularity and the verisimilitude that the form required was forcing talking chickens and related species into extinction. The satirical novel may not always have had a more nuanced tone, but it required at least a nod to realism. Tobias Smollett's *Roderick Random* (1748), for example, often described as picaresque rather than realist, has a full complement of strangely-named characters, implausible circumstances, and hyperbolic language. At its core, however, is a depiction of the disastrous 1741 Battle of Cartagena that repeatedly crosses back and forth over the line between unsparing realism and exaggerated satire. The voyage is not entirely imaginary either since Smollett had taken part in the battle after having lived for some time in Jamaica, which appears as a backdrop to some scenes in the novel. Unlike many satirists of the early Caribbean, however, Smollett has no criticism of slavery or the slave trade—indeed, the eponymous hero of the novel restores his fortune at the end of the book by trading in slaves.[28]

By the late eighteenth century, Atlantic voyaging had become too routine to be often satirized, but there are exceptions. One example is *The Adventures of Jonathan Corncob*, written anonymously in newly postcolonial Massachusetts in 1787. The book is mostly set in Massachusetts, Rhode Island, and New York during the revolutionary war, and is an important early-American satire. Toward the end of the book, the protagonist Jonathan Corncob voyages to Barbados, arguably during the great hurricane of 1780—certainly a major hurricane is described in the book.[29] Corncob's first impressions of Barbados are favorable; he is only sorry to hear that the island is so subject to "hurricanoes."[30] As he reads deeper into Barbadian society, however, his initial optimism is overturned. He witnesses the drunken brawlings of the plantocracy, the sexual hypocrisy of the slaveholders, and, above all, the wanton cruelty directed toward the enslaved people on the island. He begins to wish for a good hurricane to punish this iniquity, and is rewarded. The book concludes with a deadpan statistical reckoning of casualties set out in a table which foregrounds the indifference toward human suffering that the Barbados plantocracy's economic imperative implies:

Men, women, and children, buried beneath the ruins of buildings – –	527
Drowned – – –	134
Total	661
Loss of black cattle.	
Oxen lost by different casualties – – – –	745
Which, with 4273 head of negroes, – –	4273
Makes the amount	5018

This table may seem exaggerated in its depiction of the cold and brutal reckoning of human lives, but it was not unrealistic. The book's Bostonian author may have read similar accounts concerning both the American mainland and the islands. He may, for example, have read *A treatise upon husbandry or planting*, written by the Barbados planter William Belgrove but published in Boston in 1755. This practical plantation management manual is liberally furnished with similar tables of quantitative data. For example, Belgrove presents a table offering "A Reasonable Valuation of the Plantation":[31]

500 *Acres of Land with all the aforesaid Buildings, Utensils, &c.* at 35 *l. per Acre.*	£. 17 500
300 *Slaves at* 40 *l. per Head.*	12 000
150 *head of Cattle at* 10 *l. per ditto.*	1500
25 *Horses at* 20 *l. per ditto.*	500
50 *Head of Sheep at* 10 *s. per ditto.*	25
The Amount thereof is	£. 31 525

It is quite plausible to read *Jonathan Corncob* as a parody, at least in part, of Belgrove's *Treatise*, although the Barbadian passages are likely also to have been influenced by accounts of the hurricane of 1780. In either case, the cold reckoning of human beings as economic units was coming under scrutiny by the time the book appeared. *Jonathan Corncob*, though largely set in the 1770s, was published in 1787 and may well have been influenced by the transatlantic antislavery movement that was most visibly active in North America through the actions of Quakers in Pennsylvania and New Jersey, but which was taking hold in a more widespread and less obviously sectarian form in Great Britain. While the abolition movement was gaining in momentum at the end of the eighteenth century, however, the satirical Atlantic voyage narrative was waning in popularity. America and the Caribbean were too familiar to be the locations for fantastic lands, while at the same time being well-enough governed that satires increasingly tended to focus on exposing and correcting the vices of people that were knowable, and known.

London Caribbean Tales

While satirical voyagers explored the real or imaginary islands of the Caribbean, another group of satirists lampooned Caribbean colonists from the comfort of their metropolitan houses. In some cases, these were stories told about colonists at a distance; in others, the behavior of the colonists as they returned to England was a source of commentary, scandal, or amusement. The archetype of the former is Richard Steele's interpretation of Richard Ligon's story of the enslaved woman Yarico, which Steele embellished and expanded as the story of Inkle and Yarico in the *Spectator* in 1711. The story is well known, and has been widely discussed by scholars.[32] Steele visits Arietta, a popular aristocratic woman who is visited by all with "any pretence to Wit and Gallantry." One of the men present recounts the story of the Ephesian Matron: an old tale of female inconstancy originally told by the Roman satirist Petronius. This so angers Arietta that she ripostes with a story of male faithlessness, gleaned from reading Ligon. In a nutshell, the English trader Thomas Inkle is saved from death at the hands of "a party of *Indians*" by Yarico, a young Indian woman who falls in love with him. The treacherous Inkle, on his return to "*English* Territories ... sold *Yarico* to a *Barbadian* Merchant; notwithstanding that the poor Girl, to incline him to commiserate her Condition, told him that she was with Child by him."[33] The tale may not offer the grotesque parody of Ward's *Trip to Jamaica* or the fantastic topographies of *Gulliver's Travels* or *A Voyage to Cacklogallinia*, but it is satire nonetheless. It exposes vice in an extreme and exaggerated form, holds it up to view, and demands its correction. Steele explicitly mentions hypocrisy and inconstancy in love as the behaviors being satirized, but greed, treachery, and heartlessness are also implied. One certainly had no need to travel to the Caribbean to encounter these, but the colonial setting adds a frisson of danger and excitement to a story being told in the heart of fashionable London. Freeing young men from the obligations and constraints of civility, the story implies, causes them to revert to their underlying savage and uncivilized state. While the tale plainly articulates anxieties about lawlessness on the colonial frontier, the danger is not merely colonial. If all men are like Thomas Inkle, the veneer of civilization is thin. In a nation that had recently experienced a century of civil war and revolution, this was a troubling thought.

Although until 1708, Steele owned about 300 hectares and 200 slaves in Barbados, he had not personally visited.[34] Others had more direct personal experience, and some visitors to the Caribbean satirized West Indian life on their return to the metropolis. One such was John Wolcot (1738–1819). Originally from Cornwall, Wolcot spent time in Jamaica in the 1760s and 1770s before returning to England and eventually settling in London, where he became a popular satirical poet under the pseudonym Peter Pindar. Most of Wolcot's poems, which are now rarely read, lampoon public figures in the London of his day, but he addressed Caribbean slavery in five of his compositions.[35] His stance is somewhat shifting. In some poems Wolcot seems closely aligned with the interests of the planters, such as in "A Poetical, Serious, and Possibly Impertinant, Epistle to the Pope" (1793), in which he compares the Pope to Quako: a Jamaican Obeahman who had been foiled in his attempt to stage an uprising. Quako reappears in a later poem, "Tempora Mutantur. An Ode" (1802), in which, in the view of James Basker, "the cruelty of a black slave to his mule is used to expose the deeper brutality of white 'Christians' holding slaves."[36] The poem's title, which can be translated as "times change," does not reveal whether Wolcot considers the change to be a positive one, and the poem itself offers few more clues:

> How like the Negro on his Mule,
> Tormenting him beyond all rule,
> Beating him o'er the head and ears;
> His spurs into the creature sticking,
> Abusing, damning, cursing, kicking!
> For Blacky like a *Christian* swears.

His *quondam* Master, passing by,
Beheld the Beast with pitying eye:
"You scoundrel, hold; is *murder* your design?"—
Quako turn'd round, with a broad grin,
Not valuing the rebuke one pin:
"Massa, *me* was *your* Nega; *dissy mine*."

Whether this really does "expose the deeper brutality of white 'Christians' holding slaves," as Basker asserts, is difficult to tell. Although the poem relies on the familiar satirical trope of reversal, it is not clear that Wolcot thinks the change is progress, nor that he wants to expose "Christian" cruelty. He is quite possibly arguing the reverse; that emancipation does not end cruelty and that abuse and violence permeate the chain of being, regardless of race—or species—since presumably the mule would kick too, if it found the opportunity to do so. Whichever way we read it, however, this is poetry written about the Caribbean from a distance: a poem created by a Londoner for Londoners and telling us more about metropolitan conceptions of colonial life than about the realities of Jamaican plantations.

Some London tales poked fun at gauche Caribbean colonists returning to the metropolis. This kind of satire appears frequently in newspapers and journals, and as vignettes in some novels, but the archetype is Richard Cumberland's 1771 satirico-sentimental comedy *The West Indian*, about Belcour, a naïve colonial let loose in London with a considerable fortune, and no idea how to spend it with propriety. The humor is largely derived from Belcour's rough manners and clumsy interactions with others. When he arrives in London, "accustomed to a land of slaves, and, out of patience with the whole tribe of custom-house extortioners, boat-men, tide-waiters, and water-bailiffs, that beset me on all sides, worse than a swarm of musquetoes, I proceeded a little too roughly to brush them away with my rattan." Bringing Caribbean violence to the metropolis in this way inevitably leads to "a furious scuffle"; a scene that satirically reminds the audience that colonial manners are not merely inappropriate in London, but potentially dangerous.[37] Nevertheless, the satire can work both ways. Belcour's naïveté also exposes the absurdities of London, with "such a crowd, and such a hurry, and such a number of shops" that Belcour understands "no more than if I was in the blue mountains." Despite acting inappropriately in many situations, the audience is invited to sympathize with this stranger in a strange land, and by the end of the play Belcour's generous spirit and good nature prevail. The play's satire of West Indian manners is relatively light, and colonial idiosyncrasies are largely forgiven. In many ways, indeed, we can read the play more as a satire of London life than of Caribbean character—something that many London Caribbean tales have in common.

ABOLITIONIST SATIRE

A critique of slavery permeates satirical representations of the Caribbean in the long eighteenth century, but while satirists seem largely (although not exclusively) sympathetic to abolitionism, the reverse is less obviously true. A great deal of writing was produced to explicitly support the abolition of the British slave trade, particularly between 1785 and 1795, with another wave of material appearing in the 1820s and 1830s to promote the end of slavery in the British Caribbean. One can extract satirical, or at least sardonic, asides in much of this literature but it is otherwise difficult to characterize abolitionist writing as satirical. In the later eighteenth century, the predominant mode is sentimental, and considerable critical attention has accordingly been paid in recent years to charting the relationship between political abolitionism and literary sensibility.[38] Sentimental literature rarely manages to be satirical, perhaps because its intense concern with personal suffering means that it has to take itself seriously to avoid descending into self-parody, but there are some exceptions, such as Cumberland's *West Indian*.

Some sentimental satires are explicitly opposed to slavery. The clergyman and novelist Laurence Sterne and the butler, composer, and belle-lettrist Ignatius Sancho are among the few authors to produce antislavery writing that was both satirical and sentimental. When Sancho wrote to Sterne in 1766, "beseeching you to give one half hour's attention to slavery, as it is at this day practised in our West Indies," his inspiration was one of Sterne's sermons rather than any satirical passage in *Tristram Shandy* and his mode was sentimental.[39] Sterne's response, "a tender tale of the sorrows of a friendless poor negro-girl," which appeared in the final installment of *Tristram Shandy*, is similarly sentimental without any hint of the whimsical satire that occurs throughout the book.[40] Sterne's treatment of slavery in *A Sentimental Journey* is, however, arguably more satirical. Hearing a caged starling calling "I can't get out," Sterne meditates on slavery and imprisonment. He then buys the bird for a bottle of Burgundy and brings it back to England where he soon sells it on, first to Lord A, and then: "In a week Lord A gave him to Lord B—Lord B made a present of him to Lord C—and Lord C's gentleman sold him to Lord D's for a shilling—Lord D gave him to Lord E—and so on—half round the alphabet—From that rank he pass'd into the lower house, and pass'd the hands of as many commoners."[41] As the bird remains chattel and is widely traded, we can read this as a richly ironic commentary on how deeply the British establishment are implicated in slave trading, even if it hardly qualifies as explicit abolitionism. Nevertheless, the slavery passages in Sterne's work would remain popular with abolitionists for many years to come.

Other antislavery writers of the sentimental period toyed with satire. The poet, novelist, pamphleteer, and social experimenter Thomas Day was clearly both an active opponent of slavery and the slave trade and a writer who understood satire well. His abolitionist poem *The Dying Negro* (1773) veers between sentiment and polemic, but his children's novel *Sandford and Merton* (1783–89), a work which above all is concerned with the amendment of vices, is shot through with the kind of facetious satire that adult writers always assume will appeal to children. The book begins with a portrait of Tommy Merton: the son of a wealthy Jamaica planter who is "naturally a very good-natured boy, but unfortunately had been spoiled by too much indulgence." Merton is immediately established as an exaggerated parody of a planter's child who "had several black servants to wait upon him, who were forbidden upon any account to contradict him. If he walked, there always went two negroes with him, one of whom carried a large umbrella to keep the sun from him, and the other was to carry him in his arms, whenever he was tired."[42] The boy finds little sympathy in England, and is eventually reformed following a series of adventures involving the sturdy and virtuous farmer's son, Harry Sandford. The book extols rural virtues, but is in other respects somewhat like a London Caribbean tale. It remained popular even into the twentieth century, perpetuating the parodic stereotype of a plantation-owner's child to generations of British schoolchildren, but eventually went out of favor, not least for its sententious and sentimental style which elicited little enthusiasm in the age of modernism.

One of the best-known poets of the age of sensibility, and one of the most committed abolitionist writers, was William Cowper. While Cowper is not primarily remembered today for his satirical poetry, he was in fact a master of light social satire; his most famous work, *The Task* (1782), whatever it eventually mutated into, began as a mock-heroic history of the sofa. In 1789, Cowper was asked by the Committee for the Abolition of the African Slave Trade for "some good ballads to be sung about the streets."[43]

These duly appeared and were published as "The Negro's Complaint" and "The Morning Dream." Unpublished at the time, and only coming to light in the 1830s, was a satirical ballad called "Sweet Meat has Sour Sauce: or, the Slave Trader in the Dumps."[44] In eleven stanzas, of which five are reproduced here, the poem ironically dramatizes the anger of a slave trader who has just heard his trade is to be abolished:

> A trader I am to the African shore,
> But since that my trading is like to be o'er,
> I'll sing you a song that you ne'er heard before,
> Which nobody can deny, deny,
> Which nobody can deny.

> When I first heard the news it gave me a shock,
> Much like what they call an electrical knock,
> And now I am going to sell off my stock,
> Which nobody, &c.

> Tis a curious assortment of dainty regales,
> To tickle the Negroes with when the ship sails,
> Fine chains for the neck, and a cat with nine tails,
> Which nobody, &c.

> Here's padlocks and bolts, and screws for the thumbs,
> That squeeze them so lovingly till the blood comes,
> They sweeten the temper like comfits or plums,
> Which nobody, &c.

> So this is my song, as I told you before;
> Come, buy off my stock, for I must no more
> Carry Caesars and Pompeys to Sugar-cane shore,
> Which nobody can deny, deny,
> Which nobody can deny.

This piece of abolitionist satire may perhaps be described as another London Caribbean tale. Firmly located in the metropolis, it articulates anxieties about and opposition to colonial Caribbean practice and is clearly part of a satirical tradition that aims to foreground the iniquities of Caribbean slavery, to expose the venality and corruption of the characters and personalities of West Indian colonists and the slave traders who serviced them, and to argue, ultimately, for reform of the British Caribbean. Plainly, however, it was not effective. It was dropped by Cowper and the abolition committee at the time, no doubt because the satire was richer than its audience could bear.[45] While satire might in earlier years have been an effective tool in bringing Caribbean slavery into the public eye, in closer proximity to the suffering it described it became dangerous and unstable. Sentimental representations of suffering enslaved Africans tended to contain the horror, to minimize the suffering to genteel proportions, and to repackage the cruelty and barbarity of slavery as a fashionable ailment to be cured. Satirical representations did the opposite, magnifying horrors that were already enormities, in both senses of the word. When satire becomes too painful, readers withdraw. By the end of the eighteenth century, tastes had in any case moved away from the more robust satirical tradition of the earlier century. Both the horrific nature of the subject and the literary fashions of the day combined to ensure that abolitionist satire was a marginal literature.

This chapter has merely glanced across the surface of early Caribbean satire, but has offered a tentative typology of satirical forms for the region ranging from occasional asides, through more substantial voyage narratives and metropolitan tales, to the largely abortive satire of abolitionism. While the majority of satirical representations of the West Indies were in fact composed in Europe, satires reveal that the region was a subject of lively debate, emerging stereotypes, metropolitan snobbishness, and finally a deep-seated anxiety about the cruelty of slavery. A comprehensive critical survey of early Caribbean satire has yet to be written, but would without doubt be an important contribution to our understanding of the both the literary and the political culture of British colonialism in the Atlantic world.

NOTES

1. John Dryden, "Preface to Absolom and Architophel" (1681) in *The Works of John Dryden*, 20 vols, vol. II, ed H. T. Swedenberg, Jr. (Berkeley: University of California Press, 1972), p. 5.
2. Aphra Behn, *Emperor of the Moon: A Farce.* (London, 1687), p. 60.
3. John Dryden, *Cleomenes* (1692) in *The Works of John Dryden*, 20 vols, vol. XVI, ed Vinton A. Dearing (Berkeley: University of California Press, 1996), p. 84.
4. For recent discussions of slavery and drama, see Franca Dellarossa, *Slavery on Stage: Representations of Slavery in British Theatre, 1760s–1830s* (Bari: Edizione dal Sud, 2009) and Brycchan Carey, "To Force a Tear: Antislavery on the Eighteenth- Century London Stage," in *Affect and Abolition in the Anglo-Atlantic: 1770–1830,* ed Stephen Ahern (Farnham: Ashgate, 2013), pp. 109–128.

5. Jonathan Swift, "A Beautiful Young Nymph Going to Bed" (1731) in *Swift: Poetical Works*, ed Herbert Davis (London: Oxford University Press, 1967), pp. 517–19.

6. Alexander Pope, *The First Epistle of the First Book of Horace Imitated* (1737) in John Butt, et al., eds. *The Twickenham Edition of the Poems of Alexander Pope*, 11 vols (New Haven, Yale University Press, 1939–1969), vol. 4, pp. 276–94, ll. 67–72.

7. James G. Basker, ed, *Amazing Grace: an Anthology of Poems About Slavery, 1660–1810* (New Haven and London: Yale University Press, 2002); Marcus Wood, *The Poetry of Slavery: An Anglo-American Anthology, 1764–1865* (Oxford: Oxford University Press, 2004).

8. Basker, *Amazing Grace*, p. 38.

9. Basker, *Amazing Grace*, p. 50.

10. Jonathan Swift, *Travels into Several Remote Nations of the World ... by Lemuel Gulliver* (1726) ed. David Womersley (Cambridge: Cambridge University Press, 2012), p. 31.

11. Swift, *Gulliver's Travels*, pp. 331–32.

12. Austen's attitude to slavery has given rise to an extended critical debate. The most substantial contribution is Gabrielle D. V. White, *Jane Austen in the Context of Abolition: "A Fling at the Slave Trade"* (Basingstoke: Palgrave Macmillan, 2006).

13. Francis Hickes, *Certaine Select Dialogues of Lucian: Together With His True Historie, Translated from the Greeke into English* (Oxford, 1634). For discussion, see Brycchan Carey, "'A New Discovery of a New World': The Moon and America in Seventeenth- and Eighteenth-Century European Literature," in *Literature in the Age of Celestial Discovery: From Copernicus to Herschel*, ed Judy A. Hayden (Basingstoke: Palgrave Macmillan, 2016), pp. 167–82, pp. 169–70.

14. Howard William Troyer, *Ned Ward of Grubstreet; a Study of Sub-Literary London in the Eighteenth Century* (Cambridge, MA: Harvard University Press, 1946), p. 19.

15. Richard Ligon, *A True and Exact History of the Island of Barbados* (1657; 2nd edn 1673) ed Karen Ordahl Kupperman (Indianapolis: Hackett Publishing, 2011), p. 40; Edward Ward, *A Trip to Jamaica: With a True Character of the People and Island*, 3rd edn (London, 1698), pp. 6, 7.

16. Ward, *Trip to Jamaica*, p. 10.

17. Ligon, *History*, pp. 46, 50.

18. Ward, *Trip to Jamaica*, p. 13.

19. Ward, *Trip to Jamaica*, p. 14.

20. Richard Blome, *A Description of the Island of Jamaica; with the other Isles and Territories in America, to which the English are related* (London, 1672), p. 59.

21. Hans Sloane, *A Voyage to the Islands Madera, Barbados, Nieves, S. Christophers and Jamaica, with the Natural History of the Herbs and Trees, Four-Footed Beasts, Fishes, Birds, Insects, Reptiles, &c. of the Last of Those Islands*, Vol. I (London, 1707), pp. 33–34.

22. Thomas Tryon, *The Merchant, Citizen and Country-man's Instructor: or, a Necessary Companion for All People* (London, 1701). p. 190.

23. James Grainger, *The Sugar Cane*, edited with notes and an introduction by John Gilmore in *The Poetics of Empire: A Study of James Grainger's The Sugar Cane (1764)*, (London: The Athlone Press, 2000), pp. 87–198, I, 223–24; William Belgrove, *A Treatise upon Husbandry or Planting. By William Belgrove. A Regular Bred, and Long Experienc'd Planter, of the Island of Barbados. And May Be of Great Use to the Planters of All the West-India Islands* (Boston, 1755), p. 4.

24. ΣΕΛΗΝΑΡΧΙΑ. *Or, The Government Of the World In the Moon: A Comical History Written by that Famous Wit and Cavaleer of* France, *Monsieur* Cyrano Bergerac: *And Done into* English *by* Tho. S^{t}Serf, *Gent.* (London, 1659), pp. 20–21. For an extended reading of this satire, see Carey, "'A new discovery of a new world'," pp. 175–76.

25. Ward, *Trip to Jamaica*, p. 16.

26. For a more detailed reading of this satire, see Carey, "'A new discovery of a new world,'" pp. 177–80.

27. *A Voyage to Cacklogallinia: With a Description of the Religion, Policy, Customs and Manners, of that Country. By Captain Samuel Brunt* (London, 1727), p. 15.

28. Tobias Smollett, *The Adventures of Roderick Random* (1748) ed James G. Basker, Paul-Gabriel Boucé, and Nicole A. Seary (Athens, GA: University of Georgia Press, 2012).

29. For discussion of the book's relationship with genuine events and locations in Barbados, see Francesca Brady and Jerome S. Handler, "Jonathan Corncob Visits Barbados: Excerpts from a Late 18th Century Novel," *Journal of the Barbados Museum and Historical Society*, LII (2006): 17–34.

30. *Adventures of Jonathan Corncob, Loyal American Refugee. Written by Himself* (London: G. G. J. and G. Robinson, 1787). The Barbados passages are at pp. 115–47, and conclude with the table of casualties in the hurricane.

31. Belgrove, *A Treatise upon Husbandry*, p. 42.

32. See in particular Frank Felsenstein, *English Trader, Indian Maid: Representing Gender, Race, and Slavery in the New World. An Inkle and Yarico Reader* (Baltimore: Johns Hopkins University Press, 1999) and Brycchan Carey, "'Accounts of Savage Nations': The Spectator and the Americas," in *Uncommon Reflections: Emerging Discourses in "The Spectator,"* ed. Don Newman (Newark, DE: University of Delaware Press, 2005), pp. 129–49.

33. Richard Steele, *Spectator* 11 (13 March 1711) in *The Spectator*, ed Donald F. Bond, 5 vols. (Oxford: Clarendon Press, 1965), I, pp. 49–51.

34. Rae Blanchard, "Richard Steele's West Indian Plantation," *Modern Philology*, 39 (1942): 281–285.

35. All five poems are reproduced in Basker, *Amazing Grace*, pp. 324–28.

36. Basker, *Amazing Grace*, p. 328.

37. Richard Cumberland, *The West Indian: A Comedy. As It Is Performed in the Theatre Royal in Drury-Lane* (London, 1771), pp. 7–8.

38. Accounts of the relationship between sentiment and abolition begin with Wylie Sypher, *Guinea's Captive Kings: British Anti-Slavery Literature of the Eighteenth Century* (Chapel Hill: University of North Carolina Press, 1942). For more recent contributions, see especially Stephen Ahern, ed., *Affect and Abolition in the Anglo-Atlantic: 1770–1830* (Farnham: Ashgate, 2013); George Boulukos, *The Grateful Slave: The Emergence of Race in Eighteenth-Century British and American Culture* (Cambridge: Cambridge University Press, 2008); Brycchan Carey, *British Abolitionism and the Rhetoric of Sensibility: Writing, Sentiment, and Slavery, 1760-1807* (Basingstoke: Palgrave Macmillan, 2005); Lynn Festa, *Sentimental Figures of Empire in Eighteenth-Century Britain and France* (Baltimore: Johns Hopkins University Press, 2006).

39. Ignatius Sancho, *Letters of the Late Ignatius Sancho, an African* (1782) ed. Vincent Carretta (Peterborough, ON: Broadview Editions, 2015), p. 128.

40. Laurence Sterne, *The Life and Opinions of Tristram Shandy, Gentleman* (1759–67) ed Melvyn New and Joan New, 3 vols (Gainesville: University Press of Florida, 1978), II, pp. 747–49.

41. Laurence Sterne, A *Sentimental Journey through France and Italy* (1768) ed Melvyn New and W. G. Day (Gainesville, FL: University Press of Florida, 2002), pp. 99–100.

42. Thomas Day, *The History of Sandford and Merton, A Work Intended for the Use of Children*, (1783–89), 8th edn, 3 vols (London: John Stockdale, 1798), I, p. 12. For a more extended discussion, see Carey, *British Abolitionism*, pp. 68–72.

43. James King and Charles Ryskamp, eds, *The Letters and Prose Writings of William Cowper*, 5 vols (Oxford: The Clarendon Press, 1979–1986), III, p. 130.

44. *The Poems of William Cowper*, ed John D. Baird and Charles Ryskamp, 3 vols (Oxford: The Clarendon Press, 1980–1995), III, pp. 15–16.

45. This point is explored in depth in Carey, *British Abolitionism*, pp. 102–106 and Joanne Tong, "'Pity for Poor Africans': William Cowper and the Limits of Abolitionist Affect," in Ahern, ed., *Affect and Abolition*, pp. 129–50.

CHAPTER 10

Finding the Modern in Early Caribbean Literature

Cassander L. Smith

In contemplating the contours of an early Caribbean literary history, this essay ponders two issues. The first involves the political and cultural stakes inherent in a project to map out such a history. Why does it matter, for whom does it matter and what is the critical and historical relationship between early Caribbean literature and modern-day Caribbean literature? The second issue involves complexities of authorship and authority. How do the meanings of authorship and authority transform when we consider texts that register multiple voices and experiences that do not simply appear in the texts but help to shape those very texts? To contemplate both of these issues, I examine two narratives that relate the legend of "Inkle and Yarico," a tragic tale about an Amerindian woman sold into slavery on the island of Barbados by her English lover after she saves his life.

Richard Ligon is the first to write about Yarico's story in his 1657 travel narrative *A True and Exact History of the Island of Barbadoes*. The Guyanese writer Beryl Gilroy retells the story in a novel in 1996. An intertextual reading of Ligon and Gilroy's narratives achieves two ends. First, this approach complicates conventional notions of authorship as a solo

C. L. Smith (✉)
University of Alabama, Tuscaloosa, AL, USA

© The Author(s) 2018
N. N. Aljoe et al. (eds.), *Literary Histories of the Early Anglophone Caribbean*, New Caribbean Studies,
https://doi.org/10.1007/978-3-319-71592-6_10

enterprise. As I will explicate shortly, both Ligon and Gilroy adapted a story that had already been told in an oral form, which means they function more as mediators and collaborators, cobbling together prose that is the compilation of multiple voices and experiences. Second, the texts together emphasize the intimate relationship between literature produced in the early Caribbean and in the Caribbean today, both shaped by diverse cultural interactions that defined the region then and now. Scholars seldom discuss the thematic and cultural threads that run through colonial and postcolonial Caribbean literature. Often we understand that earlier literary production as antithetical to the anti-colonial, nationalistic aims of postcolonial Caribbean literature, which emphasizes themes of resistance and oppression, displacement and exile. Not incidentally, those very themes energize Yarico's story, in its earliest iterations and in its most recent.

In this essay, then, I want to challenge certain critical assumptions about the nature of early Caribbean literature that understand the literature as mostly a record of European dominance and colonization. I argue that studying the legend of "Inkle and Yarico" as it appears in Ligon and Gilroy's texts allows us to look beyond the colonizing intent and effect of early Caribbean literature to understand it also as the product of systems of multicultural interaction that informed— indeed shaped—the literature. As such, this literature does, in fact, speak to the postcolonial recovery efforts of contemporary Caribbean studies. In other words, studying early Caribbean literary history helps us see how and why Native American (and black African) presences mattered in terms of how the cultural landscapes of the Caribbean took shape well before the region became postcolonial spaces in the nineteenth and twentieth centuries. In this way, early Caribbean literature is not antithetical but complementary to the work of contemporary Caribbean literary studies.

Yarico's story occupies a brief paragraph in Richard Ligon's narrative, which largely recounts his experiences during his three-year stay on the island of Barbados, where he was involved in the management of a sugar plantation beginning in 1647. In the narrative, he assesses the island's economic viability and its culture, noting in minute detail the people, food, flora and fauna, geography, and religious traditions that shape the island. In this way, Yarico functions as part of the cultural landscape. The following often-extrapolated passage from Ligon's narrative initiates the legend of "Inkle of Yarico":

This Indian dwelling near the Sea-coast, upon the [South America] Main, an English ship put in to a Bay, and sent some of her men a shoar, to try what victualls or water they could finde, for in some distresse they were: But the Indians perceiving them to go up so far into the Country, as they were sure they could not make a safe retreat, intercepted them in their return, and fell upon them, chasing them into a Wood, and being dispersed there, some were taken, and some kill'd: but a young man amongst them stragling from the rest, was met by [an] Indian Maid, who upon the first sight fell in love with him, and hid him close from her Countrymen in a Cave, and there fed him, till they could safely go down to the shoar, where the ship lay at anchor ... [the ship] seeing them upon the shoar, sent the long-Boat for them, took them aboard, and brought them away. But the youth, when he came ashoar in the *Barbadoes,* forgot the kindnesse of the poor maid, that had ventured her life for his safety, and sold her for a slave, who was as free born as he: And so poor *Yarico* for her love, lost her liberty.[1]

This paragraph comes at the end of a longer discussion about the island's sparse native population. We get Yarico's story here not because it is unique but because it is representative, one story of one Native American woman's plight that helps explain how Native Americans are brought as slaves to Barbados "from the neighboring Islands, some from the Main" (106).

Yarico's story is representative in another regard; she, along with enslaved black African women Ligon also describes in the narrative, illustrates the vitality of the island's labor supply. Largely through his representations of black African women, Ligon naturalizes the link between somatic features and labor. His descriptions center mostly on black women's breasts. He notes that as young women, they "have ordinarily very large breasts, which stand strutting out so hard and firm, as no leaping, jumping, or stirring, will cause them to shake any more, then the brawnes of their armes" (103). As they age and become mothers, he writes, "their breasts hang down below their navells, so that when they stoop at their common work of weeding, they hang almost down to the ground, that at a distance, you would think they had six legs" (103).

Here Ligon evokes rhetorical strategies from travel writing predecessors of representing black African women in monstrous terms.[2] The monstrosity self-perpetuates in the form of their offspring who "when they are first born, have the palmes of their hands and the soles of their feet, of a whitish colour, and the sight of their eyes of a blewish colour, not unlike the eyes of a young Kitling" (103). Jennifer L. Morgan has already noted the racial and gendered import of these moments, arguing that Ligon uses black women's bodies to signify and, through procreation, perpetuate ideologies of racial differences that rendered black Africans as subhuman and therefore fit for slavery.[3] I highlight the moments here as context to explain his descriptions of another (brown, not black) female body, that of Yarico.

If black African women are the vehicle through which Ligon conveys racial ideology, as Morgan has argued, then Yarico complicates that rhetorical strategy. Before he provides Yarico's personal history, Ligon first introduces readers to her as a house servant enslaved in the house where he lives, and her physical features are central to his description. She is a woman of "excellent shape and color" with "small breasts, with the nipples of a porphyry color" (106). Sometime during Ligon's stay, Yarico "chanced to be with child" by another servant. He relates her labor and delivery: "[she] walked down to a Wood, in which was a Pond of water, and there by the side of the Pond, brought her self abed; and presently washing her Child in some of the water of the Pond, lapped it up in such rags, as she had begged of the Christians; and in three hours' time came home, with her Child in her arms, lusty Boy, frolic and lively" (106–107). The birth is unproblematic; a simple, short, procedure that Yarico carries out alone in the woods. Although she is not represented as a six-legged creature hunched in the sugar fields, her labor evokes monstrosity in that it occurs in the wilderness, and it appears mechanical, reflecting the process of other, lower animal forms. Like her enslaved black women counterparts, Yarico is rendered both a producer and reproducer of labor in Barbados, expanding beyond a black and white binary the racial ideologies that inform Ligon's narrative and conversations about a growing Atlantic slave trade.

Ligon, though, is more than a detached observer assessing the island's human resources. His discussion of Yarico, unlike his representations of enslaved black women, turns sympathetic when he explains to readers the means by which Yarico became enslaved. A measure of compassion informs Ligon's discussion of Yarico's enslavement, which suggests his own emotional investment, or at least his interest, in Yarico and her unnamed English lover, who functions as a colonial agent ultimately responsible for her plight. Colonialism circumvents the karma that should have meant a happily-ever-after for "poor *Yarico*" who, Ligon notes, "for her love, lost her liberty." His sympathetic rendering of Yarico's enslavement contrasts the imperialism his narrative perpetuates.

The short passage describing Yarico in Ligon's text sparked the English literary imagination, inspiring what David Brion Davis calls an "early outburst of middle-class sentimentality."[4] In 1711, Richard Steele printed a more elaborate version of the story in the *Spectator*. He named the Englishman, Thomas Inkle, and created for him a fuller character profile. More so than Ligon, Steele emphasizes the young lovers' interactions, describing a period of several months in which the two live a kind of New World Edenic existence that suggests harmony between European interloper and American native. In a significant departure from Ligon, Steele compounds Inkle's treachery. Once she discovers Inkle's plan to sell her as a slave, according to Steele's version, Yarico tells him she is pregnant. The news does not ignite a paternal feeling in Inkle; instead "he only made use of that information, to rise in his demands upon the purchaser."[5] Because Steele emphasizes more their time together, he renders even more cruelly Inkle's heartless act. If Ligon's version is, as Myra Jehlen argues, a dispassionate "tale of slavery" that treats Yarico's fate as "another of life's vicissitudes," then Steele's version is much more prejudicial and emotionally invested.[6] Steele's narrator ends the story with this admission: "I was so touch'd with this story ... that I left the room with tears in my eyes."[7]

By way of Steele's more elaborate account, Ligon's narrative of Yarico manifested in more than forty subsequent adaptations, mostly in the eighteenth century and in a variety of languages and genres, including poems, plays, operas, and epistles that ventriloquized Yarico's emotional turmoil.[8] In one anonymous poem titled "Yarico to Inkle: An Epistle," printed in London in 1736, a broken-hearted Yarico laments,

> O tell me, why am I so wretched made?
>> For what unwilling crime am I betray'd?
>> Is it because I lov'd?—Unjust reward!
>> That love Preserv'd you from the ills you fear'd;
>> If twas a fault, alas! I'm guilty still,
>> For still I love, and while I live I will.[9]

Here, Yarico does not lament her enslavement so much as her lover's betrayal. English writers who retell Yarico's story de-emphasize her actual enslavement; instead, they emphasize her noble character that suggests she is unfit for slavery, which implies that there are populations fit for the institution. In this regard, "Inkle and Yarico" functions similarly to Aphra Behn's 1688 novel *Oroonoko*, in which the title character finds himself enslaved in Surinam due to the treachery of unscrupulous slave traders. His enslavement is tragic for Behn's narrator but not because of the inhumanity of the transatlantic slave trade; in fact, Oroonoko performs none of the work typical of an enslaved person in the Caribbean. Instead, his condition is so egregious because of his royal status, which manifests in his European, aristocratic features, education, and deportment.

English fascination with Yarico's story can be explained, in part, by the story's adaptability to English debates about the slave trade.[10] In the mid-eighteenth century, some adaptations began representing Yarico as African or as mixed race Indian-African. By the end of the century, her race became indeterminate. According to Frank Felsenstein, "The growing uncertainty as to Yarico's racial ancestry that develops so conspicuously in poetic renditions of the tale may reflect a wider public distaste at British involvement in the cruel and immoral transatlantic trade of Africans to the Americas."[11] This would explain why the tale's popularity waned at the turn of the nineteenth century; England abolished its slave trade in 1807. The story lost much of its political impetus though it remained part of Anglo-Caribbean culture, manifesting for example in folk songs and the landscape. There is a place, for example, in St. John's Parish in Barbados called "Yarico's Pond."

In the wake of independence movements throughout the Caribbean in the nineteenth and twentieth centuries, Yarico's story assumed new political significance, as represented in Beryl Gilroy's 1996 novel. Gilroy was a twentieth-century writer and teacher. Born in Guyana (then British Guiana) in the 1920s, she migrated to the United Kingdom mid-century to attend college. In the latter half of the century, she taught in London and wrote a number of novels that celebrated her Caribbean roots and addressed the region's colonial legacies. She was the mother of noted cultural critic and literary scholar Paul Gilroy.

Inkle and Yarico, one of the last novels Gilroy wrote before she died in 2001, follows the basic details of Ligon's story with Steele's elaborations. However, Gilroy complicates the encounter. She extends it over seven years, and Inkle is not a wholly dominant figure or a villain. Inkle tells the story as a first-person narrator. Gilroy renders him sympathetically, as a castaway struggling to survive in a new landscape. In the first half of the novel, Inkle repeatedly mourns his fate, suffering an identity crisis; survival necessitates his assimilation into Yarico's Carib tribe. When he joins Yarico's people as a captive, they strip him of his weapons and European clothes and cover him in a purple paste to ward off insects. The paste also remakes him in the image of his captors. He concedes that his knowledge and "civilized" ways on the island are useless. He says, "To understand my surroundings, I knew I would have to give up my civilisation."[12] He marries Yarico in accordance with the customs of the Carib. He learns to hunt like Yarico's fathers, and in order to become a full member of the tribe, he undergoes initiation rituals like the adolescent boys crossing into manhood. He also adopts her tribe's mores, including the practice of polygamy. In the novel, Inkle and Yarico produce two sons, both of whom die in infancy. Inkle accidentally poisons the first son shortly after the couple marries. Yarico gives birth to a second son several years later aboard the English ship that rescues Inkle. Once the ship arrives in Barbados and Yarico discovers her and her child's fate, she throws the baby overboard; it drowns.

Yarico, too, receives an extensive makeover in the novel. Gilroy complicates Yarico's ethnic and racial identities by remaking her as part Carib and part West African. In a plot twist similar to *Oroonoko* or William Earle's *Obi; or, The History of Three-Finger Jack*, Yarico's ancestors find themselves in Barbados through the duplicitous actions of slave traders in West Africa and French pirates in the Atlantic. Her West African ancestors join with the island's Carib population to create a nation of black Caribs into which Yarico is born. Also, gone is the noble savage rhetoric that previously rendered Yarico a passive, pathetic victim of Inkle's colonial ploys. Gilroy invests her with a great deal of power, self-determination, and character flaws. Early in the novel, Yarico's Carib kin discover her and Inkle's hideaway. They capture Inkle and force him into a cage. They take him before the chief and force him to kneel while a shaman performs a ritual to determine whether Inkle is a threat. The shaman then rushes toward Inkle to kill him. At that point, "Yarico broke out of line and, snatching the flower from her hair and that from two or three of the other women, she rushed towards [Inkle] and held the posy over [his] head crying, 'Lover! Lover!' in her tongue" (22). Yarico saves Inkle, reminiscent of the even more ubiquitous story about Pocahontas, the American "princess" who saved the life of English colonist John Smith of colonial Jamestown.[13] Unlike Pocahontas, whose mythology casts her as a gentle, free spirit who cares more about peace and love than politics and wealth, Yarico does not save Inkle to keep the peace or because she is enamored. She claims Inkle as a possession, something she has found "as a child finds a treasure, a shell, a distinctive plant, a crab with an unusual claw upon the sand" (19). Yarico emerges as the dominant figure through the majority of the novel, treating

Inkle as her captive lover. Of course, that power dynamic shifts when an English ship arrives on their shore, after seven years, taking a pregnant Yarico and Inkle aboard. The baby she delivers aboard ship looks more European than Carib. Inkle notes, "Everyone marvelled at the child, blond-haired, blue-eyed and very pale in colouring" (82). Yarico's decision to kill her son is an ultimate act of resistance, a reminder to readers of her freewill. According to Inkle, Yarico saw the baby as her possession and "no one would own her pet monkey" (95).

In Gilroy's creative hands, Inkle and Yarico exhibit a range of human emotions: love, compassion, jealousy, rage, greed, fear, anxiety. Yarico is no more noble than Inkle is ignoble. The two characters are complexly human, both motivated by social, cultural, and political factors that combine with their own inherent psychologies to shape their interactions with each other. In many respects, Gilroy's novel contributes to the distortion of Yarico as a historical figure. That is to say, although Gilroy presents a portrayal that is much more nuanced and reminds us of Yarico's humanity, the novel does not, indeed it cannot, reclaim Yarico's voice. Gilroy's adaptation is crucial, though, because it unsettles certain assumptions we could easily take for granted about the nature of European-Native-African contact in the early Caribbean. The novel is not so much a critique of colonialism as it is a meditation on the themes of power and humanity. We are reminded that power was not the sole and inevitable province of Inkle, as a European colonial agent. Rather, in the novel power arises organically out of circumstances and opportunities that favor Yarico at certain times, Inkle at other times. Gilroy prioritizes black and Indian subjectivities in a way not accounted for in the earliest renditions of Yarico's story. As such, she opens up a space—even if it is speculative—that invites us to consider the complex power dynamics at play in early colonial encounters—and in the narratives written about those encounters—such as Ligon's 1657 narrative.

Ligon's text has been a popular object of study among historians and literary scholars who do work on the early Caribbean. We treat his *True and Exact History* as a reference book offering minute details about the landscape and culture of Barbados. We also examine its imperial function as a scouting report for would-be English investors. If we only encounter Ligon's narrative as writing empire, Yarico's story diminishes; it becomes an anomalous albeit interesting and sad digression. If we factor her prominently into Ligon's overall rhetorical design, her representation becomes a critique of English imperial and commercial mores. Either way, she remains an object of Ligon's rhetorical manipulation, an object of English empire and nothing more. If we, however, approach Yarico's representation as the product of complex cultural encounters—an approach supported by Gilroy's novel—not only does it complicate Yarico's representation but it also complicates Ligon's entire narrative.

Most of Yarico's story unfolds off the page, so to speak, occurring outside of and before Ligon arrives in Barbados. This means that he is relating not what he observed but details as told to him. Even the information about her labor and delivery beside the river is hearsay. Yarico's story had an oral life—through Yarico, a fellow slave, her master maybe—that traveled from the coast of South America to Barbados. Ligon does not tell Yarico's story; he re-tells it and in a written form. When we position Yarico's representation within an oral tradition, it becomes a less anomalous feature of Ligon's narrative because hers is not the only life story he relates. In fact, Ligon records a number of personal histories in his text. Examples of these personal histories include that of Sambo, an enslaved man who plays a key role in uncovering a slave revolt plot on the island, then refuses his master's offer of a reward because he sees it as his duty (105–106). According to Ligon, Sambo is a man naturally curious about science and religion, and his greatest ambition is spiritual conversion. Despite Ligon's interventions on Sambo's behalf, his master denies his request to be baptized. The denial allows the slave master to avoid questions about the legality or ethics of enslaving Christians. English law at the time already prohibited the enslavement of Christians but what of cases in which the convert is already enslaved (101)? The slave master avoids this quandary and in the process, according to Ligon, denies a man's salvation. Interestingly, Ligon articulates Sambo's struggles in a tenor similar to his discussion of Yarico. He scorns English law and expresses sympathy for the plight of "poor Sambo," a man "as ingenious, as honest, and as good a natured poor soul, as ever wore black, and eat green" (101). Ligon understands Sambo's efforts to enter the church as a sincere display of piety. It could also be the enslaved man's efforts to gain his freedom through baptism, attempting to take advantage of the very English law Ligon criticizes.

Ligon relates the story of another enslaved man, Macaw, who endeavors to hang his wife after she delivers twins. Macaw suspects his wife of having committed adultery; the suspicion reflects African cultural beliefs that view multiple births as bad omens. Ligon reads the moment as a foolish myth, calling Macaw "ignorant," one "upon whom custom had taken so deep an impression" (98). The man's murderous rage is not tempered by "all the reasons of Philosophy that could be given him" by both the slave master and Ligon (98). In fact, the only way the master can prevent the murder is by assuring Macaw that "he himself should be hanged by her, upon the same bough" if he killed her (98). For Ligon, this example illustrates the cultural mores of Barbados's enslaved population. Importantly, the moment, coupled with that of Sambo, also particularizes that population, leaving textual traces of lives (and their efforts to negotiate a foreign landscape) that, like Yarico, might have otherwise faded into obscurity. These personal histories supply Ligon's text with literary texture, registering a complexity and richness in his interactions with and characterizations of the people he meets and the landscape. His narrative, then, is not just a record of imperial and commercial possibilities but also a chronicle of contact. And just as those stories serve his larger rhetorical purposes, he serves the subjects of those stories, preserving lives in a written form that might have been forgotten centuries ago and in forms that continue to speak to us.

Approaching Ligon's narrative in this way, as a compilation of stories and voices, makes the text more relevant not only in an early Caribbean literary context but also—potentially—for contemporary Caribbean literary studies. Those engaged in the writing and critical study of modern Caribbean, or more properly West Indian, literature, frequently dismiss early Caribbean texts, such as Ligon's, as the product of colonial conquest, texts written in the seventeenth through nineteenth centuries by Europeans and white creoles, mostly published in Europe and for European audiences. Narratives such as Ligon's are often viewed as irrelevant or counterproductive to the present-day concerns of West Indian literary studies that most often understand contemporary literature as an effort to define and celebrate an authentic West Indian culture. The primary concern of literature written in and about the postcolonial West Indies, as Shireen Lewis articulates it, is to "reconstruct and reconstitute" the identities of marginalized populations who "had been denigrated, distorted, and deformed by slavery and colonization."[14] The Barbadian novelist George Lamming describes West Indian writing as a "novelty" that came "to fruition without any previous native tradition to draw upon in the mid-twentieth century."[15] Lamming proclaimed that that first generation of West Indian writers were "the ... builders of what [would] become a tradition in West Indian imaginative writing: a tradition which [would] be taken for granted or for the purpose of critical analysis by West Indians of a later generation."[16] And Derek Walcott, while recognizing the inevitable pull of the colonial circumstances that shaped the Caribbean, sees the historical context as one to be wrestled with. In one of his earlier poems, titled "A Far Cry From Africa," he wonders:

> Where shall I turn, divided to the vein?
> I who have cursed
> The drunken officer of British rule, how choose
> Between this Africa and the English tongue I love?
> Betray them both, or give back what they give?
> How can I face such slaughter and be cool?
> How can I turn from Africa and live?[17]

When considering the origins of West Indian literature, orthodox approaches point to the 1930s and 1940s and the emergence of literary magazines such as the short-lived *Trinidad* and *Beacon*, both in Trinidad, and *BIM* in Barbados that provided early platforms for writers. Also, the Négritude movement emerged at this time, sparked by black Francophone writers and politicians, including the poet Aimé Césaire from Martinique, who called for a kind of cultural nationalism whereby African-descended people could recognize and celebrate a common origin in Mother Africa. Studies also emphasize the 1950s as central in initiating many of the literary traditions that would define West Indian literature in subsequent decades. In Alison Donnell's words, "The accounts of West Indian literary histories ... consolidate a timeline of cultural development and literary activity centred on a 1950 watershed and produce a narrative that persuades us to read twentieth century Caribbean literature as being in harmony with, as shaping and being shaped by, a developmental history of decolonization and cultural nationalism."[18]

While the idea that West Indian literature is a postcolonial phenomenon is orthodox, several recent studies find the literature's origins in earlier eras, suggesting a critical shift. For example, Evelyn O'Callaghan provides a survey of Caribbean women's writing between 1804 and 1939. Importantly, while her project turns our attention toward the nineteenth century, it does so with a postcolonial inflection, with the intent of "recuperating lost or silenced voices" of women from various racial backgrounds.[19] She ends her survey by contemplating the limits of colonial discourse and what early women's texts can tell us about the experiences of marginalized people in the West Indies. She concludes that those early texts do "have a place in West Indian literary tradition," but she stops short of calling those texts "literary foremothers to current West Indian women writers."[20] Instead, they are counterpoints to which women writers in the twentieth and twenty-first century speak back, creating "postcolonial" narratives that deconstruct the images and representations from those earlier "colonial" texts. Donnell, too, advocates for the importance of considering earlier literature. She insists that scholars think more critically about why it is that the "dismissal of pre-1950 writings has remained a relatively stable trait in Caribbean literary histories since the first wave of critical studies appeared in the 1960s and 1970s"[21] Still, she concedes the socio-political benefits of such approaches as they allow "the majority of critics immersed in the process of forging a new literary history" to break away from "a historical narrative coming out of colonialism," which in turn allows the literature "to be viewed within a context that assumes its own cultural wholeness."[22] All of this is to say that West Indian literature is deemed often a postcolonial product. There is a discontinuity or a divide between postcolonial and colonial Caribbean literature.

That divide is perhaps best illustrated in an exchange between Thomas W. Krise and Walcott after the release of Krise's anthology of early Caribbean literature, titled *Caribbeana: An Anthology of English Literature of the West Indies, 1657–1777*, in 1999. The anthology is one of the first attempts to explicate the literary significance and historical import of texts written in and about the Caribbean by Europeans in the seventeenth through nineteenth centuries.[23] In a review in the *New York Review of Books*, Walcott issues a rather scathing indictment of the anthology, deeming the texts included in the anthology "flourishes of amateurs delighting in rodomontade and pseudo-Miltonic trumpetings."[24] He condemns Krise's efforts to place this literature on the front end of a Caribbean literary history. To do so, Walcott argues, is "insulting, because the contributions are so mediocre, so feeble, that to appropriate them as the sources of a West Indian literature has the plaintive claim of a grateful bastard."[25] Not only is the work aesthetically weak, according to Walcott, but it is also the work of the colonizer. "Is the descendant of the victim," Walcott demands to know, "supposed to accept, because of the patina of time, i.e., history, the torturer as his ancestor? Is he supposed to accept that these documents are the beginning of our literature in English?"[26] He dismisses Krise as a "desperate archivist, eager to find anything that will give the Caribbean past dignity."[27]

What is more, he posits an alternative literary origin, one much more agentive and optimistic for Africans and other marginalized people, one that unfolds synchronously but ultimately independently (and now unrecoverable) of European colonialism. "The victims of slavery," he argues, "never stopped dancing and singing, although four million of them died in the crossing and the seasoning, and it is that meter which matches the landscape that, at nightfall by their permitted bonfires, especially at cane harvest, cane-crop time, developed something greater than tragedy, greater than the feeble iambic couplets and turgid prose of [early Caribbean literature]."[28] In other words, according to Walcott, the roots of modern Caribbean literature reside in an oral tradition that, ultimately, "will never be recognized because it is unrecordable. Besides, its language is lost. Not one of these pieces [included in Krise's anthology] can claim to be art, but they are certainly history, and if they are virtually worthless as art, as literature, our instinct to preserve them simply because they exist is the wrong instinct."[29] Walcott's understanding of the essence of West Indian Literature echoes Kenneth Ramchand, who sees in the literature a "coexistence of the modern [literate] and the archaic [oral]."[30] Like Walcott, Ramchand defines the literature as "essentially a twentieth-century phenomenon," texts written by "people who were born and who grew up in the English-speaking territories and Guyana."[31] In conceding the existence of a body of literature written in and about the region in the seventeenth, eighteenth, and nineteenth centuries, Ramchand determines those texts were written from "alien perspectives" and pursued their own "narrow interests" that illustrated a commitment to the "idea of Europe as home and center."[32]

In his response to Walcott's review, Krise counters that studying the colonial literary past of the Caribbean does not undermine West Indian literature and culture; it enriches it. "Even though the texts in *Caribbeana* were written overwhelmingly by Englishmen," Krise concedes, "just a cursory review of them offers a considerable amount of insight into the lives of Caribs and Africans, enslaved and free."[33] Krise includes Ligon's version of "Inkle and Yarico" and two other adaptations in his anthology, calling the tale an "allegory of European colonization."[34] In his response to Walcott, he also argues that efforts in the West Indies to develop "a sense of culture that is free of the mental chains of colonialism and racism," calls for the "careful development of a cultural history that takes into account all the elements that have led the West Indies to their place in the world's culture."[35] In calling for this more temporally and thematically expansive literary history, Krise cautions against viewing Caribbean literature in terms of the kind of exceptionalism that marked the study and canonization of early American literature in the mid- to late-twentieth century. Walcott, according to Krise, is indulging in a Caribbean essentialism by defining the literature according to a narrow set of standards that renders it "separate and distinct" from those early texts produced by British-born writers. Ultimately, Krise determines, "The fact that Caribbean literature is firmly rooted in a bloody history does not allow us to disregard that history; indeed, the very bloodiness of the history is an essential and invigorating element of the literature."[36]

The present essay offers a reading sympathetic with Krise's perspective; however, Walcott's critique raises a number of questions with which this essay also grapples but ultimately does not answer, the most important of which is this: how do we recognize a literary past without valorizing or overemphasizing it, especially when doing so threatens to undermine the efforts of people who have conceived of West Indian literature as an act of resistance and a coping mechanism that, in J. Michael Dash's words, has sought to "resolve the painful dilemma of a lived reality."[37] That dilemma, according to Leah Rosenberg, involved "creating authentic modern cultures for a region that European discourses had defined as the antithesis of the modern."[38] To suggest that the modern-day literary productions of West Indian writers like Walcott, Lamming and others reside in a literary past constructed by Europeans for the benefit of Europeans must seem like another kind of imperial project, a critical colonization. How, then, do we recognize the past and appreciate its literary significance, without making the present age beholden to it—or even worse, confined by it? I posit this question and others throughout the essay as caveats as we continue to think through the contours of a field of early Caribbean literature.

Perhaps the greatest value in an intertextual reading of Ligon and Gilroy's versions of "Inkle and Yarico" is that such an approach reminds us of the ways in which Ligon's narrative is the product of collaboration among multiple cultures, without whom Ligon's text would not exist in its present form. For sure, Ligon and his English patrons and editors ultimately crafted the narrative, but its significance extends beyond what it can tell us about England and its colonial project. *A True and Exact History* is not Ligon's story alone. More than an author, he is a transcriber of lives and diverse cultures that merge in Barbados in the seventeenth century. In this way, Ligon functions as what Roland Barthes terms an interlocutor. In contemplating the "death of the author," Barthes advocates a way of reading texts that reconfigures the author as a compiler, thereby reducing his authority and control over the text. The author, according to Barthes, does not create single meanings but rather compiles through the act of writing multiple meanings or discourses in texts.[39] As for Gilroy, her re-writing of "Inkle and Yarico" illuminates for us the ways in which West Indian literature of today can speak back to and help us make sense of early Caribbean literature (and vice versa). Although her novel is a form of speculative fiction, it points us to alternative perspectives and histories that complicate the ways in which we understand mechanisms of power and the ways in which people might or might not have interacted in colonial Caribbean spaces and in the literature written about those spaces. When we approach early Caribbean literature from multicultural perspectives, we construct a literary history that matters not just to a narrow group of mostly American and European scholars working in the early-modern period but that potentially also matters for those who study in and about the region today.

NOTES

1. Ligon, *A True and Exact History of the Island of Barbados*, ed. Karen Kupperman (Indianapolis: Hackett Publishing Company, Inc., 2011), 107. All subsequent references to Ligon's narrative appear in text and are taken from Kupperman's annotated edition, which is based on a 1673 reprint. The narrative was first published in 1657.
2. For example, see Richard Eden's translation of Sebastian Münster, *A treatyse of the Newe India with other new founde landes and islandes* (London, 1553). Eden describes black African women: "The women are very fruitful, and refuse no labor all the while they are with child. They travail in manner without pain, so that the next day they are cheerful and able to walk. Neither have they their bellies wrimpled, or loose, & hanging pappes, by reason of bearing many children" (91). See also Leo Africanus, *A Geographical Historie of Africa*, trans. John Pory (London: Eliot's Court Press, 1600): *Early English Books Online*, Web, April 3, 2013, in which he describes a group of Amazon-like African women who cut off a breast to improve their skills with bows and arrows.
3. See Jennifer L. Morgan, *Laboring Women: Reproduction and Gender in New World Slavery* (Philadelphia: University of Pennsylvania Press, 2004).
4. David Brion Davis, *The Problem of Slavery in Western Culture* (Oxford: Oxford University Press, 1966), 11.

5. Steele, Richard. "*The Spectator*, No. 11." *English Trader, Indian Maid: Representing Gender, Race, and Slavery in the New World.* Ed. Frank Felsenstein. (Baltimore: The Johns Hopkins University Press, 1999): 81–88, 88.

6. Jehlen, "History Beside the Fact," 189.

7. Steele, "*Spectator*," 88.

8. See Felsenstein, *English Trader, Indian Maid: Representing Gender, Race, and Slavery in the New World* (Baltimore: The Johns Hopkins University Press, 1999), in which he has compiled and annotated a comprehensive collection of the many versions of the "Inkle and Yarico" story published in England and the Americas, mostly in the eighteenth century.

9. Ibid., 112.

10. For another perspective on why Yarico's story was popular among the English, see Peter Hulme, "Inkle and Yarico," in *Colonial Encounters: Europe and the Native Caribbean, 1492–1797* (London: Methuen, 1986), 225–264. Hulme argues that the story of Inkle and Yarico, in its many eighteenth-century mutations, was part of a larger language of sentimentality and colonial discourse, easily adaptable to the popular genre of sentimental literature.

11. Felsenstein, *English Trade, Indian Maid*, 17. Felsenstein examines the story's cultural work in English society. To understand something of the tale's ubiquity in other parts of eighteenth-century Europe, see Madeleine Dobie, *Trading Places: Colonization and Slavery in Eighteenth-Century French Culture* (Ithaca, N.Y.: Cornell University Press, 2010), which examines the tale's applicability for French culture. Also, perhaps not incidentally, a French story that bears telling resemblance to "Inkle and Yarico" predates Ligon's, appearing in Jean Mocquet's *Travels and Voyages into Africa, Asia, and America, the East and West-Indies, Syria, Jerusalem, and the Holy-land* in 1617.

12. Beryl Gilroy, *Inkle and Yarico* (Leeds: Pepal Press, 1996), 28. Note, all subsequent references to the novel appear in text.

13. Like Yarico, Pocahontas's mythology is based largely on a paragraph that appears in the third version of Smith's *The General Historie of Virginia, New England, and the Summer Isles.*

14. Shireen Lewis, *Race, Culture, and Identity: Francophone West African and Caribbean Literature and Theory from Négritude to Créolite* (Lanham, MD: Lexington Books, 2006), 90.

15. Lamming, *The Pleasures of Exile* (1960) (Ann Arbor, Mich: University of Michigan Press, 1992), 38.

16. Ibid., 38.

17. Derek Walcott, "A Far Cry From Africa" in *In a Green Night* (London: Jonathan Cape Ltd, 1969), 18.

18. Alison Donnell, *Twentieth-Century Caribbean Literature: Critical Moments in Anglophone Literary History* (London: Routledge, 2006), 35.

19. Evelyn O'Callaghan, *Women Writing the West Indies, 1804–1939: 'A Hot Place, Belonging to us.'* (London: Routledge, 2004), 9. For other recent studies that stretch or challenge orthodoxy, see Leah Reade Rosenberg, *Nationalism and the Formation of Caribbean Literature* (New York: Palgrave Macmillan, 2007) and Nicole N. Aljoe, *Creole Testimonies: Slave Narratives from the British West Indies, 1709–1838,* (New York: Palgrave Macmillan, 2012).

20. O'Callaghan, *Women Writing,* 177.

21. Donnell, *Twentieth-Century Caribbean Literature,* 13.

22. Ibid., 38.

23. Also in 1999, Louis James produced an overview of Anglophone Caribbean literature, the first section of which he devotes to a discussion of those early European texts written in and about the region. Like Krise, he recognizes that early literature as essential to the historical and cultural origins of Caribbean literature, though he does not classify those texts as Caribbean literature. Rather they are part of the cultural landscape or framework out of which Caribbean literature arose in the late nineteenth and early twentieth century. See James, *Caribbean Literature in English* (London: Longman, 1999).

24. Derek Walcott, "A Frowsty Fragrance" (Review of *Caribbeana: An Anthology of English Literature of the West Indies 1657–1777) The New York Review of Books* (June 15, 2000), section 1, accessed April 12, 2014, http://www.nybooks.com/articles/archives/2000/jun/15/a-frowsty-fragrance/?page=1.

25. Walcott, "A Frowsty Fragrance," sec. 2.

26. Ibid., sec. 1.

27. Ibid., sec. 1.

28. Walcott, "A Frowsty Frangrance," sec. 3.

29. Ibid.

30. Ramchand, "West Indian Literary History: Literariness, Orality and Periodization" in *Callaloo* 34 (1988): 109.

31. Ibid., 95.

32. Ibid.

33. Tom Krise, "Constructing Caribbean Literary History" in *Literature Compass* 2 (2005): 8, accessed April 12, 2014, doi:10.1111/j.1741-4113.2005.00139.x.

34. Tom Krise, *Caribbeana: An Anthology of English Literature of the West Indies, 1657–1777* (Chicago: The University of Chicago Press, 1999), 16.

35. Krise, "Constructing Caribbean Literary History," 9.

36. Krise, "Constructing Caribbean Literary History," 6.

37. J. Michael Dash, "The World and the Word: French Caribbean Writing in the Twentieth Century" in *Callaloo* 34 (1988), 115.
38. Leah Reade Rosenberg, *Nationalism and the Formation of Caribbean Literature* (New York: Palgrave Macmillan, 2007), 5.
39. See Barthes "The Death of the Author" in *Image Music Text*, trans. Stephen Heath (New York: Hill and Wang, 1977).

BIBLIOGRAPHY

Africanus, Leo. *A Geographical Historie of Africa*. Translated by John Pory. London: Eliot's Court Press, 1600. http://gateway.proquest.com.libdata.lib.ua.edu/openurl?ctx_ver=Z39.88-2003&res_id=xri:eebo&rft_id=xri:eebo:citation:99844139.

Aljoe, Nicole N. *Creole Testimonies: Slave Narratives from the British West Indies, 1709–1838*. New York: Palgrave Macmillan, 2012.

Barthes, Roland. "The Death of the Author." In *Image Music Text*, 142–148. Translated by Stephen Heath. New York: Hill and Wang, 1977.

Behn, Aphra. *Oroonoko*. Edited by Joanna Lipking. New York: W. W. Norton, 1997.

Dash, J. Michael Dash. "The World and the Word: French Caribbean Writing in the Twentieth Century." *Callaloo* 34 (Winter 1988): 112–130. doi: https://doi.org/10.2307/2931114

Davis, David Brion. *The Problem of Slavery in Western Culture*. Oxford: Oxford University Press, 1966.

Dobie, Madeleine. *Trading Places: Colonization and Slavery in Eighteenth-Century French Culture*. Ithaca, NY: Cornell University Press, 2010.

Donnell, Alison. *Twentieth-Century Caribbean Literature: Critical Moments in Anglophone Literary History*. London: Routledge, 2006.

Earle, William. *Obi or the History of Three-Fingered Jack*. Edited by Srinivas Aravamudan. Ontario: Broadview Press, 2005.

Felsenstein, Frank, ed. *English Trader, Indian Maid: Representing Gender, Race, and Slavery in the New World*. Baltimore: The Johns Hopkins University Press, 1999.

Gilroy, Beryl. *Inkle and Yarico*. Leeds: Pepal Press, 1996.

Hulme, Peter. "Inkle and Yarico." In *Colonial Encounters: Europe and the Native Caribbean, 1492–1797*, 225–264. London: Methuen, 1986.

James, Louis. *Caribbean Literature in English*. London: Longman, 1999.

Jehlen, Myra. "History Beside the Fact: What We Learn from a True and Exact History of Barbadoes." In *Readings at the Edge of Literature*, 179–191. Chicago: University of Chicago Press, 2000.

Krise, Thomas. *Caribbeana: An Anthology of English Literature of the West Indies, 1657–1777*. Chicago: The University of Chicago Press, 1999.

Krise, Thomas. "Constructing Caribbean Literary History." *Literature Compass* 2.1 (December 2005). doi: https://doi.org/10.1111/j.1741-4113.2005.00139.x.

Lamming, George. *The Pleasures of Exile (1960)*. Ann Arbor, MI: University of Michigan Press, 1992.

Lewis, Shireen. *Race, Culture, and Identity: Francophone West African and Caribbean Literature and Theory from Négritude to Créolite*. Lanham, MD: Lexington Books, 2006.

Ligon, Richard. *A True and Exact History of the Island of Barbados*. Edited by Karen Kupperman. Indianapolis: Hackett Publishing Company, Inc., 2011.

Mocquet, Jean. *Mocquet's Travels and Voyages into Africa, Asia, and America, the East and West-Indies, Syria, Jerusalem, and the Holy-land…* Translated by Nathaniel Pullen. London: Printed for William Newton, et. al, 1696.

Morgan, Jennifer L. *Laboring Women: Reproduction and Gender in New World Slavery*. Philadelphia: University of Pennsylvania Press, 2004.

O'Callaghan, Evelyn. *Women Writing the West Indies, 1804–1939: 'A Hot Place, Belonging to Us.'* London: Routledge, 2004.

Ramchand, Kenneth. "West Indian Literary History: Literariness, Orality and Periodization." *Callaloo* 34 (1988): 95–110. doi: https://doi.org/10.2307/2931112

Rosenberg, Leah Reade. *Nationalism and the Formation of Caribbean Literature*. New York: Palgrave Macmillan, 2007.

Smith, John. *The Generall Historie of Virginia, New-England, and the Summer Isles: With the Names of the Adventurers, Planters, and Governours …* London, 1625. http://galenet.galegroup.com.libdata.lib.ua.edu/servlet/Sabin?af=RN&ae=CY3802580590&srchtp=a&ste=14.

Steele, Richard. *"The Spectator*, No. 11." In *English Trader, Indian Maid: Representing Gender, Race, and Slavery in the New World*, 81–88. Edited by Frank Felsenstein. Baltimore: The Johns Hopkins University Press, 1999.

Walcott, Derek. "A Far Cry From Africa." In *In a Green Night*. London: Jonathan Cape Ltd, 1969.

Walcott, Derek. "A Frowsty Fragrance" (Review of *Caribbeana: An Anthology of English Literature of the West Indies 1657–1777*). In *The New York Review of Books* (June 15, 2000). http://www.nybooks.com/articles/archives/2000/jun/15/a-frowsty-fragrance/?page=1.

Index[1]

---

[1] Note: Page number followed by 'n' refer to notes.

© The Author(s) 2018
N. N. Aljoe et al. (eds.), *Literary Histories of the Early
Anglophone Caribbean*, New Caribbean Studies,
https://doi.org/10.1007/978-3-319-71592-6

Williams, Charles White, 157
Williams, Cynric, 157–158
    Hamel, the Obeah Man, 8, 148–149,
        158, 162, 167n37; eyewitness
        authority in, 160; inclusion of
        black voices in, 153–154;
        pro-planter perspective, 152,
        159; slave revolt, 154–158
    Tour through the Island of Jamaica,
        155, 157, 158
Williams, James, 111, 115
Williams, Raymond, 114
Williamson, John, 74
Williamson, Karina, 155
Witchcraft, 13, 72
Wolcot, John (Peter Pindar), 183–184
Women
    assertion of agency, 152
    captured by pirates, 126–127,
        136–140
    and female empowerment, 126,
        136, 140
    non-European, 132–134, 136–137,
        195

restrained treatment by privateers,
    127–128
sexual violence against, 126,
    137–140
transgressive, 136
Women's writing, 92, 203–204
Wood, Betty, 37
Wood, Marcus, 174
World Displayed, The, 128
World-tree, the, 27
Wynter, Sylvia, 17

Y
Young, Edward, 47

Z
Zemis, 14, 16, 25–27, 33n40
    viewed as idols or demons, 25
Zimmerman, Marc, 114
Zinzendorf, Nikolaus Ludwig, count
    von, 43